NEW CHALLENGES FOR POLITICAL PHILOSOPHY

New Challenges for Political Philosophy

Gerard Elfstrom
Associate Professor of Philosophy
Auburn University
Alabama

First published in Great Britain 1997 by
MACMILLAN PRESS LTD
Houndmills, Basingstoke, Hampshire RG21 6XS and London
Companies and representatives throughout the world

A catalogue record for this book is available from the British Library.

ISBN 0–333–67870–2

First published in the United States of America 1997 by
ST. MARTIN'S PRESS, INC.,
Scholarly and Reference Division,
175 Fifth Avenue, New York, N.Y. 10010

ISBN 0–312–16476–9

Library of Congress Cataloging-in-Publication Data
Elfstrom, Gerard, 1945–
New challenges for political philosophy / Gerard Elfstrom.
p.   cm.
Includes bibliographical references and index.
ISBN 0–312–16476–9
1. Political science—Philosophy.   I. Title.
JA71.E4   1997
320'.01—dc20   96–9725
                                                    CIP

© Gerard Elfstrom 1997

This book is printed on paper suitable for recycling and made from fully managed and sustained forest sources.

10   9   8   7   6   5   4   3   2   1
06   05   04   03   02   01   00   99   98   97

Printed and bound in Great Britain by
Antony Rowe Ltd, Chippenham, Wiltshire

Contents

Introduction   **1**
   The need for conceptual change   3
   Plan and chapter summary   6
   Perils   7

1 The Emerging Global Economy   **13**

   Historical background of the global economy   13
   The pressures for continued economic unification   17
   Challenges to the global economy   23
   Aspects of the global economy   25

2 National Sovereignty   **39**

   The historical background   39
   Sovereignty in conception and practice   42
   Challenges to the traditional view of sovereignty   48
   Conclusion   57

3 National Identity   **65**

   Facets of national identification   65
   National identity in political philosophy   68
   The dynamics of identification   69
   The nation-state and the individual   83

4 The Structures of Government   **91**

   The fragmented nature of government   92
   Need for conceptual change   100

5 The Role of National Governments   **113**

   The aspects of government   114
   The evolving role of the nation-state   117

Conditions of the present day   119
Implications for philosophy   121

6 Individual Lives   133

Freedom   133
Personal autonomy   141
Distributive justice   147

Conclusion   155

Emphasis on institutions   156
The tyranny of powerlessness   159
Human alienation   163
The haves and have-nots   169

Notes   173

References   197

Index   205

Introduction

Frequently the most enduring and timeless political philosophy is written in response to the major social and political upheavals of a particular human era. John Locke and Karl Marx are excellent examples. Both formulated their ideas in periods when fundamental economic transformation spawned political and social change. Locke wrote during the period when feudal aristocracy was finally and firmly displaced by bourgeois mercantilism.[1] Marx's analyses of labor, ownership, and politics were prompted by the Industrial Revolution.[2] Their insights and concerns are firmly rooted in specific historical circumstances, yet the relevance and importance of their philosophies clearly transcend the eras in which they labored.

Fundamental economic and social transformation is under way once again, and its impact on human life and human institutions is likely to prove equal to those of the ebb of feudalism or the rise of the Industrial Revolution. The broadest current of this transformation is the global unification of human activity resulting partly from technological advances which have revolutionized communication and transportation and made technological prowess a potent source of wealth and power. Globalism manifests itself in several distinct ways. At the most elemental human level, it facilitates a vastly greater array of human contact, whether by jet travel or electronic communication. But, this contact nurtures other facets of globalism, from broad-ranging educational opportunities to the creation of global health problems. Contemporary technology has also revealed global problems, from global warming to population pressures to ecological dangers. In addition, these advances allowed a genuinely global economy to emerge and do so on a scale which would have been impossible in earlier years. Global unification has also been nurtured by ideological commitments to free trade and international cooperation, as illustrated by the support which national political leaders ordinarily give to the General Agreement on Tariffs and Trade and the United Nations.[3]

All aspects of globalization are relevant to this project. However, the global economy is the most dynamic and potent facet of global unification and will, for that reason, receive the lion's share of attention in this work. A unified, world-spanning economy began to emerge in the years following the Second World War.[4] However, its full impact

1

has only become widely felt and appreciated in the past decade or so. Global economic unification remains in its early stages; the network of economic ties which arc across national boundaries will expand and thicken as the twentieth century ends and the twenty-first unfolds. Human beings are therefore amid a process of fundamental transformation whose final shape cannot presently be foreseen. Nonetheless, it is apparent even now that human life and human institutions will be profoundly altered by globalism and the global economy. Neighborhood stores awash with consumer products from around the world are only the most visible signs of the international network of economic ties. The global economy also affects ordinary life in many less obvious but more important ways, including matters of finance and the conditions of labor. The interest rates charged for a small business loan in rural Bavaria are affected by factors as diverse as the fluctuations of Tokyo's stock market, the policies of the United States' Federal Reserve Bank, and the price Saudi Arabia charges for a barrel of crude oil. All these factors have an impact on the value of the German mark and affect the total supply of marks available for commercial loans and therefore affect interest rates in Bavaria. In addition, the unemployment level in Liverpool is affected by the cost of labor in Singapore or Taiwan. Also, a US citizen may as easily be employed by a Japanese, German, British, or Swiss enterprise as an American firm.

However, if the above were the only consequences of globalism and the emerging global economy, their impact on human life and human institutions would be relatively superficial. Consider the complex set of transnational ties found in a single instance of automobile manufacturing. The workers at the Mazda plant in Flat Rock, Michigan, produce automobiles that are sold both as Mazdas and as Fords; Mazda is partly owned by Ford.[5] Car buyers may not particularly care whether a Mazda or a Ford badge is on the final product, and the assembly workers at Flat Rock are probably unconcerned that the name on the plant gate or their paychecks is Mazda rather than Ford. Michigan's state government was very probably as delighted to gain a plant with Mazda's name on the gate as it would have been if the name were 'Ford'. Whether the corporation or its product is ultimately classed as American or Japanese matters very little in this context. Thus, if globalism were felt only in these ways, it would scarcely have fundamental importance for human life.

For example, workers at the Flat Rock plant consider themselves American rather than Japanese. They pay taxes to, attend schools in, vote in, and are citizens of the United States. These things matter a great deal, both to the workers themselves and to their neighbors. Moreover, many of the executives who oversee the Flat Rock facility are Japanese rather than American, and 'being Japanese' is likely to be very important to them, not simply because it indicates their political citizenship but also because it defines their cultural identity – a matter of extreme importance to the Japanese people.[6] So, though national identity and national borders are now relatively inconsequential for products and corporations, they remain important for individual people and for national governments.

However, there is reason to believe that the pressures of globalism will alter the importance of national identity and national citizenship and will also reshape national governments. As a result, being American or Japanese may come to matter little more than being of Irish or Spanish ancestry does for citizens of the United States, and in years to come being a citizen of Japan or the United States may matter little more than being a citizen of California or New Jersey does for those who are Americans. The prospect that global unification will have these consequences is evidence of its importance for political philosophy, since the concepts of the nation-state and of national identification are part of the bedrock of Western European political thought.

From the era of Classical Greece, political philosophers have presupposed that human life is dominated by a single type of political unit, whether the city-state, the feudal domain, or, more recently, the nation-state. Furthermore, political philosophers have presumed that individual human beings will be subjects of a distinct sovereign entity which has ultimate power over their lives. But the global economy is undermining the nation-state and eroding the importance of political bounds. Hence, to remain relevant and vibrant, political philosophy must reexamine its core concepts and issues and revise them to accord with emerging reality.

THE NEED FOR CONCEPTUAL CHANGE

In light of the above, this book aims to reexamine the relation between the conditions of the world and the concepts and issues of political philosophy. Its core argument is that, as a result of the processes of global unification, fundamental concepts of Western European political philosophy do not adequately mirror the circumstances of human life. If they do not reflect human reality, they are an inadequate basis for philosophical reflection and argument. Philosophers' arguments and analyses can only be as good as the foundation of concepts on which they rest; arguments which employ faulty conceptions are unlikely to achieve truth. In addition, the array of basic concepts shapes the assumptions which guide philosophers' reflection; hence, to the extent that the concepts are faulty, philosophical reflection will be inept.

The pursuits grouped under the broad heading of applied philosophy offer an illuminating instance of the necessity of matching basic concepts to changing reality. Medical ethicists, for example, have rethought traditional and widely-accepted concepts of 'death' and 'personhood' in response to advances in medical treatment and increased human power to sustain life, even when the body preserved has little biological life and few distinctively human capacities. In business ethics philosophers have been constrained to rethink the concepts of 'moral agency' and 'responsibility' in consequence of their efforts to employ these ideas to evaluate the activities of large institutions and determine whether and how 'moral agency' applies to individuals at work within sprawling corporations.

Unfortunately, similar collisions of basic concepts with the facts of human life have not yet occurred in political philosophy. Even philosophers such as Henry Shue, who make admirable use of factual data in their analyses, do not turn the facts of the contemporary world back on their own fundamental conceptions to determine whether these conceptions fit them.[7] In this regard the complaint of Stanley Hoffmann, a learned and able analyst of contemporary affairs who cheerfully avows he is no philosopher, that much of contemporary political philosophy is admirable for its intelligence and sophistication but completely without connection to the real world, must be taken very seriously indeed.[8] However, Hoffmann addresses his complaint only to discussions of international policy. He does not examine the more basic issue of whether there is a close fit between the basic concepts he employs, including, 'sovereignty', 'nation-state', and 'national identity' and the present circumstances of human life.[9] Moreover, Anglo-American political philosophers in the latter portion of the twentieth century have frequently sought to skirt the constraint of empirical adequacy. Instead, they have either devoted themselves to careful conceptual analysis or devised complex and ingenious deductive systems, which may employ game theory or idealized choice situations in their attempts to achieve timeless validity for their ideas and avoid encroaching on the domain of the social sciences.

However, because of the importance of employing concepts which accurately reflect the conditions of human life, political philosophers must be sensitive to changes in the world around them. Indeed, this sensitivity to altered circumstance may help explain how the greatest political philosophers acquired the insights which shaped their positions.

Furthermore, the issues which the present work will examine have not yet been addressed by other disciplines. A rich and growing body of literature examines the relations between international business activity and politics. For example, Robert Reich, once at the Harvard Business School, presently United States Secretary of Labor, has written extensively on this topic.[10] An excellent book by Stephen Gill and David Law also examines this matter, as does a recent work by Theodore Geiger.[11] Much of what these authors have to say supports the thesis that a single global economy is emerging. However, none has asked how these developments will affect political institutions, nor have they asked whether the basic concepts of our political philosophy should be altered to accommodate them.

Corporate leaders and members of the business community, including the faculties of schools of business, are keenly aware of the process of global economic unification. Political philosophers and political commentators, however, have been almost entirely silent on this matter. Writers such as Brian Barry, Charles Beitz, Michael Walzer, Henry Shue, Thomas W. Pogge, and Stanley Hoffmann have contributed important work on issues of international political relations, but none has as yet examined the impact of global economic unification on nations, national governments, or individual persons.[12]

The concepts most directly affected by the emerging global economy include that of the nation-state (the concept which lies at the core of political philosophy) and the array of ideas related to it. Foremost among these kindred ideas is 'sovereignty', for it is being fundamentally reshaped by current developments. In addition, ideas of the legitimate *role* of governments are undergoing alteration; that is, views of that which governments ought to do and that which they owe their citizens are changing, and indeed ought to change, in response to altered circumstances. However, it is important to note that these are changes in the way people ordinarily use these terms; they have not yet reshaped philosophers' analyses. Furthermore, there is evidence that national governments will decline in relative importance as a result of the pressures of the global economy and that various international governing bodies will acquire increased importance. Also, the developing global economy will erode people's sense of national identity and its importance in human life.

PLAN AND CHAPTER SUMMARY

Given the above goals of testing the traditional stock of concepts of political philosophy against the new features of the human condition and also of demonstrating ways in which these revised conceptions must reshape the basic issues of political philosophy, this project's methodology is quite simple. It begins by formulating a careful description of the emerging global economy and offering evidence to support the claim that this unification is indeed under way.

Each of the chapters following this initial exposition will examine a particular concept or set of concepts, whether 'sovereignty', 'national identity', 'legitimacy', 'government', or 'nation-state'. The initial characterization of each concept will be drawn from the views of major philosophers or theoreticians and also from the ways in which the concepts are employed in historical analyses, the rhetoric of practicing politicians, or works of political commentary. Following this initial characterization, each chapter will examine the ways in which globalization is changing the world so as to make the above concepts inadequate to reality. Indeed, in many cases the concepts are rough abstractions which have *never* adequately described human reality. The next step is to determine how this stock of traditional concepts must be revised in order to accommodate emergent reality. Finally, each chapter will offer discussion of ways in which some of the basic issues of political philosophy must be revised to reflect the changes in human circumstances and institutional reality brought about by globalization.

Following the above plan, the work is organized into six chapters. The first elaborates and defends the thesis that a global economy is emerging. It also examines the major features of globalization. The second chapter develops the argument that global economic integration has already deeply affected national sovereignty, and made it far more complex and elusive than in the past. Chapter 3 will elaborate the claim that people's sense of national identification is being recast by these same economic forces. The fourth chapter will discuss several ways in which global economic forces may spawn new types of governing structures. Various international bodies and agreements are apt to acquire many of the functions now held by national governments. The culmination of the changes examined in Chapters 2 through 4 is that the role of national governments is being recast by the process of globalization. This claim will be developed in Chapter 5. The impact of these developments on the lives of individual persons should not be overlooked, and the sixth chapter will examine these matters, with particular attention given to the matters of individual freedom, autonomy, and distributive justice.

The conclusion will discuss several of the ways in which political philosophy should change its methodology and focus in order to accommodate the new conditions of human life. It will offer arguments that political philosophy should shift its focus of analysis from single individuals to individuals' role in institutions, that it should examine the ways in which human beings will continue the process of alienation from one another and from social groups, that it should examine more directly the issue of the 'tyranny of powerlessness' (i.e., problems resulting from *lack* of clear authority and responsibility), and that it should attend to the political strains resulting from the division between those who are part of the global economy and those who are not, because much of the coming era's political and social conflict is likely to result from the tensions between those nations, or those groups within nations, who are able to function effectively as part of the global economy and those who cannot.

PERILS

Skeptical readers may well assert that this project holds a number of weighty risks. One is that a book filled with assertions about a process that is still underway and whose outcome cannot as yet be foreseen faces the significant likelihood that its presumptions about the future will be mistaken. Readers may also be concerned about the viability of an attempt to make broad assertions about fundamental historical transformations. A basic premise of this work is that it is now possible to determine that a fundamental transformation of human life is underway and that it is possible to sketch its main features. Not inconsequentially, it also presumes that it is possible to know which currents of present human life are *not* apt to be of fundamental importance.

The above concerns are both legitimate and important. It is quite true that the circumstances of human life which ultimately result from global economic unification and the human institutions which emerge in response to it may differ greatly from those which can now be foreseen. Moreover, the global economy's nature and mode of operation may also evolve as it matures. The only honest way to address this peril is to acknowledge forthrightly that it exists and vow to make every effort to remain sensitive to the limitations which it imposes.

But, if the assumptions and conclusions of this project face a significant risk of being mistaken, its justification comes into question, particularly because it argues that the concepts of political philosophy are inadequate because *they* do not agree with present conditions. There are several reasons for wishing to embark on this venture even with its risk.

To begin with, being wrong is not necessarily a fatal flaw for a work of philosophy. Few philosophers completely agree with their colleagues' ideas, and fewer, in the course of reflection, can avoid the temptation to alter their own positions. The capacity for being fruitfully wrong is a great and important gift for a philosopher; a work that is fruitfully wrong can serve as a springboard for further thought and reflection. Once again Marx is a relevant example. He was mistaken about many things. He was mistaken about the conditions of a proletarian revolution; he was mistaken about the way in which capitalism would develop; and he was very probably mistaken about the eventual triumph of his own doctrines. Nonetheless, much can be learned from studying his work.

In addition, even if many of the assumptions and arguments of this project eventually prove false, it may still be useful, because subsequent, more adequate and far-reaching, reformulations of political principles may benefit from earlier efforts. Human beings, including political theorists, do not take everything in at once. Their vision is improved if they can react against and correct the attempts of others. The present work will more than accomplish its purpose if it plays this role for future thinkers and helps initiate discussion of what promise to be extremely rich and important issues.

But there are reasons to believe the present endeavor is worthwhile apart from its possible value as a source of erroneous philosophical ideas. In particular, though its conclusions may prove mistaken over the long run, they carry a reasonable chance of being correct for the short run because they are based on information and projections which are reasonably well-grounded at the present time. Several features of the emergent global economy are currently visible and can be used to assess the verisimilitude of the principles and ideas currently employed by political philosophers. Thus, information presently at hand is sufficient to allow a fresh look at concepts such as 'sovereignty', 'national identity', and 'government', and to establish that they are inadequate to describe contemporary political reality.

Nonetheless, when global economic unification achieves maturity, it is not improbable that conceptions of politics and of political institutions will emerge which are radically different from those we presently employ.

However, the conceptual changes proposed in this work are evolutionary rather than revolutionary. They are so because global unification is not sufficiently advanced to allow the perspective necessary for more thoroughgoing revisions. Nonetheless, the proposed changes may help pave the way to far more radical shifts of perspective in years to come – though the work of the future will also have to build on the present approach of responding to the new circumstances generated by global economic unification. Hence, the project as a whole has justification even with the risk that its assumptions about the future will eventually be shown false or be superseded by unforeseen changes in global reality.

However, even if the risks of basing a work on predictions about the future are worth taking, the project has a second set of risks. It is saturated with broad claims about the world as a whole; talk of an emergent global economy is, of course, foremost among them. But sweeping claims of this sort are always at least partially false because they inevitably fail to describe all human societies and human activity. This reveals two further difficulties.

One is the possibility that the *genuinely* earth-shaking changes of coming decades will emerge from parts of the world that do not now seem particularly important. For example, much of what will be claimed about the development of the global economy does not apply to the conditions of Middle Eastern Muslim nations. In fact, many Muslims are reacting *against* the pressures of the global economy, particularly since many believe that global commerce is controlled by nations that once sought the colonial domination of Muslim nations. It is possible that the next monumental change in world history will emerge from these nations. Or it is possible that present social upheaval in South America will eventually result in earth-shattering changes elsewhere. Furthermore, much of the world presently seems to have been converted to one or another version of capitalism and to accept the predominance of the major capitalist economic powers. However, it is possible that many of these nations will become disaffected with capitalism within the next few years should it fail to satisfy their aspirations.

Hence, it is entirely conceivable that events and areas of the world that now seem unimportant will soon explode on the world scene and change the course of world history. It is also possible that developments which now seem enormously important will fizzle out after a brief glow and have little further impact. As before, the only reasonable response to these prospects is to acknowledge that such outcomes are indeed possible, but to note further that there is little way of presently taking account of them.

But, there is a more fundamental reason for believing the risk of making presumptions about the most significant currents of human life is worth taking. It is that most of the major works of political philosophy, whether implicitly or explicitly, have also been grounded on assumptions regarding the major currents driving human society. Locke works before a background in which the feudal era of Western Europe is finished. He relies on the assumption that such remnants of feudal systems as were found in much of what is now Germany and Italy, and still persist in the vest-pocket states of San Remo and Monte Carlo, are of little consequence for the overall course of human life. Locke's background assumptions on this matter have proven largely correct, though feudal systems endure in parts of the world, such as Afghanistan and several Middle Eastern nations.

Similarly, Marx's work presumes that the Industrial Revolution was the central development of his day and that, for example, the European peasantry could be largely ignored when plotting the course of world history. Again, his assumptions regarding the importance of the Industrial Revolution proved largely correct, though the Soviet Union fractured partly because of its inability to devise efficient modes of agricultural production, and this in turn was partly caused by its clumsy dealing with the peasantry in the years following the Revolution of 1917.[13]

Furthermore, much of Anglo-American academic political philosophy of the past half century or so (that is, what most of its practitioners would call liberal philosophy) *also* gains its plausibility and its projects from another significant transition, that of the greatly increased wealth and the expanded function of governments that have emerged in this century. Prior to the twentieth century, governments were relatively small and commanded limited financial resources. However, lucrative innovations in taxation, increased demand for public services, and advances in communication and transportation all conspire to balloon the size and influence of government. The spread of democracy and broadening of the franchise have also contributed to the expansion of government. New voters frequently use their influence to demand more governmental services for themselves and to improve their lot in life. In addition, socialist doctrine has had its influence, even in domains where it is anathema, as is demonstrated by programs such as Social Security in the United States and the welfare states of Europe, which owe much of their inspiration to socialist doctrine. Furthermore, politicians, of all ideological stripes, are constrained to vow that they will use their terms in office to increase prosperity – and, to attempt to make good on their claims, they must employ the resources of government. One result is that many of the contentious issues of present day societies (such as, affirmative action programs and attempts to devise a national health-care system) are the direct result of governmental activity.

Hence, contemporary philosophers generally presume that arguments about social and political issues are enmeshed with governmental policies and action. The major issues of contemporary academic political philosophy, including those of distributive justice, affirmative action, abortion, environmental pollution, civil disobedience, or the legitimacy of government, all focus on *government*, and many philosophers presume that government must be the primary instrument for addressing these issues (including many who argue that government must be the instrument for correcting problems which it has created). Government is called upon to address these through its policies, its attempts to redistribute wealth, its efforts to change deeply embedded social practices (witness the battles against segregation in the United States), or by means of statute or judicial decision. The governments of the nineteenth century lacked the resources and the ideology to address such problems. Only in the twentieth century when governments became wealthier (through more bountiful systems of taxation), larger (as a result of their increased wealth), and more active in social affairs (as a result of the demands of their constituents) could the above issues be addressed.[14]

Current political debates swirling around issues of affirmative action, environmental pollution, or abortion would have no meaning were it not presumed that governments hold the keys to addressing them. And the debates are important because it is largely *true* that governments have greatly increased their resources for shaping the lives of ordinary people and the activities of private institutions. Even the conservative critics of academic liberalism, libertarians among others, also direct their arguments at government – generally with the goal of attempting to *reduce* governmental activity in one area of human life or another. In other words, the focus remains on government, its wealth, its power, and its resources for shaping the lives of individual human beings.

Though the points of the above paragraphs may appear elementary, the importance of understanding historical context in order to gain an understanding of current academic political philosophy has been overlooked in part because philosophers have attempted to transcend it. They have often done so by attempting to devise quasi-deductive arguments which aim at Kantian timeless truth.

This point is underscored by the work of John Rawls, perhaps the paradigm of the mid-twentieth century academic liberal. (Though the point could be made equally well by reference to the work of Alan Donagan, David Gauthier, Alan Gewirth, or Ronald Dworkin.[15]) Rawls based the conclusions of his system on a method of hypothetical choice in which the participants would have no knowledge of their own societies or of their own personal characteristics. In this way he hoped to attain universal validity for his principles.[16]

In recent years Rawls has retreated from this position and acknowledged that the assumptions of the participants in the choice situation and their values will be largely conditioned by the society from which they are drawn.[17] Rawls still fails to recognize, however, that the circumstances of history will make some problems important but cause others to sink into obscurity. The issue of religious freedom, for example, plays nearly no role in Rawls' deliberations. He simply takes it for granted, and consequently so do the participants in his original situation, but complacency regarding religious freedom would have been unwarranted during many periods in Western European history and it is unwarranted in many contemporary societies, that of Iran for example.

This project's approach differs from that of the recent crop of liberal academic philosophers mainly in explicitly attending to what appear to be the transforming currents of the present age and in explicitly acknowledging that its conclusions are conditioned by these assumptions. Chief among its assumptions are that globalism, and the emerging global economy in particular, rank with the decline of feudalism and the Industrial Revolution in importance and that other movements, such as the resurgent nationalism of the remnants of the Soviet Union or the advent of militant Islam, are relatively unimportant.

It is impossible to devise a rigorous proof of these assumptions. The final assessment of their correctness must await the passage of time. However, much of the task of Chapter 1 is to delineate the forces which sustain and propel globalism in general and the global economy in particular and to present evidence to support the assertion that they are the fundamental currents of the present day and of the foreseeable future. Hence, though this project has its share of risk, there are reasons to believe the risks are worth taking.

1 The Emerging Global Economy

'Everyone,' as Jagdish Bhagwati notes, 'is in everyone else's backyard. . . .'[1] Professor Bhagwati's quip neatly captures the untidy and complex nature of the emerging global economy. It has several aspects which are in varying stages of development in differing parts of the world. Hence, analysis must isolate its major facets and explore the ways in which they interact with one another. It must also examine the pressures which are driving the process of economic unification to maturation and survey the pressures which may possibly derail it.

HISTORICAL BACKGROUND OF THE GLOBAL ECONOMY

To understand why the contemporary global economy is particularly important, it is necessary to recognize how the current pattern of transnational economic activity differs from that of earlier periods of human history. After all, Marx believed that international borders were obsolete in his own day, that the 'workers of the world' had crucial interests which bound them together, and that nation-states and national governments were merely the artificial constructs of capitalist powers who exploited national borders and national governments to advance their own interests. Unfortunately for Marx, the events of the past 150 years have largely proved that his views on these matters were mistaken, and that nationalism and national boundaries loom large in human existence.[2]

The foundation of the global economy was laid in the years following the Second World War. Of course, trade and economic links have arced across political boundaries from prehistory. Primitive trading very probably began as soon as the first human being was able to produce more than he or she could immediately use.[3] It is also very likely that trade between human groups began very early in the existence of the species simply because broader and thicker networks of trade links open more opportunities for mutually profitable exchange. Lengthy trade routes existed in the Biblical era and played a central role in the human life of the period. The desire for profitable trade, in addition to normal human curiosity, helped motivate European exploration and gave impetus to the technological advances in navigation and ship building which stretched the links of trade further and opened new opportunities for exchange. Moreover, multinational corporations predate the post-Second World War period. American corporations were heavily involved in Latin America in the nineteenth century, and their activity accounts for much of the distrust of the United States found in the Southern Hemisphere of the Americas. But American corporations were far from the only multinational corporations active in the last century; British, German, and French corporations were also large, important, and extremely active in various parts of the world.[4]

Nonetheless, the period following 1945 differs markedly from those earlier in the scope and intensity of economic relationships and in the degree to which transnational economic activity has begun to shape human life and institutions. Part of the reason for the change is that technological advances in communication and transportation made international commercial activity far easier, more efficient, and cheaper than in past years. These advances allowed a far wider array of commercial networks and broader reaching corporations than were possible earlier. These changes would very probably have brought about a global trading network even apart from other significant conditions of the post-Second World War period. However, certain features of the years immediately following 1945 gave considerable impetus to the development of a global economy.

During this period much of the industrialized world was in a shambles; the war left Europe and Japan as smoking ruins. The United States alone remained unscathed, even strengthened economically, by the Second World War. Moreover, the end of the hot war only made way for the beginning of the Cold War between the Soviet Bloc and Western nations. These circumstances generated several factors which greatly hastened the development of the global economy.

The shattered economies of Europe desperately needed goods and jobs and thus offered tremendous opportunity for the corporations of the United States to enter Europe in search of markets and to establish manufacturing facilities. United States corporations were well positioned for this invasion because the war had demanded mass production on a huge scale and gave corporations experience transporting goods across national borders. Largely for these reasons, US corporations were predominant among the ranks of multinational corporations for several decades following the war. Only in the late 1960s and in the 1970s did corporations from other nations became globally active to a significant degree – and this factor changed much of the world's view of the nature of multinational corporations.

The policies of the United States government were another crucial factor. They were largely the work of people who held a messianic conviction that capitalism and free trade were the keys to a prosperous and harmonious world. Hence, the United States forged policies that vigorously promoted the doctrine of free and unencumbered trade, and its predominant position in the world gave these doctrines great weight.[5] Furthermore, it placed the stamp of the gospel of free trade on the economic and financial institutions created by the victorious powers following the war.

Also the recovering economies of Europe and Japan were initially too poor to digest the production of their rebuilt factories. It soon became clear to them that they would have to depend on exports in order to absorb the production of their plants and channel extra wealth into their nations. It is thus no accident that, in addition to the United States, the major exporting nations of the world are Japan and Germany (with Germany leading Japan in this area by a considerable margin). Furthermore, this pattern of economic development has become the model for the developing industrialized nations of the world; the great success stories of the latter half of this century are those of nations that have devised economic policies which are heavily weighted towards exports.[6]

Yet another factor influenced the development of a global economy in the years following 1945, and this was the advent of the Cold War. It divided the major nations of the world into two competing power blocks. The competition was primarily military and ideological, but it also carried an undertone of economic competition, as indicated by Khrushchev's infamous 'We will bury you' remark of the early 1960s. And as it happened, this economic competition was crucial to ending the Cold War, since the Soviet Union eventually recognized that it would not be able to compete militarily with the West if it could not stay abreast economically. Once it acknowledged, following various attempts at reform initiated during the early period of Gorbachev's era, that it could not compete economically, it essentially surrendered.[7]

Nonetheless, even when the Cold War was seen primarily as a military confrontation, leaders of both sides recognized that economic progress was a key to eventual victory and labored to encourage the economic success of their allies. To this end they forged a dense array of economic links that now bedevil the efforts at economic reform of the former members of the Soviet bloc but work to the considerable advantage of the former members of the Western bloc.

Hence, beginning in 1945 the technological advances that made the development of a genuine global economy feasible combined with the strong motive forces of economics and politics to propel its development. In the half century after that period, the global economy has undergone several changes. Indeed only in the past decade or so has the very great importance of the emerging global economy and the difference it will make for human lives begun to be understood – mainly by leaders in business, to a far lesser extent by governmental leaders, but almost not at all by academics, other than a few scholars in schools of business and some in economics or political science.

The emergent global economy has passed through a number of distinct periods, and the distinctive features of each phase have altered perceptions of its nature. The initial phase began shortly after the Second World War. It was a period when the great majority of multinational corporations were from the United States and a policy of free international trade was vigorously encouraged by the United States government. Because of this connection, many viewed multinational corporations as agents of the US government and, given the enormous power the US enjoyed at that time, they felt relatively helpless to resist these corporations' attentions.

The next phase began during the decade of the 1960s and continued into the 1970s. At this point, the recovering economies of Europe and other nations of the world began to develop corporations sufficiently powerful and self-confident to move vigorously into the global arena. These corporations sought entry to a variety of regional and local markets and began more aggressively to construct manufacturing plants and offices in them. Hence, during this period, perceptions of multinational corporations changed in three important ways. First, multinational corporations were no longer closely identified with the United States by those in other parts of the world. But, second, their power and mobility encouraged the perception that they had broken loose from the control of *any* national government; that they had become powers unto themselves capable of challenging the authority of national governments or, at the very least, of escaping their effective control. However, third, multinational corporations were still identified with the predominant Western European nations and the United States. Nations that had newly achieved independence from European nations, or who wished to preserve their fragile sense of independence, often responded to economic intrusions with policies founded on a highly militant and wary nationalism, marking their relations with multinational corporations by suspicion and confrontation.

The third stage began in the late 1970s and continued to the collapse of the Soviet Union. Several elements changed the perception of multinational corporations yet again. One important factor was that individual nations developed skills and resources for coping with multinational corporations. A second, related, factor was that the number of corporations active in the international arena vastly increased, and nations soon discovered they could get various corporations to compete with one another to gain entry to their economies. Also, significant numbers of corporations from Third World nations became active in international commerce, helping to break the perceived tie between multinational corporations and world domination by advanced, Western, industrialized nations. But, another highly important factor intruded as well. Developing nations realized that they required foreign capital to advance their economies and that they were unable to supply their needs either through aid from other nations or loans from international financial institutions. Hence, they were compelled to seek to reattract the attention of multinational corporations in service of their hopes for economic advance.

The fourth post-war period of multinational commerce has begun with the end of the Cold War and the collapse of the Soviet empire. Thus far, it appears that these events will strengthen the pressures of the third period. For the time being the economic promise of socialism has been discredited, and the only viable alternative appears to be the capitalism of the Western nations. Furthermore, developing nations seeking to remain independent of Western nations can no longer gain space to maneuver by turning to the Soviet Union for support. In addition, with the military confrontation of the Cold War largely eliminated from international concern, decisions and policies can often be made without the distorting influence of military tension. Furthermore, the various barriers to trade caused by the stress of armed confrontation are now either eliminated or greatly truncated. Lastly, without the distorting factor of East/West confrontation, international cooperative agencies such as the United Nations have gained far greater importance and far more support than they enjoyed in previous years. Hence, it now appears that the way is open for a considerable expansion of the scope and pace of development of a unified global economy.

THE PRESSURES FOR CONTINUED ECONOMIC UNIFICATION

Global economic unification is highly likely to continue for the foreseeable future. It is motivated by three major forces. One is politics (though the political forces are generally reactions to economic developments). The second is the nature of business activity. The third is technology.

Governments are vigorously participating in the evolution of the global economy and will continue to do so, but this is because their interests and those of the ordinary people they represent demand it. An excellent example of the force of economic unification is the travails of the European nations that are attempting to stitch themselves together into an economic and political order. It is clear to the political leaders guiding this endeavor that the arrangements they are devising will require them to forfeit substantial portions of their national sovereignty, that these arrangements will result in diminished governmental control over national boundaries (including matters of citizenship, immigration, and trade), and that the arrangements which they seek may eventually result in substantial erosion of the distinctive national identity and culture of their nations. Yet, despite these factors, the Europeans continue to devise treaties and agencies designed to bring about greater political and economic unity.[8] Moreover, nations not originally members of the European Economic Community have been scrambling to become part of the process of unification, and these include nations such as Sweden and Finland that have traditionally been aloof from the rest of Europe and sought to remain free of entangling alliances.

A striking feature of European unification is that it is being propelled largely by national political leaders, individuals whose power and prerogatives are most threatened by the arrangements they are forging. There is no groundswell of popular agitation for these developments. Though the arrangements are often approved by voters in national plebiscites, ordinary citizens do not appear emotionally committed to the effort to stitch together a new unified Europe. Many, in fact, are highly suspicious of the entire process. Nonetheless, majorities voting in national referenda commonly support decisions to continue advancing the steps in the process, and national leaders generally give strong support for the process. Political leaders do so because they believe their future prosperity and welfare demands membership in the unified community, and they believe they will lose economic and political influence if they seek isolation. Their perceptions are largely supported by the abysmal poverty of nations that have sought to sequester themselves from the rest of the world, namely miserably poor nations such as Albania, Burma (Myanmar), or North Korea.

Mainland China offers excellent evidence of the way in which global economic unification is forcing nations away from policies of economic and political isolation. Its leaders are, on the one hand, attempting to preserve its strict Communist system, but they recognize, on the other hand, that they must open China's doors to the larger world economy if they are to advance the welfare of their people, and, more importantly to the minds of its leaders perhaps, avoid lapsing into international backwardness and unimportance. It is significant that the Marxist leaders of mainland China consider these goals sufficiently important that they are willing to risk unleashing forces which will undermine their own control over China and undermine the Communist order they seek to preserve.[9]

The travails of the elderly leaders of Communist China reveal the force of the second powerful impetus to the development of a global economy, that of the nature of business activity. Commerce thrives on possibilities, openings, connections, and opportunities. The greater the array of possible markets, of goods available for purchase or resale, of technologies available for exploitation and manipulation, of options for relocating plants, offices, or personnel, the more opportunities business enterprises possess for growth, for profits, and for increased power.

Business enterprises generally do not thrive by attempting to *restrict* the array of options available to them. For a given corporation at a given time, one or another of the above arrays of possibilities may be more or less important. Nonetheless, as a general rule, no corporation would consider itself to benefit if any one of the above arrays of options were closed to it.

This general rule is proven by an apparent exception. The business communities of some states (those of Chile, Argentina, and Brazil come to mind as examples) were able to gain temporary advantage for themselves by cajoling their governments to protect them by closing national borders to the activity of outside corporations. However, nearly all the nations that have attempted this course (including those mentioned above) have reversed their policies.[10] They have done so because the absence of competition encourages inefficiency, which is revealed in higher consumer costs, lower quality, and dearth of technological innovation. So the economic cost to a nation of the policy of economic protectionism is great. Further, the nation is doomed to become an economic backwater, weak and powerless in the face of bustling world trade. In addition, domestic corporations soon reach the natural limit of their size and power, those set by their national boundaries. Hence, the economy of a nation that restricts itself becomes weak and inefficient, and its business community suffers from stunted growth and limited competitiveness. The most visible solution of the present day, as the governments named above have discovered, is to rejoin the world economy and attempt to compete in its arena.[11]

Therefore, given the means to push the horizon of their activity beyond the limits of their national borders, corporations gain substantial benefit from the attempt to stretch the bounds of their business activity as far as their resources will allow. Hence, they will (scattered exceptions aside) attempt to push aside or evade the efforts of national governments to restrict their endeavors within national boundaries. This is given vivid illustration by the efforts of business enterprises to dodge the Cold War restrictions on the export of certain types of products and information.[12] Corporations have consistently sought to loosen these restrictions and have, with equal persistence, endeavored to work around them.

However, the economic pressures to expand the horizon of opportunity do not affect only corporations; they motivate labor and capital as well. Capital tends to move to the arena where it will make the greatest return, and, the more arenas available for this, the greater the opportunity for increased returns. Hence, the global market for capital has developed very quickly and is the most advanced and liquid of the global markets.

Labor is less mobile. Nonetheless, labor *does* enjoy some geographic mobility, as the governments of the United States and Western Europe have been dismayed to learn. These governments have made mostly unsuccessful attempts to restrict the movement of immigrant labor into their economies, but the pull of increased opportunity and increased wealth that drives corporations and capital across borders also affects labor.[13] Moreover, even within national boundaries, labor is mobile in ways that encourage the development of an international economy. Laborers can move from corporation to corporation and from career to career. Within a nation labor will tend to move to where the opportunity and pay are the greatest, and this will often be in the largest and most powerful corporations, those, in other words, active on an international scale.[14] Thus, the most talented and resourceful laborers will tend to gravitate to those corporations that are active on an international scale.

Educational opportunities also enable labor to move from career to career or allow new generations of labor to gravitate to those careers that hold the greatest promise. And the forces of the present day result in the most attractive opportunities beckoning in those careers that are part of the global economy. Computer technicians are an obvious example. The force of this point is readily understood by the deans of business schools, who are likely to be working feverishly to expand programs designed to suit students for careers in international business.[15] As in other areas, those disinclined to take advantage of such opportunities will cede power, prestige, and wealth to those motivated to do so, and the Darwinian pressures of the market will tend to weed out the former group.

The Darwinian pressures goading business, capital, and labor are largely the result of the past half century's advances in technology, in particular the advances in communication and transportation that have emerged at an explosive rate since the end of the Second World War. These strides allow a far broader and thicker array of ties between human beings than was previously possible. Most importantly, these advances are global in the sense that they make trans-global communication and travel astonishingly quick and easy. Hence, they allow the creation of human institutions that function globally and allow global human interconnection and cooperation – and these are basic requirements for the emergence of a global economy.

But, technology, particularly of the past 25 years, has developed in another way, one that also encourages global activity. The major technological development of this era is the computer, and easy linkage of computers in extremely complex and broad-ranging networks is among the most important features of computer technology. The leading economic advances and the primary sources of economic wealth and power of the next decades will be deeply enmeshed with computer technology.[16]

Computers will change the equation of human life and wealth in profound ways. They require comparatively meager quantities of natural resources, both in terms of the materials and energy needed to construct them and in the energy and materials needed to operate them. Also, they depend for their power and utility on their ability to manipulate technological information rather than on access to large supplies of natural resources. A result is that power, wealth, and influence in coming decades will not depend to the extent they once did on exclusive control of natural resources or territory. They will depend to a far greater extent than at any time in human history on access to and control of technology.

But, this technology is highly mobile, not merely in the sense that the computers themselves and the means to produce them can easily be transported from place to place, but the software needed to operate them and allow them to work their wonders can be flicked across phone lines to distant corners of the world in a matter of seconds, and the emergence of new fiber-optic cables and laser technology will greatly enhance and facilitate this mobility. But, in addition and probably more fundamentally, the vast quantities of data and the calculations and manipulations which computers can easily perform on this data can *also* be quickly and easily transported across vast distances.

Two features of computers – their ability to manipulate astonishing quantities of data and the fact that they become more useful as they are more fully interlinked with other computers – give them vast capacity for facilitating communication and breaking down political and economic barriers. Computers, in sum, *lend themselves* to the exchange of information and become more useful to the extent that they do so. Hence, computers facilitate making connections, tying people and institutions together, encouraging cooperation, and breaking down barriers. As a result, they are working mightily to link the world more tightly together and crumble the same barriers to human interaction that national governments must preserve in order to maintain their power and authority.

Therefore, computers place national governments in a difficult position: governments must employ computers and their abilities in order to seek wealth and influence, but computers by their nature erode the significance of national boundaries and undermine the ability of any single group to acquire and preserve exclusive control of the powers they contain. The difficulty which governments and corporations face in retaining exclusive control over computer software and computer data is vividly illustrated by the ease with which a 16-year-old British computer hacker was able to break into highly secret and restricted US governmental computing centers.[17] Another facet of the difficulty of retaining exclusive control is illustrated by the ease with which computer software and computer data are copied and pirated by unauthorized users, the difficulty with which governments have in preventing corporations from transferring sensitive technology to subsidiaries overseas, or in preventing domestic corporations with important technology from being bought up by foreign interests. Furthermore, with the demise of the Cold War, there is considerably less motivation for, and less justification for, governmental efforts to maintain close control of technology. This point is vividly illustrated by the dazzling ease with which the states of the former Soviet Union have switched from zealous efforts to guard their technologies to equally zealous efforts to sell their important intellectual resources to foreign interests. They have done so in an effort to keep their rickety economies afloat and protect the livelihoods of thousands of skilled and highly trained engineers and scientists.

CHALLENGES TO THE GLOBAL ECONOMY

Recent events in Europe and the aspirations and conflicts of mainland China offer convincing evidence of the way in which economic forces are shaping political structures, the way in which they push political leaders along, and the way in which the process of economic unification appears to feed upon itself. However, the claim that a unified global economy is emerging is not uncontroversial. Some argue that the most probable outcome of current developments is renewed nationalist mercantilism, a fierce economic free-for-all in which each nation desperately seeks its individual advantage. Others are convinced that future decades will find the global economy frozen into several trading distinct blocks, each functioning in comparative isolation from the others.[18]

While these claims are plausible, the preponderance of evidence supports the view that neither renewed mercantilism nor a system of isolated and independent trading blocks is likely given the current array of economic and political forces. This is not a claim that there will be *no* instances of mercantilist behavior by individual nations, nor is it an assertion that systems of regional trading blocks are unlikely to form. Sometimes nations will fight fiercely for their individual interests. Also, Europe will eventually become an essentially single economic unit, and East Asia will eventually develop into another arena of economic interdependence, as will the American continent. However, these processes will not prevent a unitary world economy from emerging.

The basis of this claim is the assertion that multinational corporations and individual governments abet the process of global economic integration through their efforts to advance their own interests. For one thing, regional trading groups are not being created to exclude others. Rather, they are seen as ways of increasing opportunities and opening new markets for the nations that create them. The United States, for example, has been active in promoting free trades zones on the American Continent, but its primary motivation for doing so is to open new markets. Most importantly, it and its American trading partners are *not* withdrawing from trade relationships in other parts of the world or seeking to keep enterprises in other nations from activity within their borders. The same can be said of the European nations and those of Asia. They are working energetically to strengthen their economic bonds to one another but are not abandoning ties to other parts of the world.

Economic conflict remains, of course, but even conflict often expands the network of ties rather than the reverse. In the United States, for example, economic competition with Japan has sparked a torrent of heated rhetoric. Nonetheless, individual corporations of both nations are busily initiating joint ventures, exchanges of technology, and mutual purchases of stock. US and Japanese corporations are not only competing with one another; they are also energetically cooperating and, in doing so, are creating bonds which link themselves and the economies of their home nations more closely together.

The activities of US and Japanese corporations exemplify patterns of corporate intermingling which are found worldwide. A complex array of mergers, exchanges of stock, and joint ventures has emerged to the degree that some claim that the question of whether a given corporations is fundamentally British, Japanese, or American often cannot be answered.[19] If major corporate institutions are thus intermingled and intertwined in increasingly complex fashion, it is increasingly unlikely that they will seek to *untangle* as a result of mercantilist demands or a retreat to regional trading groups. Moreover, the economic pressures that drive corporations to unite; that is, the advantages of symbiotic technological capacities, access to more markets, promise of greater resources for capital and research projects, and insulation from disruptive political forces; will remain and will continue to make such arrangements attractive.

Also, governments' efforts to protect their national economic interests have commonly facilitated the process of global economic integration rather than slowed it. Once again, the prickly relations between the United States and Japan offer an excellent illustration. While the two nations have indulged in considerable posturing and recrimination, there is no question of abandoning trade relations. The point is made tellingly by an incident of a few years ago. President Bush met with the Japanese Prime Minister Toshiki Kaifu in Palm Springs, California. While there, Bush roundly criticized the Japanese for failing to be sufficiently open to US goods and threatened to tighten US restrictions on trade with the Japanese in retaliation. However, simultaneously, outside the meeting room, many of Palm Springs' citizens were voicing hopes of gaining investment funds from the Japanese.[20]

Furthermore, US markets are extremely important to Japan, and American consumers are unlikely to lose their taste for Japanese automobiles, electronic gear, or machine tools anytime soon. This point is vividly illustrated by the fact that the US trade deficit with Japan remained essentially constant in the 1980s despite numerous efforts to whittle it away. Moreover, this occurred during a period when the US trade deficit with other parts of the world declined. The major practical consequence of attempts to restrict the flow of Japanese goods is to increase prices for American customers, who buy them anyway and are willing to pay more to do so.[21] In addition, Japan is an important consumer of several varieties of US goods, forest products among others. As a result, the two nations are immersed in a series of negotiations which are designed to erase barriers to the sale of imported goods in Japan and make US goods more competitive. The talks have the goal of reducing the trade imbalance between the nations, but notice that they are designed to nurture economic ties rather than prune them. In consequence, the friction between the US and Japan is leading to greater economic interdependence rather than a retreat to isolation by either party.

As before, relations between the United States and Japan exemplify broader patterns of governmental activity which expand and thicken economic ties rather than prune them. Political efforts to safeguard national economies by regulating international trade have resulted in various arrangements, such as the General Agreement on Tariffs and Trade and its successor the World Trade Organization, which stabilize the conditions of international commerce and maintain the conditions required for free trade. Thus, they encourage and facilitate multinational commerce rather than the reverse. It is possible that these developments will be unraveled by a spate of protectionism or global trade war. However, these outcomes are unlikely, simply because all parties, governments as well as corporations, have too much to gain by maintaining the present course and too much to lose by abandoning it.

ASPECTS OF THE GLOBAL ECONOMY

The global economy has several aspects; each of them is developing at different rates and in various ways, and in varying stages of development in diverse portions of the world. These include markets, institutions, and rules and regulations.

Markets

In several respects markets are the most fully developed of the facets of the global economy. They are so in the sense that the majority of the world's national and regional markets are generally linked directly or indirectly to a global market and also in the sense that there are few significant barriers to the operation of genuine global markets. However, several distinct global markets exist, including those for capital, for products (which include goods, services, and intellectual property, understood as patents, books, and movies), and for labor.

Of the various markets, that for capital is closest to being fully global, and it most nearly approximates the conditions of a genuinely free market. The capital markets of the world now operate nearly 24 hours a day; they are open to all who wish to participate in them; capital can be moved from one market to another via electronic transfer nearly instantly. Hence, capital is virtually completely free to move to whichever nation's exchange is expected to offer the most desirable yield.

Furthermore, these markets are able to react nearly instantly to changes anywhere on the globe that may affect the value of capital. Efforts to reduce interest rates in the United States, for example, will instantly register in the capital markets of Tokyo, or the introduction of policies intended to spur economic growth in Japan will immediately affect the markets of Paris. Hence, those seeking capital must compete with all the others spread across the world who are also seeking funds because capital is free to move to wherever it will offer greatest advantage to the seller. This is in turn possible because there are no significant impediments to global flows of capital.

The uninhibited worldwide flow of capital has several important consequences. One is that it is forcing local markets to develop more uniform rules of operation because investors will not be particularly interested in placing capital in markets whose rules of operation are unsatisfactory.[22] Hence, the free flow of capital is pressing for the creation of regulations, regulatory bodies, and institutions which both facilitate the free flow of capital and create roughly equivalent market conditions in which it can be traded. No transnational regulatory organization mandated this; it is emerging in response to the pressures of a free and vigorous market. Moreover, it is prompting the creation of capital markets in places that did not previously possess them, such as the nations in the former Soviet empire, and the pressures of the global market are forcing these new markets to conform to the modes of operation of the older markets.[23]

The fact that any who seek access to substantial quantities of capital must compete on the global market also has a result that the various national economies are under pressure to conform to the requirements of the global market; they must do so in order to gain access to needed funds. Even governments must conform to the demands of the global capital market if they are to compete for funds or attract capital into their economies. Governments have sometimes changed policies in response to the perceived demands of the global market. They will pursue anti-inflationary measures, for example, if they believe that it is necessary to do so in order to attract capital to their economies or if they are to successfully borrow capital on the global market.

The above is a potent force: few nations on the globe are now self-financing in the sense that they are able to meet their requirements for capital using only the resources of their domestic economies. Japan and several of the wealthier oil-exporting nations of the Middle East may still have sufficient resources to remain financially independent, but most other nations of the world must seek capital from the global capital market. This is particularly true of the developing nations, who generally have a greater need for outside funds to allow their economies to be able to grow sufficiently to simply keep pace with population increases or if they are to gain greater prosperity for their citizens.

In addition, institutions that control vast amounts of lending capital, such as the International Monetary Fund and the World Bank, generally impose stringent requirements on nations seeking development funds from them. These policies often result in considerable hardship for the citizens of nations who conform to these requirements, and these hardships commonly result in political turmoil; however, nations are often willing to accept even these exacting requirements in order to gain access to necessary development capital. A particularly livid example of this stress is now found in Russia, which ardently sought admission to, and finally gained membership of, the International Monetary Fund. However, Russia is now required to impose demanding economic restrictions on its populace in order to gain loans from the IMF.[24] It has chosen to do so because it cannot generate required capital internally and hence must meet the IMF's demands if it is to have a chance of economic progress.

The capital market is currently the most potent of the forces of the global economy. It has a direct impact on the economies and governmental policies of many nation-states. Its power results largely from its ability to react instantly to changes in government policy and exert significant pressure on nations to conform to its demands. Its power also results from another feature: investors can effortlessly exert their will by simply pulling their money out of a particular market or by refusing to allow their money to be used there. The power of the capital markets is far easier to utilize and far less amenable to outside pressure than the modes of influence available to other institutions.[25] Labor must employ strikes or boycotts, while the methods governments must use to attempt to gain influence, those of negotiations or threat of coercion, are notoriously cumbersome, as are the methods used by corporations, which are generally the methods of negotiation and contract.

In addition to capital, there are global markets for a wide variety of products, though the extent of the development of global markets varies from product to product; there are global markets for particular types of products, such as computers or aircraft, rather than a single global market for all products. Furthermore, while the global markets for products do not have the direct impact on nations and governments possessed by the capital market, they are important and do have significant effects on national governments, national economies, and on the corporations and individuals forced to compete in them.

The existence and importance of global markets for several types of manufactured goods is now vividly understood by most people. They are keenly aware that there are essentially single global markets for aircraft, automobiles, armaments, electronic equipment, textiles, and sporting goods. Though global markets for manufactured goods may be less significant from a broad perspective than other facets of the global economy, they have received considerable attention because the goods themselves bring their country of origin to the attention of the consumer and because of the impact of global markets on local manufacturing concerns and hence of jobs.[26]

However, the self-sustaining power of global markets for manufactured goods is displayed when they confront protectionist pressures. A significant element of this power is that nations often hesitate to impose protectionist measures because *their own goods* will then be vulnerable countermeasures in other markets.[27] The fact is that a substantial portion of the economies of the industrialized nations of the world depends on international trade. The figure generally given for the United States is that approximately 15 per cent of its Gross Domestic Product results from international trade.[28] Comparable figures for Japan and Germany would no doubt be much larger. Hence, efforts to restrict trade will encounter resistance from powerful segments of national economies that are crucially dependent on international trade for their livelihood.

But technology which makes transport of goods easy and relatively cheap opens a way for consumers to exert pressure to preserve and expand international trade. They generally desire the cheapest or highest-quality products they can find. When such are made available to them, they will very probably buy them – and the nation of origin will likely be of small consequence. In fact it has often become quite difficult to determine the nation of origin of many consumer products, whether they be automobiles, computers, or electronic goods, simply because these products may be assembled from components shipped from several nations, the assembly process itself may take place in various nations, and it is often difficult to determine the nationality of the companies themselves.[29]

In response to customers' desires for attractive goods, retailers will seek such products to offer for sale. At that point a considerable group of people has a stake in preserving international trade; witness the activity of the automobile dealers whose franchises include foreign cars. This group has a vested interest in preserving international trade and will struggle to do so.

Global markets for goods exert pressures in other ways. Once a global market for a particular product emerges, there is intense pressure on manufacturers of that product to enter the global market simply to survive. Furthermore, there will be conjoint pressure to deposit manufacturing and management facilities across national boundaries once global markets are established. This pressure results from the economic imperatives to gain the lowest possible labor costs, secure convenient access to local markets, and insulate corporations from protectionist measures. Hence, the global market generates forces to make manufacturing global, and will therefore expand and thicken the web of ties of the global economy.

A global market for labor also exists, though it is less developed than other markets. Moreover, the global market exists primarily for the *buyers* of labor. It is global in the sense that prevailing wage rates are among the factors corporations consider when making decisions about location. Laborers in one locale therefore often find themselves competing for jobs against laborers in other parts of the world. Moreover, corporations commonly use the threat of relocation when negotiating with labor.

The market for labor is less fluid and responsive than that for capital or other types of global market. This is in part because it is not easy even for a major corporation to move its operations to a different location, particularly when the preferred location is in a different country. In addition, the cost of labor is but one factor which corporations weigh when making decisions regarding plant location. Frequently it will be less important than concerns for political stability, labor skill, location of raw materials, convenience of markets, or the business climate.

Those selling labor, the workers themselves, are generally less mobile than corporate enterprises. Apart from scientists and technicians and, to a lesser degree, management, workers cannot easily move anywhere in the world where they can get the best return for their labor. However, laborers do sometimes have mobility, as is illustrated by the influx of Mexican workers into the United States and that from Eastern Europe into Western Europe. To some degree official channels of immigration allow laborers to move to areas where their prospects are brighter. Many of the Jewish people migrating from Russia to Israel, for example, appear to be motivated more by a desire for economic improvement than by religious concerns. Moreover, even laborers who are not physically mobile compete in the global labor market by accepting lower wages, fewer benefits, or more flexible work rules in order to attract potential employers to the areas where they live.

Nonetheless, a nascent global market for labor exists, and it has somewhat diminished relative wage levels in industrialized nations and elevated them in developing nations. This tendency has not equalized wage rates across the globe; enormous differences remain. Even within the United States, where there are no significant political or social impediments to labor mobility and people migrate easily from state to state, there remain significant differences in prevailing wage rates in various areas of the nation. Furthermore, the threat of relocation or the promise of entry can be potent factors motivating politicians to attempt to reverse corporate relocation plans and make equally determined exertions to tempt corporations to locate in their domains. This prospect has given multinational corporations influence over politicians which they have not been slow to use to their advantage. Moreover, the fact that there is a global market for labor is helping to fuel the development of a global economy in the sense that corporations will be tempted to move to nations partly by the prospect of lower cost labor, and corporate relocation will thus help to expand the number of areas of the world participating in the global economy.

In addition, a global market for various sorts of services, including financial services (particularly those of banking and accounting), law, and advertising is emerging. In part the global expansion of the market for services is parasitic on the global activity of other domains. The demand that advertising agencies be able to mount worldwide advertising campaigns, for example, results from the fact that their clients are often multinational corporations whose products are offered in many parts of the world and who wish to develop coordinated advertising strategies for them.

In similar fashion legal and financial services are being pressed into international service by developments in other markets. Once again, large multinational corporations are likely to demand that firms working with them be able to function across the entire range of locales where these megaliths are present. Also, the evolution of large, extremely complex business arrangements requires legal and financial services able to match their scope and complexity. In the area of financial services, the development of a global market in capital has pushed banking into the global arena. As before, pressures of the market require it. And, as in the case of advertising, the operations on a global scale favor increased size and the creation of close business contacts with smaller, largely regional firms, and this in turn is likely to spawn additional opportunities for global activity.[30]

Though the rush of various services into the global arena is parasitic on developments in other markets, this development is also likely to feed upon itself by creating opportunities and giving advantage to firms able to function on a global scale. Hence, an autonomous global market in services of these types is apt to emerge.

But entry of various service firms into the global arena is likely to have another consequence. Services tend to devise their own standards and regulatory institutions. Hence, as various services enter the global economy, they are apt to broaden their standards of professional procedure and stretch the range of their regulatory institutions to encompass the world. This will help standardize the market but will also open the market for others, since common and uniform standards will make entry to the global arena less difficult. Moreover, it will remove some of the authority local bodies now enjoy and transfer it to the global arena.

In addition, an ever-broadening global market also exists for what is loosely called 'intellectual property'. Two main types of intellectual property exist; one is what can be broadly termed technological information and the second is what can loosely be called cultural products.

Commercially traded technological information commonly takes the form of patented or copyrighted material, the latter including such things as computer software. These are commercially important elements of the current revolution in technology. Nations and corporations lacking important patents and copyrighted technical material are keenly aware that they must gain access to them if they are to hope to become active participants in the global economy.

The trade in technological information has a two-fold impact. On the one hand, there are enduring pressures to formulate technological information into a common currency so that it is easier to transfer and put to use. The reason is that such measures expand the potential market for these products. Akin to this pressure is the attempt to establish universal rules governing the transfer and use of technology by seeking universal agreement on patent laws and licensing agreements. Thus far, there has been no significant global agreement on these matters, though a number of individual nations are working to gain broader acquiescence to patent and copyright laws.

However, another aspect of the global market in technological information is that the scientists and engineers who produce it are anxious to keep in touch with one another and exchange information. Keeping abreast of new developments and consulting with others are vital facets of scientific activity. Scientists are keenly interested in foreign scientific journals and have been quick to employ computer technology to keep in touch with one another. However, there is now conflict between those who wish to preserve the traditional free flow of scientific information and those who are eager to exploit its economic value and therefore wish to restrict its dissemination.

Hence, people across the world are keenly interested in gaining technological information and also keenly interested in exchanging it. Moreover, the language of technology is increasingly universal, so barriers of language or culture are diminishing. To the extent that such barriers remain, they will soon be eroded by the many advantages to be gained by broadened access to scientific information.

However, there are also efforts to regulate the flow of this information by establishing global rules controlling patents, royalties, and licensing fees. Thus far, there has been no significant global effort to establish such rules; the endeavor has largely had the form of bilateral dealings of particular nations, most often the United States, attempting to gain agreements on such matters. US efforts have met with mixed success because many nations have lively interest in gaining access to such technology as cheaply as possible, and some nations have made bold to proclaim that knowledge is the universal right of mankind and thus should not be subject to legal control or commercial restriction. An additional factor is that many governments simply lack the resources to adequately enforce such agreements even if they should accept them.

The cultural aspect of intellectual property has its distinctive impact on human life. Movies and television programs are now exchanged on a global basis, books to a lesser degree. The overall impact of this activity is difficult to gauge. Partly this is because the market is somewhat distorted in that American films and television programs dominate the global market to the exclusion of the products of those in other nations. Thus far, only American efforts, for better or for worse, appear to have formulated a genuinely global idiom that transcends the bounds of language and culture and appeals to all (the idiom, unfortunately, consisting largely of soap operas and violent adventure films). This may generate a global, commercial, consumer culture; though it is unclear what impact, beyond the creation of common tastes for consumer products, this will have on the deeper attitudes and beliefs of the various peoples of the world, whether it will result in greater international understanding and cooperation or remain the fluff of commercial endeavor. It is most disturbing, of course, that the universal idiom is thus far composed of films awash in violence, but once again it is not clear what the further impact of this may be.

Institutions

The basic institutions of global commerce can be sorted into two types. One is, of course, multinational corporations. The second is the various official and semi-official institutions that have emerged since the Second World War in response to the pressures of global commerce. Each type of institution has made its distinctive imprint on global commerce and on the nation-state.

Multinational corporations have received a great deal of attention in the past twenty years, and the response to them has been strongly polarized, either enthusiastically in favor or doggedly against. They are clearly among the most visible of the agents of global commerce. Their corporate logos are, as those of Coca-Cola or Toyota, familiar sights and their products intrude on many lives. As often as not, they arouse fear, because their often enormous size, vast financial resources, and political influence gives them considerable power over workers, local economies, and national governments.

It is difficult to determine whether the conditions that existed following the Second World War spawned multinational corporations or whether the corporations existed first then worked to create circumstances to suit their activity. However, it is clear that multinational corporations have been the primary vectors which spread and nurture the global economy. They have done so by pushing their way into one local market after another, then stitching them together to create a global market. They have also played a major role in knitting the world together into a unified economic whole by establishing manufacturing centers, research and design centers, as well as corporate offices in a wide array of nations.

Their ability to skip from one nation to another has given multinational corporations considerable power, since they can threaten to move operations elsewhere if conditions in a nation do not suit them, or they can dangle the lure of investment and jobs to gain significant advantages from nations that seek their presence. Their mobility often allows them to skirt the control and supervision of host nations. For example, clever accounting procedures can shift tax liabilities from one nation to another, or can shift them out of the gaze of tax collectors altogether.[31] More significantly, their size, power, and resources sometimes enable them to overawe developing nations where they invest.

Because multinational corporations in the 1960s and 1970s were thought to possess great power, many also believed that they had completely escaped the control of nation-states and perhaps become more powerful than nation-states. These fears have largely subsided. In part this is a result of the growing number of multinational corporations who compete with one another to gain access to markets and manufacturing sites and allow nation-states to play one off against another in seeking business arrangements. In another part, fear of multinational corporations has subsided because nation-states have become increasingly skilled at bargaining with them to gain advantages for themselves. Nations have also learned to establish collective sources of information and expertise to enable them to cope more effectively with multinational corporations.[32]

But something else has occurred as well. In the past two decades the corporations of ever increasing numbers of nations, including significant numbers of developing nations, have also begun to engage in significant multinational activity. In fact some of the largest and most successful multinational corporations now originate in developing nations, such as Thailand and India. Part of the power and distrust that multinational corporations spawned several decades ago resulted from the fact that they were seen as the representatives of the powerful nations of their origin. The burgeoning number of multinational corporations and the greater number of nations serving as home nations of multinational corporations has worked to erode the perception that multinational corporations are the cat's paws of one or several powerful nations.

An additional feature of the developing global economy is that there is a significant global market for corporations themselves; they are bought, sold, combined, split asunder, and recombined in a complex and bewildering array of arrangements. This complexity and fluidity of ownership and corporate structure has often made it nearly impossible to determine precisely whether a given corporation is American, Japanese, British, or German in origin or ownership.[33] Hence, corporations have often become independent of particular nation-states in one important sense, that in which they are no longer obviously institutions *of* one particular nation or another. This complexity of ownership and erosion of national identification results in other complexities, since it may no longer be clear which nation controls which technologies of particular corporations or whether the best interests of the nation are most effectively served by favoring a particular corporation or keeping it at arm's length.[34]

The other set of official and quasi-official institutions active in the global economic arena is far more diverse, but it has significant effects on global trade and the activities of the governments of nation-states. Prominent among these are the World Bank and the International Monetary Fund, which are able to wield enormous influence over national governments by virtue of their control of enormous funds of investment capital. However, an array of other institutions also play important roles, roles which are likely to grow in importance as the global economy continues to develop. Of primary importance among these is the World Trade Organization, the body charged with overseeing the transition to a free world economy. It evolved from the General Agreement on Tariffs and Trade, a series of multilateral negotiations among the various major economic powers of the world devoted to establishing guidelines on policies regulating international trade and serving as a forum for addressing trade disputes – the ultimate goal of which is to remove all significant barriers to free trade among the nations participating. The very existence of the WTO and GATT is significant because they have no supernational authority. Their function and continued existence depend completely on the good will, cooperation, and interests of the nations who support them. However, it is also important because nations have generally viewed it to their advantage to participate – to be part of a system working toward completely free trade – even at the cost of forfeiting some of their own ability to control national trade policies.[35]

Other, lesser known, institutions include the various legal and quasi-legal organizations designed to aid in the resolution of conflicts between nations and corporations. Such institutions play an important role in the development of a global economy because they help fix and regularize the rules which regulate international commerce. By doing so, they make such interactions predictable and remove some of the barriers to participation. But, they also have the effect of creating a body of procedures, rules, and de facto laws to govern international trade; this in turn encourages more participants, whether nations or corporations, to enter the arena of international commerce; they are encouraged because they have a clear understanding of the rules of the game.

Laws and regulations

There is presently no international body or set of bodies with indisputable authority to unilaterally establish or enforce laws and regulations to regulate the varied facets of multinational commerce, nor are any such institutions likely to emerge in the foreseeable future. The reason for this is the creation of institutions with definitive sovereign authority is unlikely to be accepted by the nation-states of the world. Nation-states thus far appear to be willing to parcel out portions of their sovereignty in piecemeal fashion, but they are unlikely to countenance an overt, official abdication of their sovereign authority.

Instead, it appears that a complex array of rules, agreements, oversight bodies, and quasi-governmental bodies, such as various bureaus of the United Nations, are emerging in ad hoc and piecemeal fashion to meet the needs of the various participants in the arena of multinational commerce. In this sense the rules and regulations are parasitic on the development of global markets, on the emergence and activity of multinational corporations, and on the appearance of problems that must be addressed by the majority of the nations of the world if they are to be managed effectively. (Arms control and environmental destruction are salient examples of these sorts of difficulties.) As a result of this complexity, problems of global commerce are managed by a variety of differing, though sometimes overlapping, devices. Conflicts regarding contracts, for example, may be referred to the International Court of Justice in the Hague or the International Arbitration Panel. There is no one set of rules governing multinational trade but a variety of treaties, common practices, and multilateral agreements.

Nevertheless, as global commerce continues to develop and the need for regularized methods for setting standards of conduct and resolving disputes becomes more apparent, it is likely that this array of rules and treaties will be expanded and also that it will come to have more of the force of sovereign law, because of the enuring effect of longstanding practice but also because the participants will come to desire that the rules have greater force. The demands of global enterprise will force them to do so.

None of the developments sketched in this chapter are irreversible. Neither is it the case that the continued emergence of a global economy is inevitable, nor is it the case that the stitchwork of regulations and institutions devoted to sustaining and nurturing it must continue to develop and thicken. A collapse of social order resulting from environmental disaster, resource depletion, or exploding population growth may suffice to reverse the process. Political developments, such as a triumph of Islamic fundamentalism, resurgent xenophobic nationalism, or revived socialist revolution could also derail the developments of recent decades. A loss of political will might also effectively halt the process. Nonetheless, the argument of this chapter supports the view that the continued evolution of a global economy is by far the most probable of the prospects for the future. Moreover, the forces that propel it are apt to make any setbacks resulting from the above possible counter-developments temporary rather than permanent.

2 National Sovereignty

The modern nation-state and the concept of sovereignty emerged together. There is no necessary conceptual link between the two, since the idea of sovereignty could as well have been devised by the citizens of the Greek polis, but they are tightly linked in Western European history. However, recent history has begun to prise the two apart and erode conditions which have supported them and made them significant for the past several centuries. Because they are changing, our ideas about them must change as well.

THE HISTORICAL BACKGROUND

The nation-state is several hundred years old. It emerged as the feudal era of Western Europe was pushed aside by a new social and political order in which the predominant role of nobility and kings was supplanted by a rising class of tradesmen. The impact of the change required several hundred years fully to emerge; it awaited the revolutionary movements of the seventeenth and eighteenth centuries to replace monarchies with republics, mostly liberal and democratic and mostly under the sway of the rising bourgeoisie class. A salient feature of the new order is that it allowed an overtly secular state to emerge, a state independent in power and authority from the Medieval Church of Rome. The conception of sovereignty was developed to account for this distinctive feature of emerging nation-states.

The Medieval states of Western Europe, at least in theory, were subservient to the Medieval Church. Hence, they were not, in theory once again, independent entities but were constituents of a larger body. Furthermore, the legitimacy of these states depended on their relation to the Church; they gained authority to rule only if they enjoyed the sanction of the Church. This set of relationships was complicated by the distinction between sacred and secular authority; sacred authority belonged to the Church while the secular was the domain of feudal princes. However, secular authority, if it was to be legitimate, had to receive its warrant from the sacred authority of the Church.

The distinctly modern nation-state could emerge only after this link between sacred and secular authority was severed.[1] Its claim to sovereignty does not derive from the authority of any other body; it possesses sovereignty in its own right. In addition, the significant extramural relations of nation-states are with other nation states; they deal mainly with their peers and do so on equal terms (at least in theory).

Nation-states are the predominant political institutions of the present age. No other institutions have authority over them, and in one way or another all others are subject to their control. For this reason the political philosophy of the past several hundred years has focused on them and their relations to individual persons. A central feature of the nation-state, shared with the dominant political structures of every human era, is that it stand alone and is independent. The presumption that the predominant political system of a given age must be self-sustaining and free-standing can be traced back at least as far as Aristotle, who claimed that a *polis* must have resources sufficient to exist alone.[2] The basis of his assertion is simple and obvious: a body lacking the wherewithal to be self-sustaining and independent would soon cease to be a distinct entity; it would either disappear or be absorbed into a more robust polity.

Furthermore, a political body must be a genuine unity and not an undifferentiated mass, such as a heap of stones or pile of leaves. Part of what makes it a unity is that its citizens have a sense of being part of a distinct whole, in modern terms they must share a sense of national identity, a sense of *being* British, Japanese, Egyptian, or American.[3] Another part of what makes a nation-state a unity is that it is able to *act* as a single unit. To do so, however, it must possess a structure which allows it to function as a whole. This organizing structure is provided by a national government, which must be able to control the organism if it is to carry out its function of causing the body of the nation to *act* in coordinated fashion.

Political philosophers have diverse opinions on the matter of what the government should seek to *do* with this controlling power (whether the government is that of the nation-state, Greek polis, or Medieval monarchy). Locke thought the ultimate function of national government is protecting private property.[4] Aristotle thought the ultimate function of government must be to establish good lives for citizens and to make them *good* people.[5] Marx believed the function of national government is to serve as the instrument of oppression of the dominant class within the state.[6] However, all agree that government must be in firm control of the state; otherwise it would lack organic unity and would either fly apart or come under the control of another state. Thomas

Hobbes held the extreme view that this function of retaining control and thus preserving the unity of the state can be the *only* function of the government.[7]

Unlike organisms of other sorts, the state is immobile. Though it can act and make its presence felt beyond its borders, it cannot transport itself through space; it is confined within its recognized boundaries. Its boundaries, in the normal course of events, are fixed and commonly acknowledged, particularly by other nation-states.

The state therefore is a free-standing and independent political unit located within clearly defined political boundaries. It is regarded as a peer by other states and not subservient to any other institution. It is controlled by a sovereign government whose authority is acknowledged by its citizens. However, these qualities do not distinguish a nation-state from a Greek polis or a Medieval monarchy. It is distinct from these political entities in that its citizens share a sense of national identification; they (and their government) share the sense of being a people with a common way of life, language, and culture which is located within particular geographic boundaries.

It is possible that the above conceptual features of the nation-state are no more than theoretical presumptions which have never described any actual state with complete accuracy. For example, only a very few nations, such as Japan or Iceland, possess the sort of homogeneous national identity associated with the concept of 'nation'. Moreover, the forces of the emerging global economy are profoundly affecting each of the commonly accepted features of the nation-state and are pressing it to evolve into a significantly different type of entity. As a result, in coming decades the traditional conceptions of the nature of the nation-state will become even further removed from reality. In fact, the pressures of the global economy have already begun to alter central features of the nation-state and make the traditional conceptions less obviously applicable to them.

This chapter will examine the pressures which the global economy has placed on the sovereignty and territorial integrity of the nation-state. Chapter 3 will investigate the ways in which the global economy is eroding, and will continue to erode, the sense of national identification which has molded groups of people together into single political units and allowed governments plausibly to proclaim that they are governments of *a people*. A succeeding chapter will address the ways in which the global economy is reshaping the basic role of the nation-state and its relations to other nation-states. Another chapter will canvass the ways in which the pressures of the global economy are breaking national governments apart into various smaller, less formal governing units.

SOVEREIGNTY IN CONCEPTION AND PRACTICE

Western European political theorists, beginning with Jean Bodin and continuing via Hobbes and John Locke to present day practitioners, generally presume that the most significant feature of national governments is that they are sovereign.[8] In contrast to Bodin and Hobbes, however, latter day theorists have come to recognize that sovereignty is complex and multifaceted.[9] It encompasses, as one facet, the relationship of a national government to its citizens and, as a second, its relationship to other governments. The internal aspect of the sovereignty of states includes physical control over citizens made possible by monopoly control of the instruments of violence, but it also includes something very different: ultimate legal authority. Legal authority is distinct from physical control; it has the attribute of *legitimate* authority which may differ entirely from physical control, as when a government in exile is deemed to have legal authority over its citizens though it lacks the wherewithal to achieve physical control.

The external aspect of sovereignty, the relation of national governments to other states, is the claim to freedom from exogenous coercion and meddling. In the twentieth century, this feature of sovereignty is considered sufficiently important to have been specifically endorsed in the United Nations' charter.[10] Moreover, it has become the foundation of the relations of states to one another. (Though the principle is frequently violated in practice.)

External Sovereignty

The internal and external aspects of sovereignty are closely related not only conceptually but also by the circumstances of world affairs. For example, successful violent revolutions generally must gain physical supremacy first and can only then attain legal authority. The world is such that legal authority usually counts for little without physical control, but physical dominance commonly brings legal authority in its train. Though these two facets of sovereignty normally go hand in hand, they are nonetheless *conceptually* distinct and, given appropriate circumstances, may go their separate ways. This occurred in 1990 when numerous governments of the world continued to recognize the government of Kuwait and maintain embassies in Kuwait City even though Kuwait was under the firm control of Iraq. Similarly, many governments retained formal relations with the governments-in-exile of the Baltic States of Latvia, Lithuania, and Estonia during the fifty years when these nations were under the firm control of the Soviet Union.

Nonetheless, the usual practice of the twentieth century is for nations to acknowledge the sovereignty of governments (in the sense of recognizing their claim to immunity from external meddling) that have, by whatever means and whatever their character, come to enjoy sovereign dominion over their citizens. Because of this, a plausible claim to external sovereignty is dependent on at least de facto possession of internal sovereignty. This linkage is not inevitable, however, as the case of the regime of South Africa illustrates. The South African government clearly enjoyed both legal and physical control of its citizens during the entire period of apartheid, and most governments of the world maintained relations with South Africa and recognized its government. But these factors did not prevent them from intruding in its affairs to motivate it to change its policies.

The usual diplomatic practice of linking external sovereignty to internal sovereignty is based partly on expediency and partly on the sorry history of the relations between nation-states. The pressure of expediency is due to the fact that governments generally find it very important to have relationships with national governments whom they detest or with whom they are bitter foes. The world generally grants recognition to governments formed after successful coups, even when the resulting government and its leaders are unsavory. Hence, the United States and much of the rest of the world recognized the government of Saddam Hussein of Iraq and, prior to the Gulf War, provided it with considerable material assistance. They did so even though they were keenly aware of the repressive and brutal nature of his government and that he had gained power through treachery and violence. They overlooked his faults because Iraq is significant; it is a nation that is militarily powerful, has control of vital material resources, and is located in an important and fractious part of the world. Moreover, before the war, the recognition of Hussein's government was also an acknowledgement of that government's entitlement to freedom from external meddling. It is a considerable irony that the United States and other governments of the world are now attempting to overthrow Hussein and his government and have been meddling as much as possible in his internal affairs.[11]

However, expediency is not the only reason nations have for lauding the principle of sovereignty, nor perhaps the major reason. The history of the past several hundred years is filled with wanton intrusion by nations in the affairs of others, even to the extent of using physical force or its threat in the attempt to work their will. The most extreme manifestation of this intrusion is the explosion of imperialism in the last century when many of the nations of Europe rushed to gain control of other sectors of the world. The excesses of nineteenth century imperialism were vividly echoed during the Second World War when Germany and its allies contemptuously disregarded the sovereign prerogatives of other nations and subverted them to their rule. Still sore and raw as a result of these abuses, the governments creating the United Nations placed respect for sovereignty high on the list of principles that should govern the relations among nations.[12] A further irony is that the history of the past several years has worked to undo this lesson. It has done so by showing that intrusion into the internal affairs of nations is sometimes necessary to protect the citizens of a nation from their own government, as in the case of South Africa, or from the violence and brutality of their fellow citizens, as is the case in the fragments of what was once Yugoslavia.

Though the practical and emotive connection between possession of internal sovereignty and external sovereignty has now been addressed, the conceptual connection between the two facets has not yet been established. This is no simple chore because the conceptual link between them is customarily taken for granted. Intuitively however, the link appears to be as follows: a government in control of a particular domain is charged with the responsibility of representing its people in their relations with the remainder of the world and also of tending to their interests. Hence, to meddle in the internal affairs of a sovereign nation is wrong because it interferes with the right of self-determination which all peoples possess.[13] However, it is not clear why a people or any other human group should have the right of self-determination.

Internal Sovereignty

Even though the phrase 'the will of the people' is regularly bandied about in political rhetoric and 'respect for the will of the people' is a staple of political speechifying, some foundation must be given for these sentiments if they are to have normative force. It is generally believed that individual persons have the right of self-determination. However, a group differs from an individual person, and the desires of the group may be at odds with those of the individual, as when the individual disagrees with the firmly established customs or habits of the group.

Therefore, an additional presumption must be that the group, whether an ethnic group or the citizens of a nation-state, serves to express the interests and desires of the particular individual.[14] This presumption is required because a government, considered in and of itself and without any connection to the concerns of individual persons, does not have any special claim to be free from meddling, whether internal or external.[15] Therefore, a government's claim to external sovereignty does not stand alone; it must be linked somehow to the concerns of individual persons.

Articulating the chain of presumptions required to give external sovereignty its claim to normative force reveals how tenuous the connections are.[16] Governments frequently gain power by force or subterfuge without displaying any concern for the wishes of their citizenry. Even regimes that can plausibly be said to have come to power as the result of a popular movement do not necessarily have the firm support of all or even a majority of a nation's populace; the 'popular' movement may be simply a mass, though minority, movement which was fortuitously situated to gain political power. Furthermore, even governments with considerable popular support do not always consult the will of their people. In fact, governments with significant popular support not infrequently do things that are distinctly unpopular – the attempts of President Yeltsin's government of Russia to reform its economy is a salient example.[17] In addition, governments are often involved in endeavors for which the general public has no particular concern one way or the other. The efforts of the government of the United States to gain free trade agreements or gain secure international protection of intellectual property rights are signal examples of governmental activity which is of very little concern to the ordinary citizen.

If the conceptual link between the will of the people and the activity of government is at best tenuous, the connection between the concerns of a group and the concerns of particular individuals is even more so. As hinted above, there is often no obvious sense in which 'will of the people' can be identified. Voting, for example, whether on referendums or for the election of political leaders, seldom achieves unanimity and rarely results in a complete turn-out of the eligible electorate. Furthermore, voters generally can choose only among the options listed on their ballots, and these options may not accord with their genuine desires. Opinion polls, another device often claimed to reveal 'the will of the people', seldom reveal unanimity on any given issue, and polls taken at varying times give varying results. The will of the people, if such exists, is clearly a moving target. Also, as mentioned earlier, many of the projects and policies governments undertake are of little concern to the populace as a whole, or, if they are of concern, it is often because political leaders have undertaken to *build* popular support for their policies. George Bush's effort to generate popular support for the war in the Persian Gulf is a signal example; the American people were initially lukewarm to the prospect of military involvement in the Middle East and came to support the effort only after several months of effort by the Bush administration. There is little reason to believe that the mass of people always gives form and expression to the concerns of the particular individual.

Therefore, there is little reason to believe that simply because a government enjoys internal sovereignty, in the sense of physical or legal control over a population, it is also entitled to external sovereignty. A desire for external sovereignty is often less a concern of ordinary citizens than of the individuals with positions in government – who seek a free hand for their activities and desire the respect and deference of other national leaders.

This feature of the psychology of political leaders may partly explain why nations facing no military threat from abroad yearn to have armies, and the bigger the better. Armies are a potent symbol of nationhood, a sign that a nation is capable of resisting the will of others and of attempting to impose its will on others.[18] Armies are a symbol that a nation capable of standing alone, is self-sufficient and self-dependent in Aristotle's sense. But for weak and impoverished nations that can afford only minimal military forces, symbolism may be all their defense budgets can buy.

Hence, the genuine and defensible reasons nations have for making a guiding principle of respect for the sovereignty of nation-states may reduce to the practical and emotive reasons after all. This result may help explain why concern for the sovereignty of nations has been swept aside so easily when, as when the world is dealing with Iraq, Yugoslavia, Cambodia, South Africa, or Peru, the decision is made to override the concerns of a sovereign government and to attempt to impose the will of the world community on an errant nation-state.[19] When the world community is moved to action and determines it has good cause for intervention, the rhetoric of sovereignty is not sufficient to derail the effort.

The 'Whole Cloth' View of Sovereignty

Though the multifaceted character of sovereignty is apparent to several political theorists, political leaders and the public at large generally do not recognize its complexity.[20] However, all, including political theorists, appear to believe that sovereignty is of a piece, that governments must possess it entirely or not at all. This can be termed the 'whole cloth' view, and it has two facets. One is that sovereignty cannot be held by degrees; that is, sovereign control must be total or it cannot exist at all. The other facet is that sovereign control must range over all domains of political affairs, or, once again, it cannot exist at all. The whole cloth conception of sovereignty is the traditional conception dating from the time of Bodin and Hobbes, though it has recently begun to receive critical examination.[21]

Where sovereignty is in the hands of a single human 'sovereign', that is, the monarch or dictator of a nation whose government is sufficiently simple and small to be under the entire control of a lone, supreme individual, the whole cloth conception of sovereignty has some prospect of according with reality. However, these circumstances rarely exist at present. Governments are now large and complex, and sovereignty is not held by a single individual but is spread, in varying layers of thickness and thinness, across a variety of persons and institutions. Part of what obscures this complexity is the fact that sovereignty has become a legal term and to some extent a legal fiction. That is, when nations recognize a government, they pledge to respect external sovereignty. There is no provision in contemporary diplomacy for the partial or conditional recognition of a state; it is granted recognition or not. Similarly, from a legal standpoint a government is either a nation's ultimate legal authority, or it is not; as before there is no conceptual space for partial, limited, or conditional sovereignty. The same bifurcated thinking applies to physical control. Governments are deemed either to have complete physical control over their populace or not, with no thought given to the prospect that there may be degrees or fractions of physical control.

The pressure of circumstance, however, occasionally forces practicing politicians, and ordinary students of world events, to recognize some of the complexity of sovereignty. Hence, in the days when Margaret Thatcher was Prime Minister of Great Britain and in the habit of jousting with other members of the European Economic Community, she frequently complained that portions of British sovereignty were at stake, and she was very often entirely correct in her view. For instance, for a number of years the European Economic Community has held discussions aimed at establishing a central banking system and common currency.[22] If these proposals are ever put into practice, the sovereign prerogatives of the members of the Community will be substantially reduced. This is because control of a nation's currency is among the most important facets of its sovereignty, since control of currency is central to regulating the economic affairs of a state. Nonetheless, even in the heat of her battles, Margaret Thatcher was very probably perfectly well aware that, if she were outmaneuvered by the continentals, the result would not drain *all* the sovereign prerogatives from her island, nor even a major portion of them.

The whole cloth view of sovereignty, embedded in conventional wisdom and flaunted in the rhetoric of politicians, is a serious misconception, and a more complex formulation must be introduced as a corrective. National governments, as a matter of fact, possess greater or lesser degrees of sovereignty, whether in terms of physical control, legal authority, or freedom from outside meddling. Governments may, in addition, enjoy sovereign control in some areas but not in others. Also, sovereign authority is occasionally held jointly by a number of agents. Furthermore, nations that profess to acknowledge the sovereign autonomy of other governments nonetheless commonly intrude in their affairs. It is highly unlikely that the whole cloth conception of sovereignty has ever accurately reflected the world's political reality. Certainly it does not at present. Moreover, the pressures of global economic unification accentuate its deficiencies.

CHALLENGES TO THE TRADITIONAL VIEW OF SOVEREIGNTY

National governments must relinquish portions of their sovereignty when they take collective measures to curb arms transfers, combat environmental pollution, regulate international finance and commerce, or strengthen economic ties with one another. Each agreement that commits national governments to act in concert to address such matters diminishes their control over their individual policies and fates.

Some may argue that the sovereignty of national governments remains intact even in these cases, since they are free to withdraw from their agreements or simply refuse to honor them. However, many of these abrogations of sovereignty will eventually become permanent and irreversible. After multinational agreements have been in force for long periods, it will become very difficult for individual governments to reclaim the prerogatives of their sovereignty. In matters such as the protection of the ozone layer or regulation of hazardous waste disposal, agreements must, if they are to be effective, stipulate that individual nations make firm commitments to honor them. In some instances, as the efforts of the European Economic Community to create financial and commercial union, the agreements are designed to be permanent, and the odds are that they will eventually become so. It is highly probable, however, that the current array of collective endeavors is the tip of the iceberg of international initiatives; new areas requiring joint action and joint restraint are likely to appear in the future. As difficulties of multinational scope multiply and become more pressing, nations will discover that they must sacrifice ever greater portions of their sovereignty.

Furthermore, as economic activity spreads more thickly across national borders, governments' ability to effectively control and manipulate commerce for their own purposes will diminish. Nations' efforts to control patents and intellectual property of other types offer an excellent example of this. In years to come, the strength of individual nations will depend to a considerable degree on their ability to amass and control information, whether in the form of technology, basic science, management techniques, or financial statistics. Yet commercially valuable information is difficult for governments to control and manipulate for their own exclusive purposes.[23] Moreover, the proliferation of global computer and communications networks enormously facilitates the instant transport of information to the far corners of the globe.

In response to this challenge, governments have sought to preserve their control of intellectual property via licensing agreements, treaties and revisions of international law. However, these political maneuvers have resulted in legally sanctioned channels for the transfer of technology and, therefore, have *facilitated* the exchange of information. The problem is exacerbated by the fact that private enterprises often have strong commercial incentives to whisk technology across national borders. Furthermore, governments themselves frequently discover that their interests are best served by dispatching technology abroad. Recently, for example, the United States and the government of South Korea agreed that the ROK would buy a US fighter plane for its military forces. However, South Korea was willing to do so only if it could manufacture the aircraft under license. To reach agreement the United States government had to accept this condition and agree to the transfer of technology required for the manufacturing process.[24] The efforts of national governments to retain control of technology developed within their borders, therefore, are under continual pressure from private enterprise, from the measures governments themselves take to regulate its transfer, and also from the demands of their other interests.

The global integration of economic relations has eroded the perquisites of national sovereignty in yet other ways. Successful economic endeavor, as the nations of Eastern Europe have discovered, requires free movement of people and information within and across national boundaries. At present a necessary condition for active participation in the international economy is that nations open their borders. However, to the extent that governments relinquish the means to closely regulate the flow of people, information and commerce, a portion of their sovereignty slips from of their grasp.

The pressures of global economic interdependence are therefore affecting the ability of governments to physically and legally control their citizens and are pressing them to intrude more vigorously in one another's affairs. This erosion of sovereignty sometimes occurs in piecemeal fashion, when governments cede control of one area or another of governing activity, and sometimes takes the form of pressing them to relinquish some degree of control over their internal affairs.

So long as individual persons, governments, and political theorists accept the whole cloth view of sovereignty, they will have difficulty grasping the reality of the present era and addressing its problems. The whole cloth view has blocked recognition that the sovereignty of governments has already been significantly eroded in some areas and is under siege in others. Moreover, the pace and scale of erosion is apt to increase in future years as the economic integration of the globe progresses. As this occurs, present conceptual inadequacies will become more serious, and the need to remedy them will become more evident.

However, it is unlikely that governments will explicitly acknowledge a wholesale diminution of their prerogatives and their authority; they are more apt to continue to barter away bits and fragments of their sovereign authority as circumstances require but still seek to avoid making the explicit conceptual changes that would allow them to address these developments in forthright fashion. It is likely that more adequate conceptions of sovereignty will gradually creep into ordinary language and ordinary practice – simply to meet the requirements of the changes in human life that are taking place.

Internal Sovereignty

Nonetheless, it is important to devise a more adequate conception of sovereignty, partly to better address future problems but also to allow a firmer grasp of present reality. Consider the changes that would have to be made in the traditional view of sovereignty if it were recognized that governments will not be able to retain their customary degree of control of their national borders or of the individual persons resident within these borders. It appears inevitable that sovereignty under such circumstances can no longer be adequately described in simple terms as unconditioned and self-sustaining authority.

National 'sovereignty', or what remains of it, will likely come to resemble the remnants of sovereignty presently held by the individual states of the United States. The federal government formally defers to the prerogatives of individual states, as required by the US Constitution; states can enact and enforce legislation, but they cannot override the explicit provisions of the Constitution, nor can they override federal laws. Early in the history of the United States, the states made vigorous efforts to retain the lion's share of governing authority and keep the federal government as a thin overarching shell. However, this effort has long been abandoned.[25] The federal government presently has supreme authority in the United States, and the states retain a measure of free movement and authority only in the space uninhabited by Federal authority. Moreover, states cannot – beyond certain narrow limits – control the movement of people, goods, or institutions across their borders. They are allowed administrative control over such matters, but the ultimate standards which guide their efforts are controlled by the federal government. 'Sovereignty' for individual states of the United States amounts only to administrative control which is limited and subject to federal oversight. In particular, states cannot violate the provisions of the Constitution (the interpretation of which is left to the federal courts), specifically including those of the Bill of Rights of citizens and the succeeding amendments.

The difference between the status of individual states of the United States and the probable future lot of nation-states is that the sovereign power lost by nation-states will not necessarily be transferred elsewhere. In contrast, the sovereign power lost by individual states of the United States is generally transferred to the federal government. The authority of individual nation-states to control the movement of people, goods, or institutions across their borders, once lost may often not be transferred elsewhere; it will certainly not gravitate to some form of world federal government. Instead, it is most likely that the ability to control borders and the movement of people will largely vanish, and there will be less political restriction of the movement of people, goods, and institutions than previously.

Some aspects of internal political authority may well shift to particular international bodies. It is highly likely, for example, that some type of international institution will be needed to control the transnational flow of hazardous wastes and devise standards to regulate the production and disposal of such wastes. It is also likely that an international body will eventually be established to deal with matters of global public health and transmission of disease, concerns which will become more obviously global in character as people become increasingly mobile. Problems of these sorts are too broad to be handled by individual governments or bilateral agreements of governments. They will have to be addressed by genuine international institutions, and those institutions must have power and authority over individual states if they are to function effectively.

However, these international governing bodies are not likely to emerge as portions of an encompassing world federal government; it is probable that they will be free standing and that they will be created by the collective action of nation-states themselves. Nonetheless, once created such institutions are likely to take on lives and authority of their own. That is, they are apt to discover more things to do, and they are also, over time, likely to gain the habit of obedience from individual nation-states in those areas subject to their jurisdiction, and this authority is likely to become more deeply entrenched – particularly as the array and importance of multinational problems increases.[26] Hence, a portion of the sovereign authority now possessed by individual nation-states will simply vanish and another portion be transferred to multinational bureaucratic institutions with jurisdiction held narrowly over one particular area or another.

The above discussions reveal ways in which the internal sovereignty of governments is likely to be challenged and to erode. The inability to regulate borders, and hence the inability to control the movements of citizens, products, and institutions across national borders erodes the ability of governments to physically control their citizens. Moreover, the events of the previous decades and those of decades to come will also have consequences for the legal authority of national governments, that is, their ability to enact and enforce legislation and to make decisions about how to interpret statutes. Increasingly, as previous discussions have shown, laws, regulations, procedures, and quasi-judicial bodies will become international in character, and the legal systems of particular states will be subservient to them. National statutes regarding intellectual property, environmental controls, professional standards, mechanisms for settling disputes which cross national borders, and even the protection of citizens' basic rights are all likely to come under international jurisdiction of one sort or another.

Another development also looms on the horizon; citizens of particular nations cannot now press charges against their own government in international tribunals. Proposals to allow this were made when the United Nations was founded.[27] However, they were soon abandoned in the face of hostile response by national governments loathe to accept an overt rein on their sovereignty. In future years such proposals are likely to be revived and, given a continuation of the present climate of international cooperation and emphasis on collective action, it would be safe to wager that such proposals will eventually be accepted and, with the passage of time and the accretion of a body of international judicial opinion and practice, the scope of such challenges is likely to expand.

External Sovereignty

Also, there will be significant changes in the external aspect of the sovereignty of nation-states. The external sense has two faces: that of the nation (under the guise of its agent of action, its national government) which demands respect for its integrity and freedom of action; and that of other nations who acknowledge an obligation to respect the freedom of action of individual states and refrain from meddling in their affairs. Each of these aspects of external sovereignty will be transformed but in differing ways.

In future years it is likely that individual nation-states will be unable to demand complete freedom from external interference by others, whether individual nation-states or the world community. This is partly because the claim to total immunity from external influence will become increasingly meaningless; as institutions, products, and individual people become more mobile and gain more numerous ties to others in foreign nation-states, governments will have diminished ability to control them. Such movements will be inherently more difficult to control, since easy cross-border travel and thick transnational ties of business, culture, or society are more difficult for governments to regulate. In addition, institutions and people will be increasingly able to 'vote with their feet', that is, leave, if they disagree with the policies of a particular government. Even if they do not leave, the possibility of emigration may serve as an effective rein on governmental power.

The above matters, however, may only make claims to sovereignty into increasingly hollow shells; it is possible that they will not directly challenge the idea of sovereignty. Other developments are likely to place explicit limits on the reach of external sovereignty. Salient among these are international agreements to control pollution, disposal of hazardous waste, or infectious diseases. Effectively addressing these matters requires mandatory compliance by individual nation-states. In addition, the practical requirement of commonly accepted standards and regulations to govern financial and commercial activities will effectively reduce the power of individual nation-states to do so – and increasingly dense ties of global commerce will correspondingly broaden the array of matters best governed by transnational regulation.

On a slightly loftier plane, the spluttering halt of the Cold War has removed the distorting factor of East/West rivalry from international relations and has opened space for international bodies such as the United Nations to begin claiming some of the role and authority which their creators intended.[28] The nations of the world are now more likely to be able to agree on a genuinely effective set of minimal standards to guide the conduct of national governments. There are grounds for hope on this matter because many of the new governments of the remnants of the former Soviet empire are particularly anxious to honor such standards and make them genuinely effective. Hence, nation-states in future years may come under considerable pressure to adopt minimal standards of rights for their citizens, and perhaps even feel substantial pressure from international bodies should they fail to do so. Recently, the newly revived United Nations has taken several steps in this direction by inserting itself more vigorously into several areas of crisis in the world. It is particularly significant that it has done so with the full encouragement and assistance of the major world powers.

Another development is also likely to reduce the importance of external sovereignty; it is that the significant power of the world has become economic rather than military. The United States is the remaining military superpower of the world, but this status has become quite hollow. The real powers of the world will increasingly be the economic powers, of which Japan and unified Germany are the salient instances. Lacking military tension, control of military power becomes less relevant. Furthermore, the effort to maintain military power has become outrageously expensive and can only be maintained by a vigorous economy.

However, military force is under the direct control of government in a way that economic power is not. Economic power is diffuse, and, in the era of a global economy, surges across national borders and beyond the supervision of national governments. Hence, military forces, the symbols of nationhood and instruments of national preservation, are less important to power and are being replaced in importance by economic factors. But economic forces drain the vitality of national sovereignty rather than nurture it. Hence, to the extent that sovereignty is dependent upon control of military forces, its significance is ebbing.

The demise of an era in which one or a few states enjoy the ability to physically coerce other states with impunity has another consequence. This ability was partly responsible for keeping the whole cloth conception of sovereignty alive; only if powerful states rely on the rhetoric of sovereignty to validate their prerogatives of influence and freedom from coercion can the unadulterated idea of sovereignty remain viable. Lesser states are largely without the resources to withstand the collective efforts of other nations to influence them. To the extent that the United States' lofty status as a military superpower is of diminished consequence, it must learn to deal with other nation-states as peers and address common problems via cooperation, conciliation, and compromise. In the past it often sought to coerce other states but then sought refuge in the perquisites of sovereignty when the world community wished to influence its own policies. The rising economic powers of Japan and Germany lack this lofty and unapproachable status. Though they are first among equals, they are not likely to become more than first among equals and must therefore compromise and conciliate like everyone else.

In addition, for much of the era of the nation-state, political boundaries have also been economic boundaries. People within one nation-state could anticipate economic opportunity of one sort or another simply because they were members of that nation-state, and they could generally expect to be more or less prosperous simply because they resided in one nation-state rather than another. Hence, the economic system of a given nation-state was generally confined within its borders and could be controlled by its government. This coincidence of economic and political boundaries is crumbling; the economies of the world are increasingly interlinked, and governments have less control over economic endeavor within their borders because commerce within their borders is increasingly shaped by events and decisions outside them. In fact, the governments of the most powerful nation-states now recognize that they cannot control their economic destinies alone; hence, nation-states have grouped together to jointly address economic issues that the individual states could not hope to manage by acting singly.

Thus, in future years nation-states' claims to external sovereignty are unlikely to be claims to complete immunity from external interference; nation-states will be forced by the pressure of circumstance to acknowledge explicit limits on their claim to be free of external coercion.

It is also likely that the perspective of nation-states in position to acknowledge the external sovereignty of others will also change. In part this is because the nation-states of the world have become sufficiently closely knit to compel all to recognize that developments in other nations often have repercussions in their own. Hence, they will be forced to recognize that it is no longer possible to isolate the affairs of one nation from those of another. It is also less likely that nation-states will be disposed to consider the diplomatic recognition of the government of a nation-state to be tantamount to a pledge to refrain from all attempts to intervene in its affairs. In order to protect the intellectual property rights of its citizens, for example, the United States has worked diligently to pressure the governments of other nations to enact legislation which recognizes legal rights to intellectual property and is pressuring these governments to enforce these rights. Or, when the government of one nation determines to raise its interest rates, the governments of other nations will often recognize that their own economies will be directly affected and make vigorous protest; nation-states no longer accept the view that the monetary interest rates of one nation are strictly an internal matter and of no legitimate interest to others.

Furthermore, to the extent that nation-states come to accept the view that each individual human has a particular minimal set of rights which ought never to be violated, they have an incentive also to accept the view that nation-states *lack* entitlement to freedom from external coercion in matters of human rights. However, nation-states need not accept the view that they as individual governments are thereby entitled to intrude in the affairs of other nation-states once they have made the judgment that a government has violated the rights of its citizens. Rather, governments are coming to believe that such concerns should be the *collective* interest of the world community, whether they are addressed by the United Nations or some other international group, such as the European Conference on Peace and Security.[29]

Hence, diplomatic recognition of the government of a nation is no longer equivalent to acknowledging an obligation to entirely refrain from intrusion in its affairs. The pledge of non-interference is likely to be hedged in various ways – though the primary mode of interference, should the occasion arise, is likely to be collective action rather than the solitary initiatives of individual nation-states. In part, the emphasis on collective action is likely to allay the fear that governmental intrusion is being carried out for selfish purposes whether under the guise of altruism or that of protecting the vital interests of the intruding nation. However, another reason is that single governments commonly do not want to bear the full responsibility for such actions, or do not want to accept the risk of getting bogged down by undertaking solitary action in an area of crisis. So, for various reasons the idea is gaining currency that such efforts ought to be collective, even though the implication is that this will result in a further erosion of the sovereignty of individual national governments.[30] This is because an emphasis on collective action implies that single, sovereign nations do *not* have the claim to such intrusion and also that they must acknowledge the prospect that collective pressure will be employed against *them* should they transgress international standards of conduct.

CONCLUSION

The erosion of various facets of sovereignty examined in the discussions above has already become apparent – and it is highly likely that this crumbling will continue as a result of the pressures of globalization. Nonetheless, these changes are not clearly understood; most people appear to feel them rather than grasp them conceptually and some changes may not be felt at all, whether by political leaders, ordinary citizens, or academic theoreticians.

This lacuna is more than a theoretical difficulty. It will have practical consequences if politicians, theoreticians, or ordinary citizens confuse relinquishing a portion of governmental sovereignty with forfeiting all of it, if they fail to recognize that the several aspects of sovereignty may have greater or lesser importance, if they fail to recognize that in many important ways the sovereignty of governments has *already* been seriously eroded, or if they fail to recognize that 'sovereignty' has always been an abstraction which has accorded only approximately to the reality of nation-states. People may fail to develop the political will to accept the agreements, compromises, and regulatory machinery needed to successfully address transnational problems, such as currency regulation, pollution control, or hazardous waste disposal, *all* of which will require that individual governments yield portions of their sovereign authority.

Loss of some facet or other of sovereignty, for example, can vary in importance. Global standards regarding the emission of pollutants will necessarily impinge on the sovereign authority of individual governments to set their own standards – or to avoid any standards at all. (National governments sometimes wish to avoid adopting pollution standards, often in the belief that they may inhibit their pace of economic development or make their nations less attractive to foreign investors.) However, loss of sovereignty in this domain is insignificant when compared to the full array of powers that governments possess. In contrast, loss of control over legal statutes governing the legal rights and liberties of citizens would be a significant erosion of sovereign authority. However, if only the blanket term 'sovereignty' exists to cover the full array of governmental powers, such important distinctions may be overlooked, and public discussion or legislative debate on the issue may be framed in terms of loss of sovereignty understood in the whole cloth sense.

Moreover, the whole cloth view allows and even encourages florid rhetoric concerning the sacred status of a nation's sovereignty – as though sovereignty is a precious possession which, if partly lost, will soon drain away altogether. Hence, failure to understand that significant portions of sovereignty have *already* been lost by national governments, or that sovereignty is not of a piece, will block the further understanding that the whole cloth view is simply false.

The conceptual and theoretical consequences of misunderstanding sovereignty collide with the practical in various ways. For example, if sovereignty fragments further, and the different facets of sovereignty drift apart from one another, the matter of the relation of legitimacy and of popular consent to sovereignty must be reexamined. 'Legitimacy' is the moral title to sovereignty and in popular thought and in theoretical works has been tethered, in the Western European liberal tradition at least, to popular consent.[31] In addition, considerable literature of political philosophy has been addressed to the issue of legitimacy, that is, the conditions under which governments are morally entitled to the obedience of their citizens – or whether such a claim *is able to be* justified at all.[32]

But, if the conclusions of this chapter are correct, the above concerns are mere academic exercises at best and at worst serious misconceptions which distort the true nature of the cases under consideration, or perhaps introduce irrelevant and extraneous factors into legitimate discussions. Consider, for example, the notion of 'consent' and its relation to legitimacy. It may be reasonable to regard consent as the basis of governmental legitimacy when government holds complete power over its citizens and when government, deemed the repository of its citizens' powers, demands recognition of its sovereignty from other nations. However, if political control of citizens is fragmentary, if some of the control national governments once enjoyed has dissolved under the pressures of global economic unification, and if other aspects of political control have been passed to a motley collection of international agencies, the connection between individual wishes and desires and that of governmental regulatory powers is too tenuous to support the whole cloth view of sovereignty.

It is no longer plausible to believe, as Hobbes did, that government is the repository of the collected powers of its citizenry, since examination of present reality indicates that this is not the case. But, it is also less clear what citizens accept if they do consent to the authority of a government – for the government does not have total but only partial control over them and may in fact be in the process of losing sovereign prerogatives (or having them dissolve) under the corrosive influence of the emerging international economy.

Moreover, it is reasonable to ask whether citizen consent is inevitably necessary in cases when governments seek to transfer a portion of their sovereignty to other bodies. On occasion governments have sought popular consent for transfers of this sort. The citizens of European nations have been asked, via plebiscite, to approve measures designed to weld their nations into economic and political unity – with a resultant loss of considerable portions of the autonomy of each constituent government.[33] However, frequently national governments sign treaties, devise agreements, or create international institutions without bothering to consult their citizenry – even when significant portions of national sovereignty are transferred as a result. But, if the agreements serve useful purposes, if they do not violate the rights of individual citizens or harm them, it may be unnecessary that citizen consent be granted for such mechanisms to gain legitimate moral claim to function and wield whatever authority they may possess.[34]

A further difficulty is that international regulatory mechanisms are generally created by governments of nation states and have these governments as their constituencies. Hence, they are directly accountable to governments but not to individual persons. If national governments were simply the agents of their populations and acted only in service of their citizens' interests, this would be unproblematic. However, governments all too frequently adopt interests of their own which have little to do with their citizens' interests and may even be at odds with them.

Another way to approach the issue of legitimacy is by way of human rights; that is, to claim that governments are legitimate if they respect and uphold the human rights of their citizens but not otherwise.[35] There are several difficulties with this approach. For one, respect for human rights may be a necessary condition for governmental legitimacy but it does not suffice to grant governments full moral title to sovereignty. A government may, for example, scrupulously respect the human rights of its citizens but be so grievously incompetent in other respects that all agree that it should be removed. Under these circumstances it could hardly be said that such a government nonetheless has an overriding claim to retain its powers.

But a second difficulty must be addressed if sovereign authority is fragmented; many of the agreements, treaties, procedures, or bureaus established as a result of international agreement have little to do with the human rights of individual persons. Agreements to regulate currency rates or to establish international banking controls have little to do with issues of human rights. But this does not imply that such mechanisms lack moral entitlement to the authority which they possess.

However, the above concerns do not yet touch a more fundamental issue. In a recent plebiscite its citizens declined to accept an agreement which would have bound Denmark more closely to the nations of the European Union. The Danes demurred in part because they opposed the loss of Danish sovereignty.[36] There is a real and important issue here, but formulating it in the language of sovereignty misconstrued and distorted the matter which troubled the Danish voters. Interviews revealed that the Danes were concerned that they would be overwhelmed by the more populous or more powerful nations in the nascent European consortium; they were afraid that they would be forced to accept decisions, regulations, and modes of life and culture that they did not desire and that did not accord with their national way of life.[37]

Concerns that their wishes as a people and that their cultural identity be protected and preserved are legitimate and important, and the Danes are correct in fearing that these would be endangered by steps to forge tighter economic and political links with the other nations of Europe. The countervailing arguments that Denmark would be hurt *economically* if it were frozen out of the European Union and that the nation would be in danger of fading into impoverished marginality are also legitimate and important, but they do not address the Danes' major concerns. It is quite true that the economic and political union envisioned by the European Union will place limitations on member nations' ability to control currency rates, pollution, immigration, and possibly even efforts to protect language and cultural heritage.

However, framing the issue in terms of sovereignty obscures the fundamental difficulty – because sovereignty is the possession of governments and not of citizens. Even governments that are generally democratic and generally responsive to the desires and concerns of their citizens are distinct from their citizens and have interests and concerns apart from those of their citizens. Thus, the genuine issue that confronts the Danes is whether *their own* concerns as individual citizens and as a national group will be adequately respected by the membership of the European Union. When the issue is framed in these terms it becomes clear that the European Union should take steps to ensure that the concerns of individual citizens and the protection of language, culture, and way of life are protected adequately.

It is true that the government of Denmark will lose significant portions of its sovereignty in the new arrangement. By itself, however, this is of little consequence. What is important is that the Danish people are in danger of losing some of their ability to control their individual lives and protect the heritage of their nation. However, steps can be taken to insure that the concerns of the Danish people and similar concerns of other European people are adequately addressed by the European Union.

That said, it must also be acknowledged that the Danish people most certainly *will* lose a significant portion of their ability to control their lives when the new arrangements take effect. Thus, the Dane's concerns are well-founded, and they (and the European Union) must ask whether this loss is reasonable and justifiable. But a response to this issue depends on yet another matter, that of whether the loss is *avoidable*. If the loss cannot be avoided, then the Danes' concerns, however pressing, become moot. Consider the matter of currency control, an important element of the sovereign powers of governments, and one which can have considerable impact on the economic welfare of individual citizens.

The basic fact is that the global economy will continue to emerge regardless of what political measures are taken.[38] Hence, the government of Denmark, along with those of all the other nations of the world, has already lost a significant portion of its ability to control its currency; Denmark, along with all the other nations of the world, is forced to respond to the pressures of the global capital market. Thus, loss of control is inevitable, and the issue which must be addressed is that of whether adequate measures will be taken to manage the world's supply of capital, and these can only be achieved through the collective action of the governments of the world. Similar points can be made regarding matters such as pollution control and the disposal of hazardous wastes. These are true international issues; individual governments or peoples cannot address them in solitary fashion; the issues can only be addressed through the collected action of the nations of the world. Thus, again, the Danes do not have a choice on these matters.

Even language and culture are influenced by the global economy. Global distribution of books and films, not to mention fast food restaurants and consumer products, is reshaping the cultural practices of many of the peoples of the world. The brutal facts are that individual peoples and cultures are increasingly affected by the development of the global economy and are tied more closely to the world as a whole – with the result that they are losing the ability to control their lives and cultures, at least in comparison with years past. Thus, once again, the Danish people do not really have a choice in these matters; the pressures of the global economy will shape them and their lives entirely apart from whatever arrangements are made with the other nations of the European Community. The only choice available to them is that of how they will respond to these pressures. However, assuming they wish to remain part of the world economy and wish to avoid the stagnation and irrelevance likely to accompany an effort to remain aloof, they will have to face these issues whether or not they do so in concert with the other nations of Europe.

Nonetheless, one must assume that, in common with the other problems discussed above, an adequate response to these issues can only emerge from the collective action of the nations of the world. It must be acknowledged, however, that the Danish people *will* lose a portion of their ability to determine their own lives to the extent that they are politically and economically integrated into the European Union. Their concerns on these matters can be addressed by building safeguards into the procedures of the government of the European Union, but also by noting that this loss of national autonomy is proceeding in any case and that the only way to adequately address the difficulties which the Danes, along with most peoples of the world, face, is by means of collective action – and by noting that other nations will also have to formally cede portions of their ability to formulate their own destinies.

Hence, the whole cloth view of sovereignty must be replaced by a more fluid conception in which the authority of governments is distinguished from the agency of individual persons and it is recognized that sovereign authority is not of a piece but can be parceled out as needed to address difficulties of transnational human concern.

Nonetheless, sovereignty *is* a central feature, both conceptually and in practice, of modern national government. In this respect Bodin and those who followed him are correct. Hence, if sovereignty changes, other aspects of governments must change as well, as shall become apparent in the chapters that follow.

3 National Identity

The belief that the human world is an array of distinct peoples, each possessing a keenly felt sense of national identity, each with its indigenous national government, is among the enduring myths of conventional political wisdom. In fact, a sense of national identity follows the creation of political boundaries as often as it precedes them. Once in place, national boundaries frequently create bonds among the people within them, who, as a result, may often develop a sense of identification with the nation where they reside. However, there have been nations, such as the former Soviet Union and Yugoslavia, where a deeply rooted sense of national identity never developed, as demonstrated by the fact that each exploded into ethnic conflict as soon as the bonds of military control were removed.

Nonetheless, the ties of national identity, however they are created, have considerable impact on people's lives. The past several centuries of world history are filled with chronicles of nationalist upheaval and conflict, and current newspapers are awash with accounts of outbursts of nationalist acrimony. Millions of people have died because they were identified with one nation or another, and millions more have been willing to kill because they accepted these classifications. Moreover, some historians argue that the mass wars of the past century and a half, wars unprecedented in their destructiveness and fury, became possible in large part because of the success of politicians' appeal to national identification.[1]

At present, however, potent forces are unravelling the ties of ethnic and national identification and distancing individual persons from their nation-states. Understanding this process requires being aware of the pressures that create bonds of nationhood as well as those that undermine them. Furthermore, the conception of the relation of the individual to the nation-state is embodied in the idea of citizenship, so changes in ties of national identification are apt to prompt changes in the conception of citizenship.

FACETS OF NATIONAL IDENTIFICATION

Despite the looming presence of nationalism in human affairs, the connection between political boundaries, people's sense of national identification, and their sense of ethnic identity is loose, frangible, and frequently artificial.[2] 'Nation' refers to the common life of a politically independent and self-sufficient people along with the institutions they have fashioned, while 'government' is an institution holding sovereign authority and a monopoly of coercive force within a set of political boundaries. The political bounds which define the sovereign domain of a particular government sometimes coincide with the home territory of a people sharing a sense of national identity, but often they do not. Ethnic identity (i.e. the sense of being part of a distinct linguistic and cultural group) differs from both the above; it need not coincide with political bounds or with the domain of national identity. Those sharing an ethnic identity may or may not also believe that they are a distinct nation. Ethnic identification and nationalist aspiration are thus clearly distinct. Sometimes, under certain circumstances, a particular ethnic group will come to view itself as a nation and seek nationhood. Often, however, ethnic groups do not view themselves as constituting nations and have no aspirations to nationhood. (In fact, the idea that there should be a link between ethnic identity and nationhood is a comparatively recent invention; it is only within the last 300 years or so that those who are part of an ethnic group have developed the idea that this may imply that they should also have a distinct nation-state.[3]) Government, national identity, and ethnic identity are, therefore, different and may interact in complex and varied patterns.

For example, both Japan and Great Britain enjoy a richly defined sense of national unity and a national culture that is closely entwined with their political institutions. In Japan a strong sense of national identity coincides with ethnic identity, and these in turn enjoy a close fit with Japanese governing institutions. In Japan there exists a distinctive Japanese people, in the sense of a people sharing a common ethnic identity. This ethnic group coincides (some exceptions aside, such as a substantial Korean minority) with the group of people who consider themselves a union of a distinctive people and territory, that is, the Japanese nation; and this Japanese nation has its own particular government. Very few nations of the world can presently boast the close fit of ethnic group, national identification, and national government that is found in Japan.

Great Britain has never enjoyed the seamless ethnic unity of Japan. It is a melange of several ethnic groups, each with its unique language and culture. Nonetheless, for the most part the various peoples of Great Britain share a vivid sense of nationhood and have developed a close fit between national identification and government. (This is apart from nationalist, separatist movements in Wales and Scotland.) Moreover, immigrants from former British colonies and from politically and economically unsettled portions of Europe have created a nation comprised of far more diverse groups of people with a broader array of ethnic identities than existed in the years when British national identity was formed.[4] This change in demography has placed stress on the sense of national unity prized by the British and helped expose dormant ethnic fissures. Hence, Great Britain can no longer claim the close fit between ethnic identity, national identification, and government it once enjoyed.

In rough fashion the pattern of Britain's recent history is mirrored on a larger geographical scale in the United States. People in the United States willy-nilly have come to define themselves as American despite vast differences in language and culture. Most citizens of the United States, in other words, have a strong sense of national identity accompanied by widely divergent ethnic identities. In fact, this ethnic diversity is part of the distinctive character of the national identity held by people in the United States; it is a nation where there is little pretense of a fit between ethnic identification and national identification. The two are distinct, and the success of the United States in creating a cohesive nation is based on the possibility of this divergence; if the two could not be distinguished, the United States could not exist as a nation.[5] In this regard the United States stands in instructive contrast to the former Soviet Union.

The former Soviet Union, and the surviving republics that form the Commonwealth of Independent States, have discovered to their dismay that they are complex mosaics of people, language, and culture that never achieved a strong sense of national identity over and above their various ethnic identities. Instead, the Soviet Union was a political artifact clamped together by military force.[6] When the adhesive of military coercion was removed, the skim of soviet national identity dissolved as well, and what was once a single political body became a welter of conflicting ethnic and nationalist groups. Thus, the Soviet Union was not able to develop a sense of national identification which had vitality independent of the various ethnic allegiances which existed within it.

Similarly the governments of many of the new nations of the world, those patched together from former colonies, have also discovered they are loose agglomerates of distinct ethnic groups located within arbitrarily fashioned national boundaries and lacking a strong sense of national identity.[7] Their problem, in other words, is the same as that successfully addressed by the United States but unsuccessfully addressed by the former Soviet Union, namely, that of creating a robust sense of national identification independent of various ethnic identifications.

NATIONAL IDENTITY IN POLITICAL PHILOSOPHY

Western European political thought has not devoted much attention to issues of the ties of national identification, nor has it accorded them any great importance.[8] John Locke, for instance, believed that the free agreement of individuals is sufficient to create a state and that bonds of national identification are superfluous. Marx presumed that the common grievances and dismal circumstances of the world's industrial workers of his day transcended national boundaries and would suffice to create a global political movement.

For Locke and Marx national identification was of little consequence and could be ignored. Their perspective on this matter is representative of Western European political thought; no major political thinker in the tradition gives serious attention to issues of national identity or the political importance of ties of ethnic identification.[9] Most have been staunch individualists, assuming that the single person and the relation of the individual to the state is the fundamental issue of political theorizing. Even the pluralists, those who believe that individuals can make political differences only when they function as part of groups, give scant attention to issues of ethnic or nationalist identification.[10] Moreover, Edmund Burke, who was fully aware of the importance of tradition and history in creating political reality, offered little analysis of issues of national identification, ethnic identification, or the political difficulties they pose.[11] None of the most influential contemporary Anglo-American academic philosophers, whether John Rawls, Ronald Dworkin, or Joel Feinberg, give any attention to such matters. Even the so-called communitarians, such as Michael Sandel, Michael Walzer, or Alasdair McIntyre, give only passing attention to these matters in their analyses of the nature and conditions of human community.

However, if the history of the past several centuries (or the current spate of news accounts of ethnic turmoil) contains any obvious lesson, it is that nationalism and ethnic identification are extraordinarily potent catalysts of human events. The difficulty is that recent controversy on the resurgent nationalism of the 1990s (as occurred in the Balkans) conflates nationalism and ethnic identity. The importance of ties of national identity, and their impact on political decisions, is aptly shown by the fate of Marxism in the Soviet Union. While the Bolshevik revolutionaries of 1917 believed that they had established the first beachhead of an international worker's upheaval, the Communist Party wedded itself to nationalist goals barely a decade later when Joseph Stalin wrested control of the Party from Leon Trotsky.[12] However, the Communists seem to have fractured the connection between ethnic identification and nationalist aspiration, but this disassociation proved fleeting for ethnic identification was reattached to nationalist striving soon after the fall of the Soviet Union.

Though Western liberal political philosophy is remiss in overlooking the importance of ties of ethnic and national identification, a complementary mistake is to follow the lead of Hegel and his followers and assume that ethnic unity coincides with national unity, that this is simply a brute fact of human existence, and that there is little point in attempting to examine the forces which create or which erode ethnic and national identifications or which cause the two to merge or overlap.[13] Furthermore, Hegel presumes that the individual is of little consequence apart from an ethnic group or nation. This assumption has always been false, but the economic and political currents of the present day throw its deficiencies into high relief. Certainly focus on the current areas of ethnic unrest and nationalist fervor should not prompt political theorists blindly to follow Hegel's lead.

The key for the political philosophy is to avoid both the unthinking individualism of the predominant Western liberal philosophy and the heedless organicism of the Hegelians. This can be achieved by attending to the forces which undermine and also those which nurture people's sense of ethnic, national, or personal identification.[14] Certain conditions fix and sustain national or ethnic identification and make them *important*, while others submerge them. Moreover, some forces may enhance national identification while eroding ethnic identification, while other forces may have the reverse effect.

THE DYNAMICS OF IDENTIFICATION

For several hundred years the circumstances of human life have made nationalism and the identification of individual persons with particular nations very important. Italy and Germany became unified nations only in the nineteenth century. Prior to that era of conscious struggle for national unification, neither were nations; they were collections of more-or-less independent remnants of feudal groups.[15] National unification required *effort*. It did not develop naturally and is certainly not a primordial human condition.

The experience of Italy and Germany is typical of many nations; that is, they were *created* intentionally rather than growing spontaneously. Many nations of the world resulted from military conquest, as might occur when a prince conquered others or swept regional ethnic groups into his domain. The United States also underwent a period of nation-building which was not complete until the American Civil War finally welded it together. In fact Garry Wills believes that Abraham Lincoln's signal achievement was creating the United States' nationhood.[16] In one respect at least, his view must be correct, for the United States clearly was a nation following the war in a way which it was not earlier.

As can be inferred from the above, nationhood often conflicts with ethnic identity; for nations are commonly created by the military conquest of several ethnic groups followed by an effort to overlay a sense of national identity on the prevailing ties of ethnic affiliation. There is something natural about ethnic groups, in the sense that they are prone to develop among people of a given area who share a language, culture, and mode of life. Nations, on the other hand, are commonly *formed*, and formed most often by military conquest.

Moreover, there appears to be no natural connection between ethnic groups and evolution of the formal government which is associated with nation-states. To be sure, ethnic groups may often have governments and political leaders as well as distinctive governing procedures, but these are frequently informal and suitable only for groups of several thousand people in a relatively compact domain. When nation-states became the predominant form of political unit, formal governing bodies were needed. Furthermore, nation-states allow government of far larger groups of people spread over wider areas of terrain – and hence allow the power and wealth that result from large size. Nation-states also gained resources sufficient for the creation of modern mass armies, the most potent modern military forces. In Europe prior to the Industrial Revolution, armies were comparatively small and generally comprised of a few professionals. But, the Industrial Revolution allowed the production of vast quantities of arms whose operation did not require professional skills. Hence, massed armies composed of ordinary citizens evolved and became the most potent military forces.[17] Thus, they allowed conquest of larger amounts of territory and consolidation of semi-autonomous regions into larger more complex groupings.

Furthermore, the mechanized and large scale processes of manufacture introduced by the Industrial Revolution created a need for great quantities of natural resources to feed factories, vast labor forces to keep them operating, and large populations to provide markets for what the factories produced.

Hence, technology and economics generated pressure for larger and more complex political units. The possibilities they offered for large scale military production also made sizable political units necessary in order to become large and powerful enough to avoid being overrun by other armies and thus absorbed into other units. Furthermore, in addition to greater size these nation-states were more complex, so they required more intricate and formal governing structures than before – and they required governing structures that were sufficiently large to allow management of important sectors of the economy. Nonetheless, governments of the early nineteenth century were small in comparison with those of today, but the pressures of modernization gradually served to increase their size and complexity until they reached their present mammoth bulk.

The ideology of nationalism and national identification was parasitic on the developments in technology, economics, and military science that made nation-states predominant for a substantial period of human history. There are nonetheless some odd twists in this general picture. The imperialist expansion of the seventeenth through the nineteenth centuries established formal political borders in parts of the world where none existed previously and created governing bodies modelled after those of nation-states, once again, in areas of the world where they had not hitherto existed. Hence, following imperialism's decline and the colonies' struggle for liberation, the skeletons of nation-states imposed by the imperialist powers remained. Moreover, the colonies adopted the rhetoric of national self-determination to provide intellectual justification for their wars of liberation but then found themselves with the shell of nation-states following the wars of liberation. However artificial and distorted the circumstances of their creation, these nation-states recognized that no other political structures would enable them to function in the contemporary world.

Presently, economic currents are again reshaping the political and human landscape. Economic forces have made warfare a largely obsolete means of achieving national power and influence. The same forces are also stretching the ties of human activity and human interaction across national borders. The nation-state is no longer sufficient to manage or contain them. Nonetheless, while the emerging global economy is making the shape and structure of the nation-state obsolete, it is also eroding the ties of national identification that accompanied the past evolution and function of nation-states. The main props and catalysts of national identification, those of military conflict and economic unity, no longer nurture this identification.

The complex relations between ethnic and national identification are nicely illustrated by the contrasting experience of Jewish people in the remnants of the Soviet Union and those in the United States. In the Soviet Union the Jews were frequently victims of discrimination and persecution. As a result the sense of Jewish identity was fixed and made vitally important. It was important in part because these social abuses and animosity *made* it important, so it was important both for Jewish people and for others. Possibly significant numbers of Jewish people of that era would not have given any great attention to their Jewish identity were they not driven to identify themselves as Jewish by social conditions. For these individuals, at least, it can be said that society *made* them Jewish, by making their Jewishness important and by making it impossible for them to escape this identification.

By contrast, many Jews in the United States, where the most onerous discrimination against Jewish people has long disappeared, worry about losing their identity or are concerned that young Jewish people are losing theirs or are losing the sense that it is *important* to be Jewish.[18] Lack of social persecution or social deference may imply that this identification is not socially important, and thus allows individuals to determine whether they wish to retain this identification.

The odd dynamic of ethnic identification in the United States also works in other ways. During certain periods in the history of the United States, it was very important whether or not a given individual was a member of the group irreverently termed WASPs, the White Anglo-Saxon Protestants, because members of this group were socially, politically, and economically predominant. Hence, identification as WASP would be important, not because it carried social discrimination and reprobation, but because it bore important advantages; it offered prestige, elevated social stature, and opportunity not readily available to those of other ethnic identifications. However, the present flux of social forces in the United States has drained this identification of importance. It retains mild interest (mainly for readers of the society pages of newspapers), but it presently carries little social or economic weight. It is a remnant of a bygone social era.

However, an identification which has always been extremely important in the United States, and continues to be so, is that of being black. Being white is not considered particularly important for most of the people in the United States who are so classified; it is unlikely that most white people give the matter much thought. Being Asian is of somewhat greater importance given the social climate of the United States. It is likely more important to those who are Asian than being white is to those who are white, but being Asian is *far* less significant than being black. For those who are so classified, being black in American society is extremely important. It is a central factor in the attitudes that other people have about them. It greatly affects their opportunities for education, jobs, and health care. It makes a crucial difference for their health and life expectancy. It is unlikely that any black person is not repeatedly reminded of being black during the course of an ordinary day. Yet, in other parts of the world this classification may be far less important, even trivial. In several areas it is like the difference between being Italian or being French in the United States at the present time.[19] However, the social climate that exists in the United States makes black racial identification important.

Though identification as black or Jewish is often of great importance for those who are so labelled, their ethnic identification has only sporadically been joined to nationalist aspiration. The Zionist movement focused on founding the state of Israel served to connect Jewish identity to nationalist aspiration, but Jewish nationalism does not have a profound hold on the imagination of many Jewish people at the present time. Even Jewish immigrants who left the Soviet Union for Israel were often more concerned to improve their economic status than to become part of a Jewish state. In the United States, though black identification is frightfully important, nationalism has generally had little appeal to black people. Thus, there is no strong tie between ethnic identification and nationalist aspiration. Hence, in areas of the world where ethnic identification *has* joined to nationalist aspiration, it is necessary to ask why and how the connection occurred.

At present, however, the forces that once sustained national and ethnic identification across the globe are being replaced by others which have begun to erode the importance of these ties and will likely continue to do so in the future – though it is uncertain whether the corrosive forces at work will also replace these identifications with others. A most plausible assumption is that these identifications will *not* be replaced by others, that the rootlessness and alienation which many have felt in this century will endure and deepen under the influence of the developing global economy.[20] An adequate conception of political dynamics must acknowledge the ties that bind people together and infuse them with a sense of ethnic or national unity. However, it must also acknowledge forces which may destroy these bonds and yet others which may realign people's ties of identification.

Militarism

Military conflict generally fixes and highlights the group identification of the warring parties. Hence, if two nations are in armed struggle, the national identification of the combatants is of critical significance. When ethnic groups war with one another, ethnic identification is thrown into high relief. During the era of the nation-state, the most potent instruments of warfare became mass armies, which were under the control of nation-states. Thus, major wars were fought between nation-states, and these conflicts highlighted the national identity of the opposed parties. Hence, warfare during the era of the nation-state nurtured the ties of national identification and eroded those of ethnic identification (in nations where the domains of ethnic groups are not coextensive with the boundaries of nationhood). The so-called wars of national liberation of the past century were generally not wars in which ethnic groups sought nations for themselves. The domains that sought and eventually received liberation were colonial districts which had generally been cobbled up in haphazard fashion by imperialist powers. The boundaries of these colonies were commonly fixed without regard to the mix of ethnic groups which they contained. Hence, the wars of colonial liberation in Africa commonly resulted in nations comprised of several quarreling ethnic groups. These nations have remained unstable in part because they have not yet been able to impose a sense of national identification on these groups. War against a common foe, however, has proven a potent source of national identification. This is because national governments control military forces and employ them to achieve their purposes; military conflicts are the most visceral and desperate of national conflicts, vastly overawing economic conflict or territorial dispute in their impact on national life. When military conflict looms, national identification becomes vitally important. It distinguishes friend from foe, determines who should be protected and who should be killed, and determines which groups shall suffer together and which shall triumph together. Thus military conflict unites groups of people by causing them to share fates of life or death and suffering or triumph, and these are the most important and searing human experiences.

Many understand that, in the era of the nation-state, military conflict and its threat produced visceral surges of national identification – and stamped out dissent by generating the powerful sentiment that all must unite in the face of mortal conflict. The surge of militaristic national-ism, which seems to produce a lemming-like rush to destruction, has commonly appalled liberal thinkers, for it appears to sweep reason and the instinct of individual self-preservation from public consciousness. Furthermore, politicians are adept at employing the prospect of mili-tary struggle as an instrument to suppress internal dissent or to rouse popular emotion to fever pitch to gain support for military adventures. Hegel clearly appreciated war's power to fracture a nation's internal divisions and to reinforce its sense of national identification – and he was an enthusiastic partisan of war for this very reason.[21]

Hence, so long as war is common or commonly feared, the nations that may engage in war or manipulate the instruments of war have potent means of generating a sense of national identification. How-ever, the nature of the global economy is now such that war involving the major powers of the world is nearly unthinkable. They certainly have conflicts, disagreements, and divergent interests, but they are highly unlikely to wield the instrument of war to advance their aims.[22] The rewards and conflicts of economic activity now greatly outweigh those of military endeavor – indeed, the Japanese have learned that econ-omic prowess may well gain them the stature they unsuccessfully sought by military means in the Second World War. However, as argued be-low, economic activity is now such that it undermines rather than bol-sters the ties of national identification. Hence, governments have lost the use of a powerful instrument to forge national identification and are pressed by the global economy to become active in the economic arena, whose forces corrode national identity.

In recent history the loss of military control has often resulted in an explosion of ethnic striving and ethnic nationalist impulses in those nations that had relied upon armed might to maintain national cohe-sion. The ethnic tensions and aspirations that armed might was able to keep simmering below the surface have now bubbled into furious ac-tivity. The processes that dismantled the old artificial sense of national identification also allowed a spate of ethnic nationalism and inter-ethnic conflict. Paradoxically then, the erosion of the nation-state's power has allowed a spate of ethnic conflict and unleashed nationalist aspira-tion in many ethnic groups.

However, the central issue at this juncture is that of just how important and permanent these spasms of ethnic conflict are likely to become. There are reasons to believe that these struggles will soon dissipate and that within a decade or so the current furious clash of ethnic aspi-rations will become an artifact of the past. One sign of this is that a central arena of vicious ethnic struggle is the Balkans, an ancient cockpit of ethnic turmoil and the tinderbox which provided the spark to ignite the First World War. However, at present, there is only modest danger that the conflict in the Balkans will ignite wider conflicts. The great powers of the world have no interests in the region and, other than offering tepid gestures of ineffectual humanitarian handwringing, have been notoriously slow to involve themselves in what they see as an essentially minor conflict. The evidence that the conflict is deemed minor by the leaders of the world is that for several years they were unwilling to take serious measures to bring it to a halt. The contrast between the world's reaction to the furor in the Balkans and the Iraqi invasion of Kuwait is instructive. The leaders of the globe decided that vital interests were threatened in the Persian Gulf and responded quickly and decisively. In the Balkans, they dithered for years, though they appeared to be as abhorred by the brutality there as ordinary people.

The current spasms of ethnic conflict are occurring in areas that have no larger significance; in global terms they are neither militarily nor economically important. In fact it is largely because they are essentially backward, barely post-feudal regions that they host such conflicts. None of the cockpits of ethnic conflict are found in regions of advanced industrialization, and none are significant participants in the global economy. Furthermore, there is reason to believe, as will soon be argued, that, to the extent that these regions become part of the global economy, the importance of ethnic identification will decrease; furthermore, should they remain isolated from the global economy, their difficulties will not have larger significance for the remainder of the world and will not spread beyond the confines of their borders.[23]

Hence, the global economic forces that weaken the ties of ethnic identification for active participants in the world economy may also catalyze brief outbursts of ethnic nationalist striving. Nonetheless, these spasms are unlikely to make any great difference in the way the world works simply because control of national borders and what occurs within them counts for less in the way of power and influence. Moreover, the drive to ethnic nationalism may well be self-limiting under the influence, once again, of the global economy. As Edward Kennan notes, the connection between ethnic identification and the drive to national autonomy is a comparatively recent and artificial invention.[24] To the extent that national autonomy matters less, ethnic groups may be less disposed to seek nationhood than in the days when nation-states were the dominant actors on the global stage. So, bursts of ethnic assertiveness may continue, but they are unlikely to have any great significance for the world as a whole, and the movement itself will be undermined by the same emerging global economy that helps make its initial successes possible.

Given the present circumstances of the world, the declining importance of control of the instruments of war will therefore result in a gradual loss of the significance of bonds of national identification and hence help to erode the status of the nation-state. For the past several centuries, war has been a highly efficient generator of national identification; with its loss these ties are also less important.

Economic Unification

In addition to the ebb of military conflict, global economic unification is at work eroding bonds of national and ethnic identification. During the centuries in which the nation-state has been ascendant, political boundaries have also defined spheres of economic activity, so that people within a particular nation were likely to trade with one another, conduct their affairs in accordance with the laws and traditions of their nation, and generally prosper or become impoverished together. Thus, part of what melded individual persons into national units and gave them a sense of identification with fellow citizens was their thick network of economic ties. Part of what defined nations was that they were free-standing economic units, and the people within them created additional ties with one another through their efforts to sustain themselves and prosper. Hence, there were stark distinctions between those who were within a nation's economic system and those outside it.

The global stretch of commercial activity is gradually dissolving national economic barriers and is beginning to unravel the domestic ties that once stitched citizens together into national units. The global economy is unravelling the ties of national identification possessed by some of the largest, wealthiest, and most important institutions of nations, that is, their major corporations. Furthermore, the global economy is beginning to erode the sense of national identification, as well as the ethnic identification, of individual persons, at least those who are active participants.

1. Major corporations

Though the major corporations of the world generally retain corporate headquarters in one nation or another, their interests and concerns range to wherever they seek markets, construct manufacturing plants, distribution centers, or business ties with other firms. A McDonald's executive, commenting on its activities abroad, stated, 'Our objective is to be a local company'.[25] As a result corporations have concerns in all areas where they are active and will seek to nurture ties and advance their interests as best they can in each of them. They may retain a residual sense of identification with one nation or another, but, as one corporate leader asserted, 'Competitiveness must come first, and nationalism must come second'.[26] They do not hesitate to seek assistance from governments when it is in their interest to do so, but they are equally poised to cast the interests of particular nation-states aside when they conclude that their best corporate interests demand *that*.

It is quite probable that most corporations, even vast multinational corporations, retain the majority of their ties and the bulk of their interests within the bounds of one particular nation-state or another. Toyota remains closely identified with Japan, as do the other huge Japanese conglomerates, and most feel the strong compulsion to advance Japan's national interests through their corporate activities. Coca-Cola retains its identification as a quintessentially American corporation, as do Ford and General Motors. For this reason several observers of international commerce, including a number of bureaus of the United Nations and a number of academic scholars, prefer to speak of 'transnational' rather than 'multinational' corporations.[27] They do so because they are convinced that few corporations are genuinely international in character, even though they may seek opportunity in many nations. They argue that such corporations are still largely owned by citizens of a single nation and that most executive officers are also likely to be citizens of that nation.

However, the factors which support the view that corporations remain transnational rather than multinational are in flux and will very probably continue to change in future years. The bonds to their nation of origin of American icons such as Coca-Cola are becoming less secure and are likely to erode further in the future. Coca-Cola earned 80 per cent of its profits from its overseas operations in 1991.[28] Its products are sold in over 160 different nations. Hence, the United States is gradually becoming simply one market among many others in its strategic planning. It will trade on its association with the United States so long as it sees an advantage in doing so, but it will likely not hesitate to recast its identification should corporate interests require it. In addition, its chairman is of Cuban ethnic background, and its management generally is likely to eventually more accurately reflect its multicultural scope. Similarly, General Motors and Ford reap large portions of their profits from abroad and are not loathe to move plants and operations across the national borders of the United States when it is to their advantage. In 1992 General Motors appointed a Spaniard to one of its highest and most important posts only to have him lured away by Volkswagen within a year.[29]

Furthermore, since there is a global market for stocks, shares in large corporations are sold all over the world, and buyers are both able and eager to roam the world's stock markets seeking opportunities for investment. Hence, corporate ownership is increasingly genuinely multinational and likely to become more so. It is true that stockholders have traditionally exercised little more than nominal direction over the corporations they own, but this may be changing as well. Shareholders within the United States are becoming more assertive in large part because corporate shares are commonly managed by large institutional investors who are demanding greater voice in the affairs of the corporations whose shares they control. Moreover, at least one colorful financier, T. Boone Pickins, became embroiled in lively controversy when he bought a considerable portion of the stocks of a major Japanese corporation then travelled to Tokyo seeking a fragment of managerial control.[30] His attempt failed, but it is likely that his effort is only the harbinger of other less dramatic but perhaps more successful efforts.

Hence, corporations are becoming more fully citizens of the world, and national governments will be forced to make ambitious efforts to attract corporate attentions and retain their loyalty, no matter what the nominal nation of origin of these corporations may be.[31] So, particular national governments are less obviously governments of *them*, and thus many corporations are losing their sense of identification with a particular nation. Even if this were not the case, the pressures of global competition will force them to expand their areas of operation and also their regional loyalties.

2. Individual persons

People commonly have thicker and sturdier ties to their home nation than corporations. Nonetheless, contemporary economic forces are undermining individual persons' national and ethnic identification. As an example, something of an international popular culture is emerging, nurtured by the same economic forces as are eroding other barriers. American movie films, for example, often generate more income abroad than at home. The Russian bureaucratic elite, even before the Iron Curtain dissolved, apparently savored the same detective mysteries and spy novels that divert Western European audiences.[32] Rock music, fast

food restaurants, and informal clothing styles are the shared, ubiqui-
tous facets of an international youth culture. It may or may not be the
case that this shared popular culture is nurturing common attitudes
and values or that it is playing an important role in binding people
closer together.

Nonetheless, an emerging shared international culture *is* likely to
play its role in eroding ties of national and ethnic identification. It will
do so partly by dissolving significant cultural barriers to international
mobility; a person can now find familiar books, movies, clothing, food,
and the international youth culture in most segments of the globe. Hence,
people may feel nearly as comfortable and at home in distant nations
as when nearer their birth place. Furthermore, the speed and ease of
communication and transportation will likely continue to increase. Thus,
people even in distant corners or the world need not *feel* isolated from
their homelands, since they are unlikely to be more than a quick phone
call or a few hours' jet travel away.

In addition patterns of life seen in the United States, and no doubt
also practiced in Europe, give evidence that younger generations of
people are less culturally insular than in past years. Urban people and
younger generations in the United States are eager to sample exotic
ethnic restaurants, view foreign films, and travel abroad. In addition,
many colleges and universities of the United States have arrays of
programs that not only allow students to study abroad but give them
some first-hand exposure to differing cultures. These efforts are generally deemed part of a good liberal education, but they are also increasingly demanded and supported by the business community, because
business leaders and the deans of business schools are keenly aware
that the business community will increasingly demand people who are
comfortable in a variety of differing cultural settings and able to function effectively in them.[33]

Hence, economic forces will loosen people's bonds to their native
cultures and make them more interested in partaking of differing cultures – not only because foreign cultures are not as likely to seem as
alien to them as to their parents or grandparents but also because their
success in careers or business may require that they develop such
openness.

Moreover, the global economy demands considerable mobility of its
participants. It is now common for an executive of a major United
States corporation to have spent a considerable number of years in
various nations, gained the ability to speak a number of languages,
and to be able to function effectively in various cultural settings. In

fact, this multicultural facility may soon become necessary prerequisites for advance to the higher reaches of corporate offices.

In the near future it may be unremarkable for executives of Toyota to spend the great bulk of their working careers in the United States or Europe and pay the taxes of these nations, obey their laws, make a living within their borders, and enjoy their culture, yet remain citizens of Japan. It is even possible that they will finally retire to the coast of Spain, with their Japanese citizenship intact. Individuals whose career follows this trajectory are unlikely to maintain strong national or ethnic identification. In fact, people with this background may well be more comfortable with and share more experience with other corporate nomads than those who are nominally compatriots. The pressures of the global economy are likely to create a group of international citizens, people able to make themselves at home in most parts of the globe and retain little more than sentimental identification with any particular piece of territory – and this is the group of people likely to become influential and important in the future.

As mentioned in Chapter 1, ordinary workers' mobility is presently considerably less than corporate executives. Nonetheless, many ordinary laborers now have a considerable degree of mobility and are likely to gain more. The political leaders of the United States, Western Europe, and Japan have discovered that laborers are able to traverse international borders with disconcerting ease. Mexican laborers routinely cross the Rio Grande into the United States, and many eventually settle in the United States. Western Europe is a favored destination for workers from Eastern Europe, the Middle East, and Northern Africa. Japan receives workers from other parts of Asia. It is common for workers from India and the Philippines to travel far abroad in search of livelihood, and they often demonstrate considerable ingenuity in transporting themselves to distant places. They do so even though they are often mistreated and work under harsh conditions in the domains where they alight. Furthermore, there is reason to believe that there will continue to be increasing opportunities for immigrant laborers, greater ease for them to move to areas where there is work, and greater pressure in their native lands for them to go abroad, as well as fewer barriers to doing so.

For example, few nations are as jealous of national boundaries or protective of their homogeneous national culture as Japan. Presently, however, Japan is suffering a labor shortage. The combined effects of a diminished birthrate, a graying labor force, and a generation of younger people who, unlike their parents, no longer are prepared to work long hours and sacrifice personal life to career are conspiring to diminish the supply of laborers. However, Japan's leaders are well aware that they cannot sustain their amazing economic success without an adequate labor supply, and the managers of various manufacturing concerns are also aware that they cannot continue to prosper without sufficient labor. Hence, managers are willing to resort to illegal laborers smuggled in from other parts of Asia to keep their enterprises functioning.[34] Government, for its part, is unlikely to make serious attempts to restrict this practice because it is aware that the economy will falter if a labor shortage develops. Hence, foreign laborers are finding their way into Japan and very likely will do so in greater numbers as time passes. This will occur, despite concerns about loss of cultural and racial homogeneity, because continued economic advancement and prosperity demand it.

The nations of Western Europe have suffered labor shortages for years and relied on imported workers to keep their industries functioning and to fill jobs that are too monotonous, dangerous, dirty, or dull to attract natives. Moreover, nations with advanced economies share a number of factors that are apt to result in chronic labor shortages. Advanced economies generally have a diminishing birthrate, which sometimes drops below the level needed to sustain population. As more education is needed for desirable jobs and women enter the labor force in greater numbers, the birthrate tends to decrease. These forces pervade advanced economies and are likely to result in a sustained need for imported labor, particularly since birthrates in less developed nations remain high.

However, ordinary laborers are likely to have a different impact on bonds of national or ethnic identification than roving corporate executives. Rather than moving periodically from nation to nation to seek their livelihood, as do executives, laborers tend to take root where they land. To their dismay Western European nations have become permanent hosts of diverse non-European ethnic and racial groups, and many in these nations fear losing whatever ethnic homogeneity they may have enjoyed in the past.

To the extent that masses of alien workers continue to clump and pool together in the industrial nations of the world and become permanent inhabitants, they are apt to erode ties between ethnic identity and national identification and are likely to fray the sense of national identification – because citizens of a nation will no longer enjoy the secure sense of being part of a distinct 'people' which is matched to its particular nation.[35] Moreover, if the United States can be used as a model, the presence of unassimilated or partially assimilated groups in various nations will erode the sense of cultural insularity held by the native inhabitants, simply by exposing them in the course of their daily lives to diverse cultures and acclimatizing them to their presence.

Furthermore, in a fashion similar to that of the experience of the various states within the United States, economic considerations are prompting many of the nations of the world to begin erasing the political barriers which have prevented easy transit of national borders. Once again, they are compelled to do so to avoid becoming isolated from the developing global economy. This ease of transit, as well as the broadened cultural affinities which the global economy is generating, will also erode the barriers inhibiting migration from national state to national state. In the space of several decades, the political and cultural barriers to migration from nation-state to nation-state will very probably not be appreciably greater than whatever may still inhibit migration from state to state within the United States.

THE NATION-STATE AND THE INDIVIDUAL

If in future years individual people are not as obviously citizens of any single particular nation-state and if individual corporations are not as clearly institutions of any particular nation-state, the conception of the relation of individuals to governments will evolve in practice and hence must be recast in theory. The common thought is that national governments are governments *of* an identifiable group of people who in turn rely on their government to serve their interests and represent them in dealings with the external world.[36] To the extent that the interests of particular individual people or particular corporations are not exclusively linked to one single national government, the matter of their citizenship or formal political affiliation becomes correspondingly less important.

In coming years, in other words, citizenship of a particular nation-state may become of little greater concern than citizenship in one or another state of the United States is at present; people within the United States commonly move to a variety of locations during their lifetimes, often taking up citizenship in several different states. They become citizens of these states, but, for most people in the United States, this is little more than a minor legal and administrative chore; their ties to a particular state and its government, and their sense of identification to a particular state, such as being a Californian, Michigander, or

Virginian, is also likely to be slight, or primarily a matter of senti-mental identification.

Hence, the developments discussed in this chapter will break the connection between a particular national government and the idea of nationhood or the conception of a particular identifiable people resid-ing in a particular territory. To the extent that the people dissolves, the traditional conception of a nation will dissolve with it.

These analyses yield several conclusions regarding commonplace thinking about the nation-state. Hegel was correct in believing that nationalism was a crucially important factor in human history and human politics and that it must emerge from human ties. In this regard he echoed the insight of Aristotle, who ridiculed the idea that a viable organic political body could be created by contract; he snorted that contracts are suitable only for commercial transactions and cannot produce the unity required for an organic political body.[37] Aristotle believed that only a shared way of life can suffice to create the unity necessary for a functioning political organism.

However, Aristotle had another insight as well; that this unity of a shared way of life could only be achieved if the organic political body were small, limited to a few thousand people. Larger polities generate shears and fractures that destroy organic wholeness.[38] In this regard Aristotle is correct; ethnic groups with the organic unity of a shared way of life are relatively small, numbering a few thousands at most. Of course, this characterization would not apply to the many millions who casually identify themselves as members of one or another ethnic group and do not think to use this identification as the basis of a pol-itical order. The mere sentimental identification of these people would be insufficient to establish an organic political unity. This is because there is a distinction between genuinely sharing a way of life and simple sharing of language, race, or ethnic identification. But, as has been argued repeatedly, the nation-states of the modern era are not of this sort. Because of this, Hegel's view that nationalism is an outgrowth of a shared way of life of the people of an entire nation was an illusion, a myth created to give legitimacy and unity to a national entity that had been established by quite different means.

However, a Hegelian myth of national unity may be necessary if an organic governing body can be established only over a unified group of individuals known as a people, and this people can only achieve the requisite unity by sharing a common way of life and culture. What Hegel failed to see is that the national identity he sought depends on factors including military domination and an encompassing web of economic ties, in addition to the skim of emblems and symbols of nationhood, such as flags, anthems, and creeds. However, these do not require the existence of a people with a shared way of life envisioned by Hegel and Aristotle; they are also quite different from the bonds which create ethnic identification. Nation-states emerged and prospered for reasons quite distinct from any links, real or imagined, created by the existence of a people.

Nonetheless, none of the above implies that John Locke was therefore correct in believing that viable nations could be established on the basis of a simple contract or act of explicit or implicit agreement. Aristotle was correct in this regard, a simple contract cannot be an adequate basis for a viable political entity. Locke's views gained plausibility because he could take the existence of national government for granted; national government obviously existed, the question was how it came to exist. But, nations were not founded on a primordial contract. Even the Mayflower Compact did not found a national government. Rather, it was the formal ritual of a group of people already unified in the way that Aristotle required. Aristotle would have claimed that the Compact alone did not create a government; it could not have done so. It simply formally established the government that would have surely ensued even if the Puritans had not been beguiled by English political thought.

Locke's contract theory and current philosophical examinations of contract theory are important for a quite different reason than Locke thought; the contract provides a way of explaining how a government can be *morally entitled* to sovereign authority over the particular individual and how a government can gain entitlement to sovereign authority over a people. But the matter of entitlement to authority differs from the understanding of how government comes to exist. This distinction is often obscured by revolutions in which particular governments are destroyed and replaced by others. Sometimes, though more commonly not, these are popular revolutions in which massed citizenry arises and ejects a particular government. However, these upheavals concern particular governments only and do not address the question of how it is possible for government to exist at all, and they also ignore the fact that the revolutionary governments are often able to retain power only by resort to brutal military force. Hence, popular revolutions do not explain the existence of national identity or the ways in which nations come to be and remain in existence.

The above demonstrates that the explanation of the authority of governments cannot be found in the claim that they give voice to and are the creations of a people in the Hegelian or Aristotelian sense – because for most nations there *is no* people in this sense. National identification is created and sustained by military or physical force, the use of the unifying symbols of nationhood, and, most importantly, the bonds of economic relationships. Hegel was therefore mistaken in believing that nations emerged naturally and that they were permanent features of the lives of human beings. The most that governments can claim is that they represent the interests of those persons who reside within their national boundaries – who may be united by no more than their common national residence.

However, if this chapter's arguments are correct, nations are presently losing the ties that created the possibility of national identification. People living within given national borders now have less to unify them with their countrymen and greater incentive to create ties with people in other parts of the world. But, if an individual person's interests and concerns flow across national boundaries, the governmental activity of nation-states must do so as well if it is to serve the citizen's interests. This political necessity may be undermined by several factors. One is that citizens' international interests may be at odds with those of their government, as when citizens want to sell products to other nations that are thwarting their government's policies. But, second, oftentimes the international interests of various groups of citizens will be in conflict. A nation's consumers may benefit from lower tariff rates which yield cheaper goods, but reduced tariffs may harm businesses that must compete with imports. Third, the complex welter of multinational corporations may allow a corporation identified with a foreign nation to nonetheless hold a substantial presence of manufacturing plants and markets in other nations. In such cases it may be difficult for a government to determine whether or what interests of those multinational corporations should count as interests it is pledged to protect. Hence, it will be increasingly difficult for governments to determine whose corporate interests they are bound to serve.[39]

For the above reasons, the view that governments require some sort of unity of a people in order to function – or Hobbes' more radical view that the function of government is *only* to provide unity – is apparently false, and so Locke may have turned out to be correct after all. However, he will be correct only on the condition that the nation-state has evolved into a very different and far less consequential entity than it was in his day. A government whose mandate is mainly to keep good order in a given territory and attempt to serve the interests of those who reside within its borders (something like the sort of government Locke envisioned) does not require national unity and need not claim to represent the unified will of its people. But neither would such a government require more than a formal and perfunctory consent. Moreover, it may not require any sort of consent at all, since its functions will be quite limited.

Common views of the relation between individuals and their governments are encapsulated in the conception of citizenship. This idea, moreover, has evolved as the conditions of human life and the nature of governments changed. Those in Plato's Athens believed that citizenship was determined by birth and could not imagine that it would arise in any other way. An individual was *born* a citizen of Athens or Sparta or was not, but citizenship could not be changed any more than one's family could be changed.[40] With the advent of the Roman Empire, the idea that citizenship could alter was introduced, as people could become citizens of Rome. Nonetheless, the idea that citizenship was a fixed and long-term relation, a status that formed an important part of the identity of a person, endured.[41] It is a safe bet that the ordinary conception of citizenship still retains this implication, even though people are generally aware that it is possible to hold dual citizenship and that some people will be the citizen of several nations in the course of their lives.

With the advent of the nation-state, citizenship became joined to the idea of nationhood, so that to become a citizen was also to become part of the nation, understood as joining a people sharing a culture, language, and values. Hence, it was considered far more than a hollow legal or formal ritual but a matter of joining a culture or way of life.

Also, and perhaps in consequence of the above, citizenship was also considered a matter of pledging allegiance to the government of a particular nation-state, that is, of making a commitment to obey that government and accepting the authority of that government over oneself. In part this is a formal legal consequence of the procedure by which one becomes a citizen, though it is also more broadly conceived as the burden which *any* person must accept at the point of becoming considered legally a citizen, by reaching the age of majority, for example.

In addition, the full-bodied conception of citizenship has always held the aspect of participation in the processes of government. In Aristotle's day this was taken in a literal and robust sense, as the Athens of his time was a full participatory democracy for all of those who were citizens (though many adult residents were not citizens). At present, the idea of participation, at least for the general run of citizens, is considerably more attenuated; few will actually hold office or have a direct role in managing government. For the ordinary run of citizens, participation entails the right to vote in elections and at least the *possibility* of holding elective office. It may also include the opportunity to seek to influence the political process via lobbying or joining special interest groups. Though efforts to sway governmental decisions are important facets of political activity, they should not be identified only with citizenship because it is not necessary to be a citizen to engage in them. Foreign nationals and foreign nations regularly engage in an array of activities designed to influence policies of the United States government, activities for which they often have far greater resources and far greater influence than the great majority of US citizens.

Hence, the traditional full-bodied sense of citizenship includes permanence, cultural affinity, obedience, and participation in the political process. Liberal political philosophers have always been partial to the idea of consent, the belief that governments gain legitimate power over people only when they specifically consent to that relationship. However, the idea of consent is stretched thin when applied to the notion of citizenship. Those born citizens of a nation rarely give explicit consent to the relationship, and those occasions on which formal allegiance is pledged have more the aura of ritual than actual choice. Also, few people who immigrate to a particular nation and seek citizenship have a genuine choice in the matter – since they frequently have been forced from their homeland and have no other place to seek refuge.

The conception of client, however, is quite different from the features of citizenship listed above. A client is party to a far more limited and specific relationship than is a citizen. A client enters into a relation with another for a specific set of purposes, may give the other party sufficient authority to carry out those purposes, and when the purposes are fulfilled, or the client becomes dissatisfied, the relationship may end, or the basis of the relationship may be renegotiated. Hence, the relationship of a client to another party is not necessarily permanent and need not involve personal bonding greater than that which is necessary to achieve the client's purposes. The client remains free to dissolve or reestablish the relationship at any time and enters the relationship only as the specific result of an act of uncoerced will. If necessary to achieve his or her purposes, the client may grant a measure of authority to the other party (as in the case of a relationship with a lawyer, physician, or accountant – where the client will need to rely on the other party's professional advice), but this grant will be strictly limited and will be narrowly conditioned on its employment to achieve the client's purposes. However, once the relationship is authorized, the role of the client is generally passive; the client may cooperate or participate in the relationship to the extent necessary to bring about the desired result, but the client is not the major agent in the relationship established. The active agency of the client is normally not necessary in order to achieve his or her purposes.

Two features of this conception are worth noting. First, the idea of a client is obviously distinct from that of the traditional full-bodied conception of the citizen. Second, however, the conception of the client accords tolerably well with John Locke's view of citizenship. For Locke the citizen enters into a relationship with the state for a fixed and limited set of purposes, that is, avoidance of what he terms the inconveniences of the state of nature. The citizen gives authority to the state, but this grant of authority is conditional on the effort of the state to satisfactorily enforce the laws of nature.[42] If the state attempts to usurp more power and authority than needed for this end, the state has violated its portion of the bargain, and the citizen is free to cancel the relationship or renegotiate it.

Locke did not attend to the cultural bonds and ties of national identification that form an important part of the usual conception of citizenship. In many respects he was correct to do so, because conceptual clarity is gained by distinguishing the concept of national government from that of national identity or that of a unified, distinctive people, bound together by language, culture, or values.

However, this chapter has demonstrated that the problem of achieving national unity has been an important issue for the history of political philosophy both practically and theoretically. It is of practical importance for nations whose national government presides over a territory containing distinct ethnic groups whose interests conflict with one another. Many of the former colonies that received independence in the past several decades and many of the nations recently freed of the control of the former Soviet Union are experiencing an explosion of conflict generated between groups who see themselves as distinct from one another and at odds with one another. In these cases, some sense of national identification, it would appear, is necessary if they are to continue to exist as nations and avoid the fate of Yugoslavia or Czechoslovakia, which disintegrated as a result of ethnic disturbance.

The difficulty is also theoretical, for philosophers beginning with Aristotle have presumed that some form of national unity is necessary for a free-standing political unit to continue in existence. In Hobbes' view the issue was of central importance; for he believed that the *only* function of national government is to achieve and then preserve national unity. For Locke, however, achieving national unity was not a problem. It was not a problem because there was no need for it; a state existed so long as it had the free consent of its citizens. No more substantial ties were necessary or desirable.

Locke's view is given credibility by the experience of some nations, the United States being the salient example, holding diverse ethnic groups, each with a sense of identity and often in conflict with one another, that nonetheless is still able to function as a national whole. So it appears that a fit between ethnic identity and national government is not always required. However, the United States was able to create a robust sense of national identification which was independent of the welter of ethnic identities it contains. This chapter's argument, though, is that the pressures of militarism and economics which created this national identification are no longer able to support it. Furthermore, these same forces are undermining people's sense of national identification in all the major nations of the world. Hence, the reality which is emerging will require a concept of citizenship which is stripped of its previous rich and colorful associations and reduced to the mundane notion of the client. Part of the necessity for this transformation is found in the evolving role of governments, as will be argued in the next chapter. The same forces that are grinding away the importance of citizenship are at work transforming the nature and role of national governments.

4 The Structures of Government

Political theorists, politicians, and ordinary persons commonly believe that a government is a closely integrated unity with a single seat of power and authority holding ultimate control over political decisions and policies.[1] As noted in previous chapters, political philosophers of past centuries, such as Aristotle, Locke, Hobbes, or Rousseau, worried considerably over how to unify a nation's citizens. Nonetheless, they presumed that the governing body itself would be unified – probably on grounds that they believed that a government lacking unity could not function and would soon be torn apart by its own centrifugal forces. However, this ordinary and commonsensical belief does not accurately describe the vast majority of the national governments of the world. National governments are not single, organic entities but are agglomerations of more or less independent elements.

The recognition that government need not be, and in fact most commonly is not, a unified whole is essential for grasping the actual, as opposed to theoretical, nature of government and the way in which governments function – or fail to function as they ought. However, this recognition also opens the way for another, namely, that genuine *world* government is emerging. This has been overlooked because people presume that *all* government must fit the template of the unitary organic whole envisioned by such philosophers as Aristotle or Hobbes. But realization that government need not be monolithic allows the possibility that government may exist in guises and locations not previously expected.

Furthermore, the view that government must be an organic whole becomes more obviously and importantly mistaken if, as there is reason to believe, the pressures of the emerging global economy will fragment and scatter the function and structure of governments even more than they already are. At present the various governing bodies of each nation-state are *formally* united into one governing structure which has legal claim to sovereignty. However, the pressures of the global economy are scattering governing functions beyond the umbrellas of individual national governments. National political leaders recognize that significant elements of international government are required to maintain the proper function of the global economy and address problems that are clearly international in scope.

However, recognition that significant governing functions and governing powers may be disbursed leads to realization that the functions and powers of governing need not reside within a formally unified governing structure at all. Rather, they may be free-standing and more or less independent of one another or any other governing authority. Furthermore, it is highly likely that additional free-standing international governing entities will soon emerge and that they will also gain importance as globalization brings new problems and new demands.

THE FRAGMENTED NATURE OF GOVERNMENT

The customary belief that government must be a single organic whole likely results from several factors. One is the traditional view, which can be traced back to sixteenth century theorizing about the nation-state, that there must be a single sovereign in the state which is the ultimate locus of political and legal power and authority.[2] The traditional view is that this sovereignty must be concentrated in one place on the reasonable grounds that it would be a logical contradiction and practical impossibility for more than one ultimate authority to exist in the state. Another factor supporting this predisposition is that language allows, indeed forces, us to refer to 'the government' or to say, 'The government has decided this or done that', suggesting that it is a single whole. An additional element which leads readily to the view that government is unitary is the diplomatic practice of recognizing governments and the complex relations and maneuvering of the various governments of the world. Yet another factor is that governments generally have a formal and legal structure which in theory places ultimate authority in one body or group of bodies.

Hence, part of the reason why ordinary people and theoreticians are prone to believe that government must be unitary is that they also believe that sovereignty must be a seamless whole. However, Chapter 2 demonstrated that sovereignty need not be the possession of an ultimate political authority controlling all facets of political and legal life. Rather, differing bodies have authority over one or another segment of the full range of political activity. This occurs frequently, even where the formal legal structure of a government may indicate otherwise.

Furthermore, no great practical difficulty results if the authority of different governing bodies overlaps, because they in fact do overlap in many cases, and government does not freeze in place or fly to pieces. Rather, the reality of political power allows scattered factions of government conjointly to hold bits and pieces of regulatory and policy authority, allows these factions to do battle when their powers directly conflict, and allows them to smooth their differences, negotiate compromises, and devise common policies. The pressure which motivates these differing segments to accommodate one another is not the requirement that sovereign authority be a seamless whole. Rather, the motivating factor is the simple, practical need to be effective, to competently deal with difficulties and issues, or face public censure, ridicule, and possibly loss of power. Hence, pressure to get the job done forces accommodation rather than the cohesive pressure of a single overawing authority. But, note that this pressure to get the job done also contributes to the view that governments are unified wholes. It does so by giving the illusion of unified activity and authority.

If sovereign authority need not be a seamless whole, the bearer of sovereign authority need not be unitary. Whatever the reasons, it is easy to view government as a single unified agent, but this view is mistaken. It may have been plausible in the feudal era when governments were small and simple, and ultimate governing authority was closely held by a single prince. However, governments have long been too diffuse and complex for this simple picture to remain accurate. Most contemporary national governments are vast networks which employ many thousands or even millions of people and spread across a complex array of offices, staffs, bureaus, agencies, legislative and judicial bodies, boards and councils.

National Government

Many fragments of the motley assemblage that constitutes national governments may set policies, create and enforce rules, examine issues, and offer problems to public scrutiny. Each is likely to have some sphere in which it has ultimate authority and which it is able to protect from incursion by other domains of government, but each is also likely to periodically vie with others to expand its control. Whatever the organizational charts avow or statutes proclaim, no one of these facets of the over-all governing structure enjoys unassailable power over the others.

Even offices denominated president, chief executive, or secretary-general are often, as a matter of actual practice, unable to exercise the full array of powers which organizational charts claim for them. For example, students of politics recognize that there are a number of acts which the President of the United States cannot, as a matter of actual practice, perform even though they lie within the range of powers formally denominated presidential.[3] Furthermore, despite clean lines on organizational charts or unassailable statutory authority, the *de facto* powers of the various branches and offices of government fluctuate with time and circumstance. They carve out new areas of responsibility for themselves, intrude into areas that they had hitherto ignored, or assume additional powers to address new and pressing problems. For example, during the two centuries of the United States' existence, its Supreme Court has steadily created new domains of power and authority for itself.[4]

The President of the United States (or more accurately, the Office of the Presidency, since the Presidential Staff contains hundreds of people and numerous offices each of which is sometimes capable of acting on its own behalf and independently of the particular individual holding the title of President) has steadily accumulated additional powers, but has also lost some to other parts of government. Congress has acquired several new powers but has lost others to the White House, the Supreme Court, or to one or several government agencies. Students of government are well aware that each small bureau and fiefdom jealously guards its patch of turf, seeks to fend off the intrusions of others, and makes occasional forays into other domains.

The branches of government within the world's nations fight with one another, squabble over matters of rule and policy, and often function in happy disregard of the conflicting policies of others. It has been asserted, for example, that the United States government has no single policy regarding Japan. Rather, the Commerce Department of the United States has *its* policies on Japan, the Department of State pursues *its* policies and practices, and the Department of Defense has *its* approach to dealing with Japan.[5] The views and policies of these agencies often differ, but they appear able to function independently and without interference from others.

Nominally the American Congress or the American President has means to impose unity on these fiefdoms, but this ability is limited, both in theory and in practice (in part because these bodies are sufficiently large and diverse that they rarely speak with one voice or act from one policy). Governmental bodies' diversity of policy and practice is disguised in several ways. Hence, a news report or official news release may state that 'the United States government' or simply 'the United States' has determined that some action is to be taken or a particular policy is to be followed, or it may deplore or applaud some event or another. This nurtures the impression that the government as a whole unit has acted, but the reality is that some particular bureau or agency has made this determination, and often this body speaks mainly for itself, even if it is explicitly entitled to pronounce on such matters for the government as a whole.

Hence, to discuss *the* policies of the United States government or *the* actions of the United States government, or that of Great Britain or Japan, is frequently misleading at best, and mistaken at worst. The inescapable complexity of contemporary government infects even those few nations, such as Iraq or Syria, that remain under the sway of an old-fashioned despot. These nations do not have a single, ultimate sovereign, for each nation's tyrant must have support from many different bodies to retain and exercise power and could not function without it.

International Government

If national governments need not be unitary, emerging international government need not be unitary. In fact, there are reasons to believe that the emerging structures of international government will be less cohesive than the governments of individual nation-states. Nor need such a world government possess seamless political legal and political sovereignty over all other governments. As shall be seen, the emerging structures have no such formal overawing authority, nor are they likely to acquire it soon.

The world's national governments have been creating the patchwork of contemporary international governing structures since the final years of the Second World War. The war's end saw the creation of many of the structures which form the major portions of current international government. For the most part, no radically new structures have come into existence since the immediate post-war years; rather, the array of governing structures has increased in number and importance. In addition, as the pressures of the global economy continue to shape governmental policy and action, the issues and difficulties which these structures were designed to address have become more pressing, so the structures have become more important as well.

International governing structures can be sorted by their intended function, their form, and the way in which they are designed to work. The United Nations is first among these. It has no formal sovereign authority nor does it have formal, independent power to force recalcitrant national governments to obey it. However, a central claim of the present work is that narrow focus on formal, legal, or conventional formulations of sovereign authority are misleading, both because they contain presumptions which are inaccurate and because the world is changing in ways which make these presumptions even less in accord with reality. Hence, the important question is whether *in fact* any of these structures have the power to work their will on recalcitrant governments, whether this will is effective, and whether it is generally recognized that they enjoy this power and are entitled to it. Despite its lack of formal power, the United Nations is not without means to work its will or have a decisive impact on the world. For one thing, it has the power of moral suasion, which exists in two forms. One is the resolutions of the General Assembly. These have no legally binding authority but can serve as a powerful lens to focus world opinion (understood, of course, as the opinion of the governments of nation-states which are its primary constituents). Furthermore, the Secretary-General of the United Nations has considerable resources of moral suasion, which may be wielded with greater or less impact depending on the stature and skill of the individual holding the office. The United Nations also has a resource with considerably more clout, the Security Council, composed of representatives of the major powers of the world. It is true that the power which the United Nations gains through the exertions of the great powers is parasitic on their own power, but to the extent that they exercise their power through the medium of the UN and feel compelled to do so, the UN can be said to enjoy this power in its own right. Lastly, the United Nations has considerable influence simply because it has machinery available to address difficulties which member nations seek to resolve through an international forum. The Cold War prevented it from becoming an effective source of influence in its own right. Now, with the Cold War a grim memory, nations are coming to rely on it more than in past years. It is gaining more power on its own behalf, and its independent sources of power are apt to increase in the future.

In addition, there are a number of bureaus and commissions established under the United Nations' umbrella, in somewhat the same fashion as bureaucratic structures are erected under the umbrellas of individual national governments. There are several important differences between the United Nations' structures and those of individual national governments. Most importantly, the United Nations' structures often receive their funds directly from member nations.[6] The funds are not channeled to the UN which then disburses them as it pleases. This arrangement gives the UN's sub-agencies a measure of freedom from the central governing organization but also places them more firmly under the influence of donor nations.

Also, there are several regional structures which dimly mirror the United Nations in scope and ambition. They include military treaty organizations, which are designed to seek military goals. However, they often take on some of the functions of government and are sensitive to economic concerns because economic strength is crucial for long-term military success in the present day. Also, there are regional associations, such as the Organization of American States and the Organization of African States, which enjoy varying degrees of success in serving as regional coordinating units. However, the older associations, generally founded on military and diplomatic concerns, are being supplanted by overtly economic unions which are coming to enjoy considerable importance. The latter are constructed from economic necessity, and economic pressures are making these organizations effective in ways that the military or diplomatic efforts are not.

The most striking example of the potency of economic pressure is the European Economic Community, which is driven by economic concerns to gain expanded power over its member nations and is now pressing the European nations to forge closer political links and begin to dissolve their economic and political divisions. Once again, economic necessity rather than military, diplomatic, or political necessity is the basic motive force. As in other cases, the formal sovereign power of these bodies is limited, but economic pressures bestow genuine power in ways that other forms of pressure cannot.

In addition to quasigovernmental structures such as the United Nations, the world community has also created financial and trade structures which are gathering increased importance as global economics becomes more important. Several of these have odd and unusual configurations. For example, the Group of Seven is ostensibly a group of the major industrialized nations that meets informally to discuss economic concerns. However the meetings have become more frequent, more regular, and their agenda has broadened from economics to a broad range of military and diplomatic issues.

Another group that is exceedingly important but also highly unusual in structure is the General Agreement on Tariffs and Trade (which has lately become the World Trade Organization), which has no formal administrative apparatus, and no status independent of the nations that are party to its negotiations, but nonetheless is playing a central role in erasing barriers to free international trade. While its negotiations are in chronic danger of collapse, and crises of one sort or another

perennially arise, the negotiations somehow continue. They do so because national governments believe that they have no choice but to
make them succeed, that failure would result in world trade war which
would in turn precipitate global economic calamity.

In addition, various regional trading groups are actively establishing
closer economic ties and erasing economic barriers. In many cases,
these regional group's efforts to relax trade barriers are more sweeping than GATT's. Moreover, participants in these groupings are discover-
ing, as are the Europeans, that lowering trade barriers has important
political consequences, among them dissolving political barriers between nations and eroding the sovereignty of participating national governments. In the trilateral negotiations involving the United States, Mexico,
and Canada, for example, the effort to lower trade barriers encoun-
tered issues of the pollution laws of each nation, labor safety laws,
immigration laws, and financial regulations. In each domain individual
governments forfeited an increment of sovereign control for the sake
of lowering economic barriers, but they believed themselves forced to
do so because they were convinced that economic advance demands
economic integration. In fact, Canada, which was not originally slated
to participate in the talks, *demanded* entry on grounds that its economic future required participation.[7]

Hence, trade negotiations, driven by the demands of economics, are
helping erode individual nation-state's autonomy and constructing communal mechanisms for making decisions which will be binding on all
participants. While considerable decision-making authority lies in the
hands of individual governments, economic pressures are forcing them
to renounce much of what they previously enjoyed.

In addition to economic, military, and diplomatic agreements, a growing
number of treaties address issues that can be adequately met only on
a global basis, including arms control, environmental pollution, public
health matters, disposal of hazardous waste, and international transportation and communication. While these global issues are to some
degree independent of economics, they all have economic significance.
Furthermore, the advent of a global economy will greatly increase the
rate at which global problems arise and must be addressed by the collective efforts of the governments of nation-states. Once more, national
governments will be pressed to forfeit portions of their sovereignty
adequately to address these issues, and they will do so because they
must, because the issues will have to be addressed, and there is no
other means of doing so. However, there is an important difference
between these issues and agreements and those more centrally involv-

ing economics; it is that they do not as overtly spill over into other political issues and do not carry the same intense drive to agreement possessed by economic issues.

Visionary thinkers have long proclaimed the virtues of a world government able to prevent or halt wars, compel errant nations to mend their ways, and forcefully address difficulties that face the world as a whole.[8] However, they have believed that world government must follow the pattern which they presume shapes the governments of ordinary nation-states; that is, they have assumed that any world government must be a unitary whole with a distinct seat of sovereign power. Though elements of an international government are emerging, they do not form a sleek organic whole. Instead, as above discussions demonstrate, they are a hodgepodge of diverse elements. These various international governing structures have fragmented and overlapping authority and function. As the present conflict in the Balkans illustrates, the UN and NATO hold overlapping authority and mission. The several economic groups also have overlapping mandates. Furthermore, some, such as GATT, have no analogue on the level of national governments. Others, such as the legislative function of the General Assembly of the UN, mirror structures found in national governments. There is no coherent delineation of power and authority on the international level. Rather, a motley collection of groups created in ad hoc fashion has sprouted up. Nonetheless, these groups have effective authority because they must have it in order to fulfill the functions nations demand of them.

It is highly unlikely that these scattered fragments will soon coalesce into a single monolithic governing body. A unified world government is not likely to emerge soon, because existing national governments are not disposed to abrogate their sovereignty in the overt and wholesale fashion required to create a single institution. In part, this is because governmental leaders are generally loathe to surrender the perquisites of sovereignty which are the source of much of their power and trappings of office. In other part, it is because the fragments of international government are being crafted in piecemeal fashion by national governments. They do not do so because they are committed to the ideal of world government. Rather, political leaders *must* take these measures to adequately address many of the difficulties they face. Furthermore, the fact that they are playing this role allows them to construct the types of international governing structures that suit them best, and they are not prepared to create a governing entity which they believe is capable of challenging their own authority. Hence, political leaders are likely to continue to allow national sovereignty to be gradually nibbled to pieces by the various collective undertakings of national governments, but they will not throw it into the lion's den whole. World government is emerging, but as a fragmented and unstructured array of entities, each claiming its bit or piece of governing power and function.

NEED FOR CONCEPTUAL CHANGE

If the above claims regarding the nature of government are correct, and the above arguments regarding international governing structures are correct, then a variety of other conceptual and philosophical issues should be reexamined and reassessed. Salient among these are the conceptual issues related to governments' moral entitlement to authority ('legitimacy', in other words) and the conception of government broadly known as 'democracy'.

Legitimacy

Among the issues which have vexed political philosophers during the past half century, and which have also concerned political philosophers of earlier eras, including Aquinas, Thomas Hobbes, and John Locke, is that of legitimacy, the moral entitlement to rule, or, from the perspective of the individual citizen, the basis of the moral obligation to obey.[9] It is generally presumed that the issue of legitimacy can be settled once and for all by establishing optimal criteria of legitimacy, then determining whether a particular government meets those standards. If, however, government is not unitary but fragmentary and in continual flux, then the issue of legitimacy cannot be settled once and for all by determining whether a mythic single, unitary, and stable government has rightful claim to its authority.

Instead, a more complex and messy process must occur, that of identifying the various units and types of governmental authority, then attempting to discover which criteria are best suited to determine whether these particular authorities have legitimate claim to their powers. The discussion of legitimacy is thus put on a different plane. For one thing, usual discussions of legitimacy are based on the premise that governing and sovereignty are unitary and overawing, with the implication that a citizen of a particular government is the subject of overwhelming power and authority. However, if sovereignty and government are fragmented, then the issue of legitimacy is not single but multiple, and no one domain of legitimate governmental authority need be overwhelmingly important for individual persons or for the collective existence of the nation. Moreover, if sovereignty resides in diverse nooks and crannies of government, each holding distinct responsibility and authority, then it is entirely possible that varying criteria of legitimacy will be appropriate for each differing governing entity. If so, not one but several standards of legitimacy may apply depending on which type of governing authority or activity is at issue.

Lastly, it may be the case that the various candidates for the correct criteria of legitimacy will gain or lose plausibility if the view that government is fragmentary is accepted. The belief that legitimacy must rest on the consent of the people seems reasonable, for example, if there is only one governing entity that requires consent. However, if there are many governing entities, all loosely grouped under the umbrella of government, and, if these elements may drift into and out of existence, gain and lose authority, or shift their domain of authority from one arena to another, seeking popular consent for each minuscule shift is both impractical and probably impossible because numerous referenda would be required to certify each shift and sprouting of governmental function. Also, the requirement for popular certification becomes implausible when the power each element possesses over the individual citizen may be so slight as to be invisible.

In addition, basing legitimacy on respect for human rights (as some have sought to do) suffers diminished plausibility, since many of the diverse governing units have little impact on citizens' human rights. Agencies charged with maintaining roads, for example, while clearly important, have little impact on human rights. Of course, they are obliged to respect the rights of their workers, the people with whom they deal, and those whose lives may be affected by their activities. However, the same obligations bind any other human institution, and the obligations have little to do with matters of governance. Nonetheless, it is possible that the above points are plausible only because highway maintenance offices have the remotest relationship with governance, understood as the business of telling citizens and institutions what to do. But this employs a constricted view of governing, for these institutions are clearly part of most governments and carry out functions which most people believe are the proper business of government.

Therefore, it would seem reasonable carefully to examine each of the various individual modes and agencies of governing and, based on their particular responsibilities and powers, make specific decisions about whether each entity is entitled to its perquisites. Furthermore, it is entirely possible that many of these agencies have *no* moral entitlement to their powers and authority. But this need not be taken to imply that they are *illegitimate*, in the sense that they deserve to lose their authority. Rather, it implies that they have no moral title to their existence or activity any more than does a private organization or business enterprise. Hence, they may be disbanded, supplanted by other organizations, and have responsibilities removed or added should citizens or other branches of government decide to do so. In other words, for many types of governing entities, it may be inappropriate to ask whether they are legitimate or not. The legitimate questions would be those of whether they are performing useful functions and carrying out their tasks competently. Nonetheless, even if they *are* both useful and competent, they may have no moral entitlement to remain in existence.

Furthermore, while clarifying the proper role of legitimacy is underway, another distinction must be kept in mind, that separating the formal structure of government from the culture of politics and government and from the individuals who hold governing power. When the concept 'government' is brushed in broad strokes, these three aspects are not always clearly distinguished. Yet, the distinction is highly important, for complaints about government, abuses of its authority, or other failings can generally be traced to one or another of these facets of government – and the appropriate remedy will depend on recognizing which is in need of reform.

For example, it is very important that a judicial system be designed to protect certain human rights, and it will also be important that those within the system employ their authority so that this body of rights is protected and respected. However, a judicial system cannot seek to protect and preserve the full array of rights which it can be claimed that people ought to enjoy. Rather, it must confine its attentions to bodily security, protection of legal entitlements, and fair and proper dealing. Thus, if rights pertinent to a judicial system are violated by the system itself, it may lose its legitimacy, that is, its claim to continue to retain its functions and authority. However, it is not obvious that popular consent is the most appropriate device for determining the legitimacy of a judicial system, since political pressures often bias judicial systems and impair their ability to protect rights.

Furthermore, while it may be appropriate for a legislature to be directly accountable to popular approval, since its activity directly affects people's lives, it is also a mistake to grant a legislature a broad range of power over all segments of governmental authority. The obvious examples are that the judiciary should be excluded from legislative interference and that all citizens should enjoy rights which are not vulnerable to the will of the majority. Also, according to several prominent conceptions of Madisonian democracy (the view that citizens should have a body of rights protected from compromise by the will of the majority), there are good reasons for believing that popular will should not have unlimited reign over all facets of governing; there should be a reserve of protected rights free from popular manipulation for the very sound reason that unpopular persons, groups, or ideas have entitlements that should be protected even in the face of popular acrimony. Hence, legitimacy, founded on concern for individual rights, may appropriately apply to some offices and roles of government. Others may best be judged by appeal to popular consent in some guise or another. Yet others, however, may lie beyond the reach of legitimacy altogether.

Democracy

If the above ideas concerning the fragmentary nature of governmental structures and governmental power are correct, and if the ideas regarding the revision of the concept of legitimacy discussed above are correct, the vague, multifaceted and popular conception of democracy must be also reevaluated. 'Democracy' is among the most thoroughly abused terms in the political lexicon. During its centuries of service in political debate, it has been stretched, pulled, and distorted until it often retains little substance. This distortion is largely due to the fact that democracy has become very popular, so popular that every government of the present era (with the possible exception of several Islamic republics) claims to be democratic whatever its relationship to any reasonable conception of democratic government.

The common and crude view of democracy is that it is rule by the people. But few national governments meet this standard in any literal sense, and it is not obvious that they should attempt to do so. Certainly the governments of nation-states do not; they are too large, and the territory they rule is too vast and complex to allow anything resembling direct, participatory democracy. The era of direct participatory democracy as practiced in Athens in the day of Plato and Aristotle (and not particularly admired by either of them) is long past. So, rule by the people in any literal sense is a historical relic at best, and an idle dream at worst. Hence, the *idea* of direct participatory democracy is best considered a fondly remembered relic of a vanished era.

Furthermore, there are important conceptual difficulties with the crude view of democracy as rule by the people. One is that there is considerable difficulty in determining what constitutes a people and the more pungent difficulty of determining just what it is the people want.[10] However, a more basic problem is determining just what is meant by 'the rule of' the people.

Hence, the common rhetorical conception must be replaced by another, or possibly several others, if democracy is to retain a useful role in political analysis. The more sophisticated and subtle alternatives are democracy as rule on behalf of the people or as rule accountable to the people. At present, most of the governments of the world with some plausible claim to the title of democracy are representative governments. Hence, the world appears to regard governments as democratic if they are led by officials who gain office through reasonably free, open elections and must regularly undergo the rigors of re-election. Those so chosen are presumed responsive to the desires of their citizens and disposed to act on their behalf. However, elected officials frequently make decisions on matters about which the general public has few discernable desires or is badly fragmented. Moreover, they sometimes make unpopular decisions, that is, decisions which are contrary to the desires of the electorate. Most governments, in addition, contain agencies which are explicitly insulated from public pressure in hopes of allowing these offices to function without political influence.

Thus, the representative government of nation-states is far removed from actual rule by the people and is only sporadically responsive to their actual desires; in fact, the issues which ignite the most intense public interest are frequently of minor importance. In 1992 the electorate of the United States was incensed to learn that many members of Congress had overdrawn accounts kept in a special congressional bank even though these peccadillos cost the taxpayers no money at all.[11] On the other hand, Americans showed little interest in major scandals in the savings and loan industry which have cost the federal government many billions of dollars and promises to cost many additional billions before the affair is closed.[12]

Politicians nonetheless cling to the honorific term 'democracy' when referring to their own governments, and it is worth asking whether any of its original core of meaning remains viable. It is possible that it does, if the core meaning is recast to the view that government is democratic if it is *accountable to* its citizens. Free and open elections provide an opportunity for ordinary people to express displeasure with their politicians. In addition, the periodic ritual of elections, which demands that politicians seek the favor of citizens and apply to them for their offices, is extremely important; it impresses both politicians and citizens with the idea that the former owe their jobs to the latter.

According to the view of democracy as accountability, the significance of elections is not that they give individual voters means to elect the candidates of their choice to office. The view that elections express the will of the people or that of individual voters has been criticized by those who argue that a careful look at the way elections actually function demonstrates that people do not have occasion to express their preferences.[13] They are presented with a slate of candidates or a roster of issues which may or may not include any of their actual preferences as options. Even if their desired choices are on the ballots, these choices may fail to gain a majority of votes. The view of democracy as accountability thus holds that elections are important but not because they allow voters to exercise their will or enact their choices. They are important as rituals which compel politicians to pay homage to the electorate in quest of office.

Democracy understood as accountability thus requires that government be responsive to its electorate in those areas where it demonstrates visible concern and provide means for the electorate to voice its displeasure with individual politicians or particular political parties. However, democracy as accountability does not entirely cohere with the reality of the present day, which is that a substantial portion of the vast and complex structure of government exists largely beyond public view and interest, and the largest segments of governments, the various bureaus and offices, are almost entirely beyond direct public control.

This difficulty is underscored by the realization that government is split and fragmented, that government is not a unity which can therefore be said to stand in one relation rather than another to the people of its society. As with the conception of legitimacy, the question becomes that of how democracy should be conceived and what reasons may be given in favor of democratic government – or whether, in many cases, a mere gesture in the direction of a democratic form of government is the most reasonable course.

The difficulty is compounded in the domain of international governing structures. The international structures of government being devised will generally be democratic in several senses; they will be composed of the representatives of their constituencies, be accountable to them, and respond to their pressures. Their constituencies, however, are and will likely continue to be governments of nation-states rather than individual persons. Hence, international governing structures are twice removed from the wishes and desires of ordinary people; instead, they are accountable to their creators and constituents, namely, national governments.

Moreover, decisions to cede portions of national sovereignty to international structures are commonly made by governments alone (though this not inevitably the case, since referenda are occasionally held to approve of various measures and treaties). Also, these decisions are generally not straightforwardly linked to the wishes of their citizens. For example, several important treaties which lower barriers to free trade and create open economic trade and commercial zones have not been subject to public referenda. The reason is clear; the public would very probably disapprove, since such measures are often politically unpopular. Insofar as the public is aware of them at all, it is generally suspicious of them.[14]

So long as international governing structures have national governments as their primary constituency, individual persons will be represented in international councils only indirectly, via the agency of their national governments. Any claim to democracy these international bodies may possess is also undermined by the fact that their activities commonly affect the interests of individual persons in only circuitous fashion. That is, the most important domains of international control include currency regulation, international trade management, or environmental protection, none of which ordinarily has immediate impact on individual persons. None of them (with the possible exception of environmental pollution) are issues about which the public has displayed great interest, nor is it likely to do so at any time in the foreseeable future. Policies governing these matters will eventually affect the lives of individual persons, but will generally not directly change the ways in which individuals live, nor do they have direct control over individuals' actions.

Furthermore, matters of justice for individual persons or concern for individual rights is not likely to be directly affected by the activities of international structures any time soon, though there is some effort to establish means to allow individual persons to press charges of abuses of rights against governments.[15] Thus far governments have forcefully resisted the creation of such institutions, generally on grounds that the oversight they would exercise would be a direct assault on their sovereignty. Political leaders are willing to forfeit sovereignty in other areas but are loathe to give formal recognition to efforts to constrain their relations with their own citizens. However, this stance could easily change. If the major powers of the world were forcefully to seek the creation of such structures and attempt to insure that they would function effectively and impartially, it is quite probable that the remainder of the governments of the world would eventually approve. However, given present circumstances, it is difficult to see how international governing bodies can be judged legitimate or not, presuming that judgments of legitimacy are based on the criteria of respect or support for human rights.

While the initial impulse, given contemporary political rhetoric and the honorific status granted to the term 'democracy', is to insist that any and all governing entities, including international bodies, should be directly accountable to individual persons, this would often be a mistake. Part of the basis for this assertion is that national governments continue to wield great power in international circles and an attempt to circumvent their control would likely result only in ineffectual showcases of governmental activity. Moreover, the issues these diverse bodies must address are for the most part those of concern primarily to governments and require the cooperation and support of national governments. Matters, such as currency regulation, control of international trade, and of international law are of little concern to ordinary people. Governments appear to understand the need for these bodies and generally work to support them; in this regard governments have moved beyond the particular concerns of individual citizens.

Such matters affect peoples' lives, of course, but indirectly; hence, they are best omitted from politics and placed in the realm of international bureaucracy, since ordinary people are likely to have little interest in them and the intrusion of additional political turbulence is apt to result in less effective management of these issues and more political intrusion in them. Bureaucratic approaches to such matters are feasible because the issues they involve are largely technical and therefore best managed by those who have training sufficient to understand them. Moreover, the history of the United Nations demonstrates that efforts to make decisions are often chaotic and hobbled by politicking. Other matters, including the need to address international crises, are such that they require the direct attention of governments, who must work in harmony to address them, despite the chaos of decision-making which exists on the international level. Once more the intrusion of an extra layer of politics is apt to make their responses less rather than more effective and competent.

An additional problem is that of what form democratic structures on the international level should take. It would appear obvious that only some form of representative government would prove workable. However, the immediate question is that of the nature of the representatives. An attempt to have representatives elected directly by ordinary people and report to international governing structures, which would be independent of national governments, would risk becoming a sham. This is because national governments retain the overwhelming margin of power, both physical and that of the purse, in the international realm. Therefore, an attempt to rule without their active support would be an exercise in futility. Furthermore, most of the issues arising on the international level also require the active cooperation and resources of national governments, so they *must* be involved regardless of what formal structures of international government are adopted.

An alternative is for representatives to be chosen by national governments. Such representatives would then participate directly in the international ruling bodies and be accountable to ordinary citizens. But this response would only revive the problem of the above paragraph, since these representatives would have to gain cooperation from their own governments in order to address the issues they must face, and hence would very likely soon come under the control of national governments.

Thus, given the present circumstances of the world, the only practical course is to retain something like the present arrangement of retaining governments as the constituents of international government. This is an imperfect response at best, because the interests of political leaders frequently diverge from those of the majority of their citizens. This divergence is partly because many national governments are agents of a ruling elite which wields the machinery of government to maintain its privileged status, and also because many of the governments of the world are tyrannical, abuse their citizens' rights, and dismiss their interests. However, once again, there seems no workable alternative to this arrangement.

But there is a more basic reason for believing that resort to representative democracy is not inevitably the optimal response to matters of international government, and it is the fragmentary and limited nature of the emergent governing bodies. If government, along with sovereignty and legitimacy, were of a piece and existed either totally or not at all, then it might be reasonable to insist on some measure of direct popular control of international government. This is because governmental control over individual persons would be extensive and because it would be feasible to institute one mechanism of democratic control over a single unitary body.

But, since the international governing bodies exist as discrete entities and lack the shell of a unifying structure that most national governments possess, it is both impractical and unnecessary to require democratic accountability of them all. It is impractical and unnecessary for the same reasons as apply on the level of individual nation-states. However, the reasons are more compelling, since the degree of fragmentation and discontinuity is greater on the level of international governing structures. Hence, an attempt to impose representative democracy is impractical due to the wide diversity of international governing bodies, bodies which are disconnected and lack an overarching structure of authority. But it is also unnecessary because these governing bodies generally have little impact on the ordinary lives and concerns of individual citizens. Their duties are clearly important but are largely technical and hold little prospect of infringing on the lives or rights of individual persons. Hence, international governing structures should retain their present roles as the governments (in however a tenuous a sense) of governments.

However, the above does not imply that there is no proper or practical role for democracy, in what might be termed an extended sense, on the level of international governing structures. If democracy in the sense of concern for the interests of individual citizens or the collective interests of citizens as a whole is ruled out, democracy as an extended sense of public accountability remains, and it would appear a viable and reasonable candidate for a conception of democracy which would be workable on the level of international relations and perhaps that of national governments as well. However, the usual mechanism for achieving democratic accountability, that of elected governmental representatives, has been shown to be unworkable for international governing structures.

This does not signify that democracy as such has no role on this level, for there are other possible ways of instilling a measure of public accountability on the array of governing bodies sprouting up on the international level. In fact, the measures may be sufficiently workable that they would allow some public accountability for even highly technical and bureaucratic governing bodies.

Thus, the extended sense of democracy as public accountability would entail devising means to give ordinary citizens a voice in the international bodies where they have an interest, whether a personal interest in matters affecting their own lives or an indirect interest in what happens to others or simply the more general interest in fair and competent governance. Extended democracy would also include mechanisms for making some of these bodies accountable to individual citizens. Allowing individuals or groups of individuals a direct voice in the deliberations of some of these bodies by mandating periodic open forums for public comment and expression of concern is one such mechanism. Something like this has occurred at the United Nations' conferences on the environment and population, where many different, non-governmental groups attended and were given a voice. Another would be to require opportunity for public hearing on measures passed or policies adopted, or provide some other means of making the interests of individuals felt and heard directly on the international level and independent of the agency of their governments.

Addressing the matter of making these bodies accountable to citizens would be more difficult, since the obvious measure of filling them with elected representatives who could be voted out of office if they incur popular displeasure has been shown impracticable. However, the mechanism of representative government is compatible with the other measures for seeking accountability. There may be instances where it would be best to rely on this mechanism as a means of seeking accountability or advocacy of the interests of individual human beings. The point is that this mechanism is likely to be unworkable in many instances. It should not be claimed that a government which is composed of the elected representatives of a people is therefore automatically genuinely accountable to them.

Hence, genuine world government is developing and has been for some years. It has been overlooked because people have been unable to see it for what it is. They have been misled by the common view that government can exist only as a single, unified whole. This view is false, even as a description of ordinary national governments, and is even farther from capturing the nature of emergent world government. The simple fact is that contemporary governments are far too complex, have far too many functions, and exist in far too many guises for the view that they are organic wholes to approach adequacy. World government is being created a bit and a piece at a time and is unlikely to become anything approaching an organic unity. Nonetheless, it is acquiring an ever broader array of governing functions.

This diverse and fragmented government has clear import for the usual conceptions of legitimacy and democracy. If governing functions and bodies are diverse and fragmented, then simple, one-dimensional conceptions of legitimacy and democracy must be inadequate. In fact, for some functions, they may be superfluous. Differing criteria of legitimacy are required for governing functions of differing sorts. In the same vein, traditional conceptions of democracy do not apply to the emerging structures. In some instances, 'democracy' may not apply at all, and ought not.

It must be acknowledged, though, that there is another reason why the emergent world government has not been recognized for what it is. It is that many of the functions it is undertaking differ from those in customary views of the proper role of governments. In other words, the roles which governments (whether national or international) perform have evolved along with their structures. The work of the following chapter is to examine this transformation.

5 The Role of National Governments

For centuries political philosophers have debated the question of the proper role of sovereign governments. Both Plato and Aristotle devoted considerable energy and thought to this issue, as have Thomas Aquinas, Thomas Hobbes, John Locke, John Stuart Mill, Karl Marx, and, in contemporary Anglo-American philosophy, John Rawls and Robert Nozick, along with other academic liberal philosophers. This discussion is particularly important at present, for the forces of globalism are presently changing the role of governments.

Examination of the role of governments is crucially important for several reasons. A government that fails to perform its proper role is incompetent and therefore has lost a substantial portion of its mandate to govern. Thus, discussions of the role of governments are relevant to devising criteria used to determine which governments have plausible claim to their power and authority. In addition, understanding the proper role of government can guide discussions of which policies governments should adopt and what structure they should have. Conceptions of the proper role of government can also be used to devise political ideals, that is, goals that governments should strive to achieve, and can offer citizens criteria for judging governments' competence.

Part of the discussion of governmental roles, therefore, is a debate about what governments *ought* to seek to achieve, but this debate must be rooted in the facts about what governments do as a matter of fact seek to achieve and about what governments can or must seek to achieve. That which governments are able to achieve, or are forced by the pressure of circumstance to attempt, has undergone considerable evolution during the course of human history. Discussions of what governments ought to achieve should not be limited by what governments in fact seek. However, even idealistic views must have some basis in the factual conditions of human life if they are to be more than idle day dreaming.

THE ASPECTS OF GOVERNMENT

As in the case of sovereignty, discussion of the roles of government must examine two perspectives; the internal relation of a government to its citizens and the external aspect of its relation to other nation-states (or international political bodies or significant foreign institutions, such as corporations).

The Internal Role of Government

For most of human history there has been general agreement that a major portion of the internal role of government is to provide a stable social order for individual citizens and institutions (however imperfectly this is achieved). Government does so by protecting citizens from one another via establishing and enforcing standards of social conduct but also by maintaining conditions in which basic social institutions (such as schools, churches, medical facilities, and professions) can grow and function. Those espousing minimalist conceptions of government, such as John Locke, Thomas Hobbes, or, a contemporary figure, Robert Nozick, argue that government's role should be confined to this basic function of preserving good social order.

However, others claim that governments are also obliged to seek prosperity or good lives for their citizens. Indeed, popular sentiment, particularly in contemporary liberal democracies, has forced this goal on governments, since political leaders who fail to achieve a thriving economy are apt to be voted out of office, and politicians are keenly aware that a sure way to get voted into office is the promise of providing prosperity. Even totalitarian governments are aware that failure to achieve economic prosperity for citizens is the failing most likely to result in unrest sufficient to remove them from power.[1] Oddly perhaps, some partisans of minimalist government accept the importance of seeking a prosperous society; in their view prosperity is most likely to result from minimal government intrusion in private commerce.

A view seldom found in the rhetoric of Western liberal democracy, but which has great attraction nonetheless, is the conviction that governments should seek to make their citizens happy or good or both.[2] Both Plato and Aristotle accepted this view. Also, it was a basic principle of the Leninist rule of the Soviet Union during the 75 years that it enjoyed power. The Leninist state sought to improve both its citizens' character and their material welfare.[3] Moreover, though the goal of happiness is not part of the official liberal ideology of most Western liberal democracies, they, as a matter of actual twentieth century practice, have adapted some of its elements. Hence, the welfare states currently predominant among Western liberal democracies provide various services designed to improve the lives and well being of their citizens.

The United States, in popular lore a bastion of frontier independence, has also become a welfare state, and popular sentiment is unlikely to allow a significant retreat from these policies. Beginning with the New Deal of the 1930s and continuing with Lyndon Johnson's 'Great Society' of the 1960s, the United States has created an array of social programs designed to improve and protect the lives of its citizens. These include education, job retraining, ambitious health care programs, a vast array of public health and safety regulations, and public welfare programs. The obvious goal of these efforts is to improve the lot of ordinary citizens. Moreover, these programs were established in response to public demand, and it is likely that a political leader who attempted seriously to curtail or eliminate any substantial portion of these programs would be tossed out of office. This partly explains why even conservative politicians ideologically opposed to such programs have left them largely unscathed and in some instances have expanded them.[4]

External Role of Government

The external role of national governments has played a lesser role in the thinking of most political philosophers; in fact, they have been largely silent on the matter. In part this is because they have generally presumed that the business of governments is properly confined to the area within their national boundaries. Government, after all, is largely a matter of the relationship between those holding power and those governed.

But there is another reason for political philosophers' reticence; they have assumed that there was little to say. For most of human history, the international arena is best described as a state of anarchy. Philosophers have generally viewed it as state of nature, a condition where there is no government, no law, and hence no principle guiding relations between states other than brandishing arms.[5] Government could exist over nations only when military power allowed one nation to subjugate its rivals. But, when nations could not subjugate one another, there was no government among them, and the resort to arms was the ultimate foundation of their relations.

Thus, for the most part governments of various nation-states have had relatively little to do with one another. In past centuries trade was a salient exception to this rule (though the spate of imperialist expansion of the last century may rival it in importance). However, these relations were relatively peripheral. Transnational trade generally played no great role in national economies, and trade relations did not have any great impact on the lives of most citizens.

Nonetheless, the most important and constant of the interactions between nations has been war or military posturing. Hence, the primary external role of governments has been either that of protecting the nation from external incursion by means of the use of military forces or the protection and expansion of national interests abroad, once again, via the deployment of military force.

Thus, however civilized they may have wished to appear, the mutual dealings of national governments, in the final analysis, have been based on military power. Its importance is exaggerated in periods of military tension, as during the era of the Cold War, when the military preeminence of the United States and the Soviet Union allowed them to dominate lesser military powers. The significance of military power may ebb in periods of relative peace, but these have been few and mostly brief. For instance, some years after the American Civil War, Brevet Major General Emory Upton of the US Army calculated that the United states was at war for one year in three of the first century of its existence.[6]

Though several nation-states' wars have involved control of trade routes, the great majority of wars have been fought over the control of territory. In large part this is because control of territory and of people has long been the key to the power, wealth, and influence of national governments; though this power, wealth, and influence may directly benefit only the governments themselves and the people who control them. Military success does not always benefit the ordinary people of a victorious nation, who are often as poor in a wealthy and powerful state as in a poor and uninfluential state.[7] Though the direct consequence of military violence is destruction, whether that of armies, citizens' lives, or property, destruction generally allows control of land – and of the people residing on the land thus gained.

Given the above general and broad gauge description of the usual roles of the governments of nation-states, it is apparent that a key element of governments' ability to play these roles is their control of armed power. It is used to gain control of the territory of a nation-state, to keep its citizens obedient and compliant, and to exercise influence over other nations. Hence, during the period of human history when nation-states have been ascendent in human affairs, their central importance has largely been the result of their monopoly control of armed force. This has shaped the relation of national governments to their citizens and defined their dealings with other governments.

In addition, governments' monopoly control of physical force has shaped political theorists' perceptions of the nature and role of government; theorists in the tradition of Western European liberalism have generally presumed that the key to governmental authority is found in its coercive power.[8] Hence, they frame the issue of governmental legitimacy in terms of government's entitlement to demand obedience from citizens.[9]

THE EVOLVING ROLE OF THE NATION-STATE

Early in this century governments' role within their national borders gained an added dimension. The introduction of wildly successful methods of taxation (among them the income tax, a brilliant invention for transporting huge sums of money from citizens' pockets to the coffers of government) played a major role in this change. Prior to the twentieth century, governments were small, their functions limited, and their finances slender, at least when compared with the present. The bounty created by new modes of taxation helped change all of this.[10] The size and expense of military forces ballooned, as did the cost and complexity of the equipment they employed. The number of government employees multiplied, and, because they needed something to do, the functions of government also multiplied. The impact of governments on the day-to-day lives and activities of citizens and institutions, including business corporations, greatly expanded in consequence.

Governments shaped the economies of their nations by removing vast sums of money from the hands of private citizens and also by the way they spend their largess.[11] An enlarged tax bite gave them significant influence on the growth and shape of domestic economies. Tax laws had an additional impact on national economies, since they determined which segments of society would bear the burden of supporting greatly enlarged government.

In addition, the increased size of government and the requirements of modern industrialized economies spawned arrays of regulations, along with bureaus to enforce them, for the oversight of business activity and of human life in general. These efforts also shaped and directed the flow of commercial endeavor. Regulatory efforts eventually resulted in national central banks and agencies to oversee financial markets and institutions. As these were put in place, it became apparent that the decisions of the various bureaus of government would have a substantial effect on national economies, and many regulators determined that their decisions should aim at sustaining the growth and economic vibrancy of their nations.

These efforts were given legitimacy and focus by twentieth-century economic theories, such as those of John Maynard Keynes, which described the effects that governmental policies are likely to have on the economy of a nation and prescribed measures to ensure that such policies would nurture economic vitality. In addition, advances in communication and transportation, along with the development of new academic disciplines in economic and social sciences, allowed governmental agencies to acquire vast quantities of information regarding national economies and the global economy. Most importantly, this information could be used to determine whether the economy was prospering or floundering. Hence, business, governmental, and financial circles await the periodic dissemination of governmental economic statistics with the eagerness functionaries of ancient Rome awaited periodic analyses of entrails.

Knowledge brings power, but it also brings responsibility to address the problems it reveals and gives means of assessing the performance of those who claim to bring economic prosperity. Once the Pandora's box of economic data comes open, it cannot be shut again. As a result, civil servants and political leaders have accepted responsibility for nurturing prosperity, and, as an additional result, have also made themselves vulnerable to censure when their nation's economy deteriorates.

The pressures which compel political figures to accept responsibility for their nation's economic prosperity have become overwhelming. Politicians are keenly aware that, if they do not pledge themselves to enhance national prosperity, others will, and may push them out of office as a result. Further, all politicians, of whatever ideological stripe, appear to accept the view that they must employ the machinery of government to honor their promises, since, in part, they have no other instruments available for this purpose. Ronald Reagan in the United States and Margaret Thatcher in Great Britain committed themselves to nurturing the prosperity of their nations, and to do so using the instruments of government, even though both pledged unswerving allegiance to principles of *laissez-faire* and limited government.

This change in the role of governments is reflected in the work of twentieth century academic philosophers. As exemplified by John Rawls' *A Theory of Justice*, many came to presume that theories of distributive justice were central to political philosophy.[12] They continue discussions of the traditional topics of citizens' rights, the principles of democratic society, and the nature of human freedom. However, philosophers now commonly analyze these topics in terms of their relation to distributive justice, and they have presumed that the locus of these issues is the activities and responsibilities of national governments. The questions that absorbed the political philosophers of the seventeenth through the nineteenth centuries, those of the proper limits of governmental power, have generally moved to the background, while theories of distributive justice and basic human entitlements have moved to the foreground of philosophical examination. This shift has occurred at least in part because of the changes in the role of government which have taken place in this century.

CONDITIONS OF THE PRESENT DAY

The emerging global economy is spurring yet another change in the role of governments. To a far greater degree than in past years, the economic destiny of nations, even very powerful ones, is controlled by events elsewhere. Their destiny is also shaped by the compelling need, presently shared by all nations, to compete effectively in the global arena. As previous chapters note, what were once strictly domestic political decisions regarding banking controls, the cost of capital, the transfer of technology and the exploitation of natural resources now often directly affect other nations. Even decisions about labor regulations or pollution control now commonly affect foreign nations.

The globe is no longer chopped up into numerous more or less independent economic zones confined within the borders of single nation-states; the world is an interdependent network in which events in one part of the system can immediately affect the other parts of the system. Individual national governments must function and seek prosperity within this network; they can no longer afford the attempt to remain independent.

National governments have also discovered that they must vigorously seek to protect and advance their interests in the international arena.[13] Their efforts can no longer be sporadic, nor are they peripheral to national welfare. The regular meetings of the Group of Seven, the creation of international bodies such as the Organization for Economic Cooperation and Development, the swelling international traffic of economic ministers, delegations and committees, as well as the proliferation of international economic conferences, all testify to the importance of the role that national governments must play in advancing their nation's fortunes in the international arena.

Governments' attention is no longer predominantly focused within national boundaries; it is increasingly directed outward. The success and competence of governments will increasingly be judged by their aptitude for furthering their national economic interests in the global arena. They will be evaluated in terms of their success as facilitators, regulators, and sustainers of the emerging global economic order.

Competition among the major nations of the world remains, but it is now predominantly economic rather than military. For the most part nations' struggles for economic success or predominance are no longer aided by military confrontation.[14] As the Cold War evaporated, the ascending economic powers, Japan and (a reunited) Germany, discovered that their influence in the world is increasing, while that of the great military powers, the United States and the former Soviet Union, is ebbing. Indeed, the superpowers' commitment to preserving their military superiority is now something of a liability. While such matters are notoriously difficult to predict, it now appears extremely unlikely that the major powers, whether economic or military, will soon find themselves at war with one another. This view is reflected in the titles of a series of recent works; one that is representative is John Mueller's *Retreat from Doomsday: The Obsolescence of Major War* (New York: Basic Books, 1989), which, note, was written *before* the events of 1989 (that is, before the events which clearly signalled the demise of the Cold War).[15]

Hence, the role of governments is increasingly defined by the pressures of economics, whether within their own borders or in their relations with other nations. Though they retain their armies and police, controlling instruments of physical coercion is no longer of overwhelming political importance; certainly it is not important in major powers' dealings with one another. National governments' relations with one another, furthermore, decreasingly resemble those of the desperate and treacherous competitors in Hobbes' state of nature.

The above developments have an important implication. The tie between military force and government is strong; substantial military force is almost invariably linked to some form or another of formal government. However, for better or worse, the important international relations of the present day are those established by the emerging global economy, which is based on private commerce and the principles of free trade. Economic institutions and activity are not bound to governments by tight links of the sort that connect military forces and governments. Moreover, the conditions of the emerging global economy make it increasingly difficult for governments to completely dominate economic activity; certainly they cannot do so to the extent that they dominate military forces (or are dominated by them). As a result, insofar as economic prowess rather than military force is the major source of power in the world, the importance of the governments of nation-states will decline. National governments will retain great power, and they will have the central role of coordinators and regulators of the global economy, but they will not remain the unparalleled masters of human affairs that they have been in the past.

IMPLICATIONS FOR PHILOSOPHY

If the above conclusions are roughly correct, and if they become more obviously correct as the global economy continues to evolve, they have several important implications for political philosophy. The central and most obvious implication is that the attention of political philosophers can no longer focus primarily on national governments as it has been for the past several centuries. If the governments of nation-states decline in importance and other institutions take over some of their powers, or if a substantial portion of the authority that they once enjoyed over individual persons and private institutions simply evaporates, then political philosophers must look beyond them to attempt to discover the genuinely important loci of power and authority.

Complexity of Governing Structures

A major difficulty which will confront philosophers is that of where to find the loci of governmental power and authority. If it appeared that the power and authority of national governments were simply transferred to a formal unified world federal government, this new institution would become the central focus of political philosophy.

However, as claimed in Chapter 4, it is highly unlikely that a unified world government will emerge any time soon. This is because the governments of nation-states are loath to formally and finally surrender the perquisites of sovereign power to a global governing authority. National governments have been willing, under the pressure of circumstance, to barter away bits and pieces of their sovereign authority. However, they have always done so reluctantly, and they are unlikely to countenance a large-scale surrender of their sovereign authority. Furthermore, the movement to international governing structures has occurred on a piecemeal basis, as national governments find themselves confronted with difficulties they cannot adequately address in solitary fashion.

International governing structures have been devised with a narrow focus and limited perquisites because they are generally created to address specific issues. At least for the foreseeable future, those who seek an international government modelled after the unified governing structure of national governments are likely to be disappointed.

Hence, as the discussions of Chapter 4 revealed, political philosophers' analyses must become more complex. Governing power and authority is likely to become diffused across a wide variety of governing structures, both national and international. When, for example, philosophers wish to address a particular conceptual issue, such as that of legitimacy (the question of which conditions must be satisfied before governing structures gain moral entitlement to their authority) they will discover that the criteria must differ with variations in the nature of the governing structure in question and the sort of responsibilities which it carries. Legitimacy can no longer be applied in global fashion as though it applied only to a single, coherent, all-powerful, government modelled on the traditional view of the governments of nation-states. International financial structures established to control currency flows and oversee exchange rates, for example, may have enormous power over the economies of individual nation-states and the people within them, but it hardly seems relevant to assert that such structures are only entitled to their powers if they respect human rights. Yet entities of this sort are likely to be established in the near future, and theoreticians must learn how to think about them.

Interests Protected by Governments

Another issue is that of whose interests national governments should seek to protect and who will be the beneficiaries if national governments compete successfully in the international arena. It may seem that there is a clear and obvious answer to this question: governments are obliged to protect the interests and welfare of their citizens and those of the institutions their citizens create. During the greater portion of human history, this would have been the obvious and adequate answer. Of course, there has always been discussion of just *who* should be counted as a citizen, whether only adult males born to parents who were citizens, as in ancient Greece, or adult, non-slave males, as in the early years of the United States. Nonetheless, it has always been presumed that once the question of who counted as a citizen was answered, it would be clear that government should concern itself with the interests of citizens and that individual citizens should believe that their governments were charged with seeking to protect their interests. This response remains plausible even if, as was suggested in Chapter 4, the conception of citizenship is becoming attenuated and has come to resemble that of a client.

However, this definite and seemingly obvious relationship between citizen and government is being strained by the pressures of the global economy.[16] As individual persons or private institutions become increasingly mobile and accumulate ties and interests across the globe, their narrow loyalty to the particular government of a nation-state is likely to fade and become less relevant to their daily concerns and to the reality of their existence. Already, there is clear evidence that multinational corporations are slipping away from this identification. If so, governments' claim to represent the interests of a fixed and identifiable people must vanish as well, and the crumbling of governmental unity mentioned earlier is matched by a crumbling of citizenship and national identification.

Should the above erosion continue, national government will become primarily a government of territory rather than of a determinate people, just as the state governments of the United States are presently governments of territory rather than a unified and distinctive people. American state governments compete with one another to lure people and corporations to their domains in the effort to enrich the territory over which they have jurisdiction. Their success or failure in this endeavor, however, may not matter particularly to the people residing within their borders. This is because state residents will simply leave to seek brighter futures or more comfortable conditions elsewhere if they are dissatisfied with their government or the condition of its economy.

Furthermore, as pointed out earlier, the significance of national borders is eroding as well; hence, control of a particular patch of territory will lack the importance in future years that it enjoyed in the past, simply because governments will lose their ability tightly to control border traffic. In this regard, national governments are coming more closely to resemble the states of the United States. The latter also have nominal control of their state borders, though the control they may exercise is in fact severely restricted by both the law of the United States government and by the unified economy of the United States.

Hence, the role of national governments must alter significantly. The function of maintaining domestic order and protecting citizens from one another must remain. However, it is unlikely that governments will retain the power to enforce substantially greater restrictions on citizens' lives than those minimally required to maintain public order, simply because citizens and the institutions they work for may emigrate if they find governmental control onerous. Thus, governments may be dissuaded from tyrannical impulses but also from concerted efforts to mold the lives and characters of their citizens to a particular plan, as the Soviet Union attempted to do, and as Aristotle and Plato believed they should attempt to do.

Nonetheless, national governments may be pressured to offer the array of educational, medical, and social services that have become associated with the welfare state in order to attract and retain workers and corporations. They will be vastly more involved in relations with other nation-states than in past decades but not in the guise of violent military confrontation. Rather the governments of nation-states will become more deeply embroiled in competition for economic advantage and prosperity. Nonetheless, they will also be forced to continue cooperation to manage the complex array of systems required to keep the global economy afloat. Oddly, they will be required to do so because they will be clearly aware that the welfare of each individual nation-state depends on maintaining a healthy and smoothly functioning global economy. Given the present state of global interconnectedness, when the economy of one nation falters, those elsewhere soon suffer in sympathy.

In this regard Marx may have been right to claim that government would eventually reduce to bureaucratic and administrative functions, though he was mistaken about the context in which this deflation would occur. National governments will remain obliged to maintain good social order within their boundaries, will compete with one another to attract people and corporations, and will cooperate to manage the world economy, functions none too different from those Marx envisioned for the Communist utopia.

The preceding account of pressures and counter-pressures does not address the question of which goals governments *ought* to seek. However, if the claims of this chapter are correct, this traditional formulation of a perennial issue of political philosophy is inadequate to present and emerging circumstances. The issue of what governments ought to strive to attain can only be addressed, by first attending to other, more basic, matters. One is that of just who or what the governments of nation-states should be expected to serve; this is joined with the related issue of what should become of the traditional conception of 'citizen'. An additional question which the above analysis pushes to the surface is that of to whom or to what the questions regarding goals should be addressed, because solitary governments of nation-states will not be the dominant political units of the near future, and certainly they will not be the ultimate channels of political power.

Nature of Governments' Obligations

If the discussions of Chapter 3 are correct, governments of the future will be related to their citizens more as service-providing professionals (such as lawyers, physicians, accountants, or advertising agencies) are to clients than in terms of the traditional conception of the relation of government to citizen. In the former case government provides services for groups of people residing in a certain area rather than having dominion over a group of people established as a nation. The legal status of being a citizen will no doubt remain, in at least a formal sense, but mere legal citizenship is a hollow shell of the full-bodied conception of citizenship. If it is merely the legal entitlement to vote or run for political office, legal citizenship may count for little, since those who are not citizens will also be able to function within a nation, exert pressure on government, enjoy many governmental services, and make use of whatever advantages a state has to offer without taking on the status of citizenship. Citizenship may not matter at all, particularly if, as argued in Chapter 3, the link between government and cultural identification is broken.

However, the answer to the question of exactly who or what national governments should serve must be complex. In part, of course, national governments will be required to serve the interests of whichever particular individuals happen to be residing within their borders. Their relationship to these residents will be more that of professionals to clients than that of the traditional view of the relationship as that of government to citizen. A result will be the loss of the rich array of associations which have clustered around 'citizenship' as a result of centuries of reflection on politics. In particular, there is likely to be the full eclipse of the modern day remnants of Plato and Aristotle's view that the activities of citizenship, understood as direct and active participation in the affairs of governing, constitute essential constituents of the richest and most satisfying human life.

A group of theorists influential in recent years, known as communitarians, appears to be seeking a revival of the traditional conception of citizenship which involves active participation by individuals in the public life of a nation, understood as an identifiable group of people with shared culture and shared values.[17] While there is much to admire in the conception of human life embodied in these views, the difficulty is that the conditions necessary for the creation of the genuine communities sought by communitarians do not exist in the present era. The mobility, specialization, and fragmentation of contemporary life prevent the creation of communities which can make this ideal viable. Moreover, as claimed in Chapter 4, government itself is fragmenting, and fragmented government with modest responsibility is unsuited to play the grandiose role past thinkers envisaged for it.

In addition, and perhaps more importantly, contemporary advances in communication and transportation, along with huge increases in the earth's human population have resulted in the creation of vast and sprawling institutions. The power and efficiency of these institutions will cause them to crowd out the smaller human groups that boast a more intimate scale. Huge institutions do not allow close personal contact among members of the organization nor do they allow individual members to believe that they can make significant differences in the way the institution functions or hope to make changes in the major policies or practices of the institution.

These large structures stretch beyond the scale needed for immediate human empathy and sense of genuine belonging that are necessary to create communities in the classical Greek, romanticist Rousseauean, or the contemporary communitarian sense. Yet large institutions are the looming reality of human life. However cold and unappealing they may be, the realities of human existence will not allow them to be dismantled. Consider the federal government of the United States. As recently as a century ago it was a rather small and close-knit affair, needing relatively little in the way of funds and able to rely to a considerable extent on tariffs for its budget.[18] At present it is a sprawling and complex structure employing millions of people and is spread, literally, across the earth. The cozy human scale of the federal government of a century ago is not available to today's government. There is irony here, for larger government appears to loom smaller for ordinary persons than in past years; the Census Bureau or the Environmental Protection Agency, though they are important for individual lives, do not capture the imagination in the manner of the princes and conquerors of earlier periods of history. Yet there is no possibility of a return to the past; people demand too much from the federal government, and it needs to do too much, for its nature to change fundamentally. Similar claims can be made regarding other human institutions; the large, powerful, and complex will tend to drive out the small and intimate.

Hence, active citizenship involving direct participation in the affairs of government in a communal setting is no longer viable for most people, not even as an ideal. The present reality of human life is that of huge and imposing institutions. Nonetheless, human beings remain social creatures who gain satisfaction and comfort from association with others. The difficulty is that they may be forced to seek these values outside the domains of life that make a genuine difference in the way the world works; they may have no option other than to seek them primarily in their private lives. Thus, a major challenge for philosophers and for human beings generally is to determine how satisfying human lives can be achieved in this setting.

This is no longer the age of giants, not so far as individual human beings are concerned; it is the age of those who must function as small cogs in large and complex machines. The challenge is to determine how satisfying lives can be devised for these small cogs. As far as political philosophy is concerned, the implication is that the old rich and alluring conception of citizenship is no longer available, and human beings must make do with the thinner, hollower conception of something like clienthood.

But the obligations of national governments are also directed toward the institutions within their national boundaries; governments will be obliged to maintain and preserve an environment in which these institutions can prosper. Moreover, part of the obligation of the governments of nation-states must be directed back on themselves; that is, to nurture government and maintain its own institutional integrity and proper functioning. Governments' obligation to preserve themselves must ultimately derive whatever moral force it possesses from a link with the welfare of individual human persons, and the argument can easily be made that such institutions *are* necessary for the achievement and maintenance of satisfactory lives for individual human beings. It would also appear that the relevant individual human lives in this instance are those of the persons who are citizens. However, this must be only part of the truth. As shall be seen below, there are good grounds for believing that national governments must come to have increasing obligations, in one form or another, to humanity as a whole.

In future years, the belief that the government of a nation-state has obligations *only* to its own citizens will no longer be viable. In part this is because, as noted above, the future bond between government and citizen will be far more tenuous and fleeting than in past centuries, so that there will no longer be a huge divide between citizen and non-citizen; today's citizen may soon become a non-citizen, and those who are non-citizens may shortly become citizens. But, also, there will be circumstances in which the obligations of national governments to human beings in other parts of the world outweigh their obligations to their own citizens. This is because a substantial portion of the obligations of the governments of nation-states will be directed outward, toward other nation-states and the world community; the governments of nation-states are gradually taking on the collective responsibility of maintaining the good order and smooth operation of the world economy.

Furthermore, the interdependence of nation-states and national economies that the global economy is nurturing will cause national governments to have direct responsibility to the governments of other nation-states and to the citizens of those other nation-states. The reason is that the policies and decisions of national governments commonly directly affect the people and governments of other nations, and with these effects comes responsibility to control and take account of them. National governments will have these obligations because, once again, the welfare of individual persons will depend on it.

Moreover, because of the importance of the global economy for the entire world and because of the possible effects of decisions and policies of one nation on the people of another nations, it will sometimes be the case that governments will be obliged to give greater weight to the concerns of those in other nations than to their own citizens. This may occur, for example, if allowing power plants and manufacturing plants to produce emissions resulting in acid rain will benefit the economy of the polluting nation, but also greatly harm people and commerce in other nations. Or, if radiation emissions from nuclear power plants, themselves important for the economy of one nation, endanger the health of those in other nations. In such instances, the national governments in question would have a clear obligation to the people in other nations whose lives were harmed by such practices, and the obligation might be sufficient to outweigh obligations of that government to serve the interests of its own people.

Moreover, because much of the governing of the world economy and of world affairs will be carried out, in one fashion or another, by the collective agency of national governments, individual governments may have the obligation to seek policies and institutions that will benefit the entire world rather than only their own citizens. Once again, this may occur when the nations of the world attempt to devise policies or institutions for controlling the emission of pollutants.

Bearers of Responsibility for Achieving Goals

In previous centuries the question of which institutions had ultimate responsibility for achieving political goals could receive a quick answer: the burden would fall to the governments of nation-states. This is because they were the predominant political institutions of human kind. Now, however, and to an increasing degree in future years, these political functions will not be undertaken by the solitary governments of single nation-states. In large part this is because single governments will be incapable of addressing them adequately. On matters of international currency regulation, trade laws, regulation of multinational corporations, environmental pollution, or international public health matters, individual governments are already incapable of effective action. Such issues will be adequately addressed only by the collective action of national governments. They will do so via treaties, creation of international regulatory institutions, or greater reliance on the agencies and structures of the United Nations.

Hence, when appeals for action on one or another of the issues of global consequence are made, they cannot be addressed only to individual national governments but to international mechanisms for addressing the issues or to the world community as a whole. At present the United Nations is the major forum for addressing transnational issues. The UN's shortcoming is that its membership is limited to governments, and they have been loath to create avenues to allow individual persons direct access to the world community's ear.

Hence, pleas for action must be addressed to whichever body is best suited for dealing with them. The difficulty is that most international bodies are the creations of national governments and remain their creatures and their captives. However, it is likely that these bodies will come to gain an authority and legitimacy of their own as the world community becomes accustomed to their activity and comes to rely upon them for services. It is also likely that, as such bodies shuffle off their dependence on national governments, they will also become more open to pressure and pleas from private individuals and non-governmental organizations. Furthermore, huge transnational corporations are likely to play a role in pushing for greater international government. They will do so because they generally prefer to operate in accordance with a single set of laws and regulations rather than various differing sets. They have displayed this proclivity in the United States, where they have often sought national regulation in order to avoid the prospect of being subject to differing regulations by each individual state. Hence, they may soon press for single global regulation in order to escape the welter of differing systems of regulations found in individual nation-states.

Goals of National Governments

It should now be apparent that in the future the responsibilities of national governments must range much wider than in the past. National governments can no longer justify limiting the range of their responsibility to the edge of their national boundaries. At the very minimum, they are responsible for insuring that their acts and policies do not cause undue harm to the persons or institutions of other nations. They have this obligation because they now have both the ability and the knowledge to be aware of the impact of their activities on those beyond their borders, and, further, the pressures of the global economy will cause the range of impact to be far broader than previously. National governments can no longer claim that their responsibilities are simply to their nation, considered as an identifiable group of people found within a specific set of national boundaries and more or less independent of the events and circumstances of the rest of the world.

Hence, just as the ability of the governments of nation-states to control their national borders and what occurs within those borders is eroding, their ability and responsibility to concern themselves with what occurs beyond their borders, indeed what occurs across the globe, is vastly increasing. It may therefore be said that what national governments are losing in intensity of concentration of authority and power, they are partially regaining in the range of their responsibility. This is because national governments now have the responsibility to maintain and nurture the world economic system and also to maintain international structures for addressing global issues. National governments have this responsibility because they are presently best situated to meet these demands and because the well-being of the individual people of the world increasingly depends on the effective function of these global structures.

At present it may be said that national governments owe this responsibility primarily to their own citizens, but secondarily to the people of the entire world. However, this balance may change in future years as the interdependence of the globe increases and the distinction between citizen and non-citizen of a particular nation-state decreases; that is, the obligation of national governments to the people of the world may increase as their obligations to their citizens decrease.

Oddly perhaps, expanded human knowledge and technological ability have unveiled problems that would have gone unnoticed in past years but which can only be adequately resolved via governmental activity. The effects of pollution or viral disease transmission on public health and welfare would have been unrecognized only a few years ago, simply because human beings did not have the resources to gain such knowledge; people would sicken and die, and such occurrences would be accepted as the facts of life. Or, people recognize occupational or product safety hazards that could not have been recognized or understood a few years ago. But with the increased knowledge also comes increased responsibility; recognizing a problem also carries the responsibility to attempt to do something about it. But, advances in technology have also broadened the scope of problems which human beings can understand and the problems which human beings themselves cause – such as pollution.

Global problems, such as are isolated above, also require global and organized responses, which only governments can provide. Hence, they will have the global responsibility, due to all the people on the globe, to address them. Furthermore, they will have a responsibility to all human beings to maintain the global economic structure in good order. Once again, they have this responsibility because the role of governments in economic matters has greatly expanded in this century and because they are best situated to address it.

There has been little emphasis on human rights in the above discussion and more emphasis on addressing global problems and maintaining global prosperity. The reason is two-fold. One is, as mentioned above, governments, because of their decreased power over individual persons, will have less opportunity to violate human rights – or, indeed, to subject individual persons to undesirable governmental control of any sort. Hence, violation of basic human rights is likely to be a less important issue in the future than it is now. But, furthermore, with the decline of the Cold War and the decline of the importance of military control as a means of national power and influence, the collected governments of the world are more likely to be interested in international measures taken to protect individual human rights.[19] As often happens in world affairs, as a problem becomes less important and difficult, the resources for successfully addressing it increase and become more effective and popular. Furthermore, the necessary reduction in the governmental role of making people better human beings or providing them with a sense of community or belonging also implies that government will intrude less into their lives and hence be less likely to abuse their rights.

However, the primary focus of this chapter and those preceding it has been on governments, their responsibilities, and the way in which they are changing. The pressures of globalization have also generated changes in the lives of individuals and their relations to their governments. These matters will receive scrutiny in the next chapter.

6 Individual Lives

The symbiotic currents of global economic unification and advances in communication and transportation are changing the lives of individual human beings as well as altering nation-states and national governments. In particular, these currents are reshaping the relation between individual persons and political institutions. They are recasting personal and political freedom, individual autonomy, and distributive justice. As argued elsewhere, these changes must be accommodated by altering the relevant concepts so that the emerging reality can be understood and addressed competently.

FREEDOM

As noted earlier, a global economy expands the personal freedom of participating individuals and also reduces governments' ability to restrict it. Following Isaiah Berlin, many find it useful to distinguish between negative and positive freedom.[1] Negative freedom is simply the ability to act as one desires without intrusion by others, whether the others are other persons or social institutions. Hence, negative freedom is maintained simply by letting people alone. Positive freedom is more demanding, for positive freedom is secure only when people have the means to achieve their goals successfully. Furthermore, positive freedom is commonly thought to entail a moral claim on others (the 'others' in this context can be either other individuals or social institutions) to provide the wherewithal to secure these ends should the person lack them. Positive and negative freedom can be understood in both a factual and a normative sense, because there is a distinction between the amount of positive and negative freedom various individuals or societies *in fact* possess and the amount they *ought* or are entitled to possess. Positive and negative freedom may both play a role in political freedom, individuals' ability to participate in political processes. Globalization will also affect this freedom in several ways.

Negative Freedom

The pressures of the global economy are *in fact* expanding the negative freedom many individuals will enjoy. They will increase negative

freedom in two ways. One is by corroding the social and cultural relationships which bind individuals to particular ways of life, and the
second is by pressing national governments to allow their citizens greater
leeway to conduct their lives as they wish. Governments will be forced
to grant *de facto* negative liberty in significant amounts because economic pressures will give them strong incentive to open their borders
to the free movement of people, goods, and capital, and this will sap
their resources to control the lives of individual persons. A significant
facet of this development, moreover, is that it need not be restricted
only to those people who can directly participate in the global economy.
The deterioration of political means to control individual human beings is a benefit that will accrue to all.[2] Nonetheless, the benefits of
the global economy will tend to flow to those people directly participating in it in some fashion or another, since they are best situated to
employ their global connections to gain freedom for themselves. As
noted above, this will primarily be true of nations and individuals able
to participate fully in the emerging global economy. Nations whether
by choice, such as North Korea, or by circumstance, as Afghanistan or
the nations of sub-Sahara Africa, that do not participate in the global
economy, may also escape pressures to enlarge their citizens' sphere
of negative freedom. Such nations must recognize, however, that a
price must be paid for preserving the conditions which allow this eva-
sion, (a price which North Korea is apparently beginning to recognize); the price is the poverty and impotence in world affairs that attend
isolation from the world economy.

Moreover, nations, such as mainland China, that are keenly aware
that they must join the global economy to gain increased prosperity,
will also be forced to yield to their citizens' considerable portions of
de facto negative freedom. It will become necessary for them to do so
as a condition of participating fully in the global economy. Mainland
China's leaders will feel pressure to cede this freedom whether or not
they also abandon their Marxist ideology. However, the increased negative freedom will primarily benefit Chinese participants in the global
economy. But, negative freedom is not held in the manner of chastity,
that is, either entirely or not at all; rather, possession of negative freedom is a matter of degree, and those most vigorously active in the
global economy will enjoy the highest degree of negative freedom,
while those less involved will generally have correspondingly reduced
amounts of negative freedom.

Also, citizens of nations lacking formal commitment to negative freedom, those who do not participate in the global economy, or par-

ticipate in only marginal fashion, may be able to enjoy very little of this freedom, because their government will escape pressure to yield it to them. Hence, the degree of negative freedom available to differing people will vary, and there will remain a distinction between those who function as part of the global economy and those outside it. This is the first of several divides separating those who are active participants in the global economy from those who are not.

However, changes in human circumstances will often carry their own pressures for yet more change and development, and it is possible that the people who become accustomed to expanded negative freedom will become dissatisfied with its simple *de facto* enjoyment and will demand *de jure* possession of them as well. Mainland China's elderly rulers are concerned about this possibility and are actively seeking ways to gain the benefits of participation in the global economy while avoiding the price of political liberalization.[3] The grizzled Chinese autocrats are right to have this concern because there are signs that this is occurring in other nations of Asia.

South Korea and Thailand offer evidence to kindle the anxieties of the elderly veterans of the Long March; they have plunged vigorously and successfully into the global economy.[4] However, the resulting prosperity has created a confident middle class in each nation that is dissatisfied with authoritarian governments closely controlled by military leaders. Hence, in both nations there is considerable pressure to evolve toward more genuinely liberal democratic governments.

South Korea has advanced considerably farther along the path of liberalization than has Thailand, but the political pressures in both nations are strong and increasingly difficult to ignore. Furthermore, the pressures are likely eventually to be successful because the governments cannot afford to suppress or ignore these classes of people – since those pushing for reform hold the keys to these nations' prosperity. If substantial numbers of these middle class professionals and managers leave for other nations or are oppressed to the extent that they cannot contribute to their nations' economies, the momentum of economic advance will evaporate. Hence, over the long term, new middle classes are apt to prevail, and, once they prevail, *de jure* political protection of negative freedoms is likely to become the legal entitlement of all citizens in these nations. In this regard the newly developing nations of the world are caught up in the same dynamic of the bourgeois push for liberal government that rippled through the nations of Western Europe several hundred years ago. Though conditions differ in various nations, the rough outlines of the dynamic remain the same.

An additional factor that will play a substantial role in broadening the vistas of negative freedom is the fact that a significant portion of international commerce now consists of, and depends upon, the uninhibited flow of information. International trade requires accurate information on the production rates and resources of nations. It also demands unfettered exchange of what is called intellectual property. The technocrats, engineers, scientists, and managers who sustain these developments must be able to communicate freely with one another if they are to avoid drifting into the backwaters of global commerce or of global science and technology.

Also, the *laws* regulating business activity must become open and stable in order to accommodate global commerce. Commerce requires that a nation's statutes be clear, stable, and public; otherwise corporations will lack sufficient confidence in the stability of the business climate to risk entering a nation's market. The importance of this factor is amply demonstrated by the nations of the former Soviet Union. Foreign corporations and investors are intrigued by the potential of this vast market but many are unwilling to make firm commitments until a body of law is established which makes the regulation of business relationships clear and dependable.[5] Moreover, once a legal system is established and statutes are made clear and enforceable, the benefits become available to all citizens and all institutions, not simply those who directly participate in international commerce.

The ebb and flow of people across national borders, as well as the eroding distinction between citizen and non-citizen, will also diminish governments' ability to monitor the activity of people within their borders and control them. Porous borders will also allow those who are dissatisfied with a particular government to leave.

Open borders, uninhibited communication, legal reform, and diminished political control, all fruits of the pressures of the global economy, will therefore result in expanded personal freedom in the sense of an increased negative liberty for individuals. But these are aspects of freedom from *government* intrusion into the life of the individual. In addition, the flux of the global economy will erode the ties of culture, community, and family which sometimes pinch and channel individual lives. Hence, negative freedom in the sense of freedom from intrusion by society or family into the life of the individual will also increase. Oftentimes individuals are more closely tethered by family and community ties than by governmental meddling. In fact, social bonds are commonly felt more deeply and relentlessly than is governmental constraint. The global economy frequently requires individuals to leave their home nations in order to advance their careers or simply to find suitable employment. In fact, many people will hop from nation to nation numerous times in their careers. As this occurs, the pressures of local constraints will dissolve. The confining ties of family and local culture will also be frayed by the fact that the global economy is also likely to draw aliens from other parts of the world, many of whom will reside for significant periods of time and make their imprint on local culture.

Moreover, the international economy has also begun to introduce its own culture and has done so in several ways. One, of course, is the international consumer culture, the movies, books, music, food, and dress which, with minor variations, are found across the world. But, a second and perhaps more important and influential culture, is that of business, that is, the values and standards of behavior inculcated by commerce. The business climate presently requires a common educational background of those individuals who participate in it. No matter what their national background, they are trained to analyze issues in the same manner and make the same assumptions about what constitutes good business practice and which goals business endeavor should seek. In many respects, the American MBA degree is the contemporary archetype of international business education and the culture it embodies. Moreover, the assumptions and practices the business culture engenders about how organizations should be structured, how problems should be addressed, and how personal relations should be conducted are apt to spill beyond the domain of commercial relationships and shape personal life. Hence, not only are indigenous commercial cultures likely to be displaced (such as the traditional commercial cultures of the Middle East and of Japan), but local social structures may undergo modification. Once again, a result is that particular individuals will tend to be freed of the constraints of local and family ties, with a resulting increase in negative freedom, that is, the absence of external constraints in the way of leading one's life as one wishes.

It is also true that the emerging global economy will often have important consequences for the positive freedom of the individual, the ability of the individual to acquire the means to secure his or her ends.

Positive Freedom

Positive freedom entails the present ability to achieve one's desires, rather than the simple lack of restraint which is embodied in negative freedom. An impoverished peasant farmer in Bangladesh, for example, may face no legal restriction on travel abroad, but this is largely irrelevant, since he lacks the means, the finances, education, and information, which would allow global travel. He has negative freedom to travel but lacks positive freedom to do so. Positive freedom, therefore, overlaps personal autonomy, the ability to lead a life of one's own choosing.

Individual's positive freedom will be affected in two distinct ways by the emerging global economy. One is the direct benefits the economy offers those able to participate in it. The second is the competitive pressures which will likely force governments to provide services for their citizens as they compete with other governments to attract members of a mobile and transient business community and others whose abilities are needed to make them function.

For active participants, the global economy promises impressive benefits of material wealth, physical mobility, and the personal status and influence that results from association with prestigious and successful institutions. Furthermore, the education, managerial skills, technical facility, and ability to function in various cultures required of participants in the global economy are also valuable instruments that individuals can employ in their personal lives to gain whichever ends they seek. In other words, the competitive pressures of the global economy will require that individuals become certain kinds of people, those with a number of well-honed abilities, and these abilities will be useful in individuals' private lives.

However, there are several negative aspects in this picture. One is that these benefits will be available only to those able to participate in the global economy directly, as workers or as those able to benefit in other ways from the presence of multinational corporations. Those unable to do so are apt to be left by the wayside. A second is that, to the extent that the global economy channels individual life in certain directions, it forecloses other avenues of personal development and initiative. The predominant way of life will be that required to function in big business or in business activity compatible with the international commercial system. The career of the small shopkeeper, individual entrepreneur, or family farmer will likely be squeezed from the spectrum of viable ways of life.[6]

The global economy will make an important contribution to positive freedom in another way. As mentioned earlier, individual nation-states will increasingly have to compete with other nation-states for the attentions of multinational corporations and the individual persons necessary to make them function. Given the choice, and the influence to make their choices felt, those in advanced industrialized nations have pressed their governments to provide the trappings of the welfare state; that is, the array of educational, health, retirement, cultural, and social services generally associated with contemporary advanced societies. These social welfare benefits are particularly important elements of positive freedom, not simply because people desire them but, more importantly, because they are frequently necessary for living the sort of life people desire and for attaining their ends. In the United States even those purporting to favor minimal government and to be adamantly opposed to governmental intrusion into personal life are eager to take advantage of governmental pension programs and health care services and complain loudly when these programs are threatened.[7]

In addition, an especially important requirement of the global economy is an educated labor force, and nation-states are already aware that they must provide adequate education for their citizens if they are to hope to attract multinational corporations. The particularly significant feature of this pressure is that education is valuable to all strata of societies and, in fact, is most crucially important to the relatively disadvantaged. Thus, it is a requirement quite likely to make an important difference in the positive freedom of those who take advantage of it.

Political Freedom

Political freedom is complex. Many believe it includes negative freedom and nearly as many believe it includes positive freedom of one variety or another. Nonetheless, political freedom contains a third aspect which will be the focus of this section. It is the ability to actively participate in a nation's governing process. Political freedom contains both a type of negative freedom (in the sense of a lack of political inhibitions to participation in the process of governing) and a type of positive freedom (in the sense of participating in a way that makes the individual's voice and desires effective). Political freedom thus understood is obviously an aspect of democracy. However, the pressures of the global economy are apt to have quite different implications for the negative and the positive elements of political freedom.

The greater negative freedom discussed earlier is likely to result in increased negative political freedom. This is because the mobility and erosion of national ties engendered by the global economy will allow individuals to evade governmental control and pressure governments, via their ability to leave for more hospitable circumstances, to refrain from creating barriers to political participation. The global economy therefore is likely to result in diminished political control over private property and the speech, actions, and beliefs of individuals. Furthermore, just as national governments will feel pressures to offer the trappings of the welfare state, so they will feel pressures to offer the trappings of democracy, such as free and open elections, political accountability, and the rule of law. As the experience of Thailand and South Korea indicates, emergent middle classes will not hesitate to demand such perquisites, and governments will come under considerable pressure to accede to their demands.

However, the factors of individual mobility and eroded ties of national identification may also result in diminished opportunity for individuals to take an active role in political processes. In part, this is because the individual mobility and transience of a global economy will erode local political cultures which give individuals means to enter public life. Persons cannot act in a vacuum. They need social structures that enable them to channel their concerns and energies. But communal political structures may be worn away by increased personal mobility. This would occur if the continued flux of individuals and corporations erodes the personal and social ties needed to create an effective political culture. Or, what is perhaps more likely, the communal political structures of nations will be captured by a small elite with little interest in allowing outsiders access to its workings. Such privileged groups may then manage nations for their own benefit and grant only such concessions to the global economy as are necessary to maintain the presence of economic institutions.

Furthermore, people may simply *care less* about their government's actions if they are able to elude direct political control or avoid governments that dissatisfy them. Eroded ties of national identification will also diminish individual persons' attachment to their nation. Also, if, as claimed earlier, national governments decrease in importance because they have reduced control over what occurs within their borders and the functions of governing are taken up by international governing structures, people's interests may simply focus elsewhere.

An additional factor which may also erode political participation is that personal mobility provides an important safety valve by opening a ready avenue of escape for those who are at odds with their government. The middle classes of South Korea and Thailand have been battling authoritarian government in their nations. But, if the global economy should significantly increase their personal mobility, they may well be tempted by the easier and safer course of migration. If people can avoid being manipulated by an unsavory government, they may lack the motivation to press for change, and incompetent or corrupt governments may continue unopposed.

Hence, as a result of global unification, governments may lose some ability to control their citizens, but citizens may simultaneously lose some of their means, and also their incentive, to shape their governments. Governments and citizens may go their separate ways. In consequence, problems such as national deficiencies of education or medical care of corruption in government may go unchallenged simply because alert, energetic, and influential people are not motivated to address them.

PERSONAL AUTONOMY

The developments which accompany global economic unification may hasten the emergence of what might be termed 'mass man', that is, people (both men and women) in 'mass society' who are free of external constraint but lacking a clear sense of self-identity and self-direction.[8] They consider themselves helpless to change the world and are content to drift along on the social currents of the day. Many aspects of contemporary human life fit the template of mass man. Consumer products, political campaigns, opinion polls, popular culture and communications media are designed to appeal broadly to all segments of society. People become 'mass persons' partly because they feel powerless to resist the force of these currents, partly because they can conceive of no alternative, and most importantly because they gain fulfillment by merging themselves with larger social currents. The conditions of several of advanced industrialized nations approach those of mass societies, and their political campaigns are designed to appeal to mass psychology. Furthermore, the emerging global economy is apt to expand the scale of the development of a global mass society, since the commercial, popular culture it nurtures is modelled on those of the advanced industrialized nations.

Another important social current runs through the twentieth century and will very probably be strengthened and broadened in the twenty-first. At present many people find themselves closely affiliated with large organizations that demand intense labor and highly-developed skill, reward them handsomely with material goods and social status, but leave them with the sense of being enmeshed in a giant, impersonal mechanism. In other words, people increasingly must function within, and by means of, large, complex institutions. Individual human lives consist of a series of encounters with large, sprawling institutions, whether governments, places of employment, insurance companies, hospitals, or chain stores. Furthermore, they must live their lives in accordance with the strictures established by the institutions, whether they are attempting to get a driver's license, health care, a job, or food for their table.

Hence, a second important model for understanding human life as it is presently lived may be termed 'institutional man' (including both men and women). Moreover, people whose lives are lived within sprawling institutions cannot function in the way foreseen by the Western European conception of personal autonomy; they do not control their lives and destinies as the traditional conception of personal autonomy envisages. The advances in communication and transportation that have nurtured the global economy also allow the creation of large and intricate institutions. Advances in communication allow larger, more sprawling networks of control and cooperation. But, in addition, factors such as this century's exponential increase of the earth's human population have resulted in the creation of, and need for, large institutions; more people generate more demands, more complex problems, and hence require more ·complexity as encapsulated in large corporations.

In addition, because of their size, power, wealth, and efficiency these institutions are crowding out other, smaller and more personal structures and will likely continue to do so. The effects of these pressures were visible in the frenzy of corporate buy-outs of the 1980s; successful small firms were bought by larger ones, while the less successful often simply failed. In addition, some of the more vigorous smaller firms sought ties with larger firms because they recognized the need for greater resources of capital and human expertise in order to remain competitive. The pressures which demand large size or enormous resources are visible when huge corporations with immense resources seek to join forces with bitter competitors. They do so when they acknowledge that they lack the resources to carry out some program or another.[9] There is ample reason to believe that these pressures will intensify and broaden in the future. Successful business activity requires far greater resources for finance and development than in the past. Hence, institutions are pressed to grow, fail, or create a thick network of arrangements with other institutions in order to acquire resources that will allow all to expand and hence survive.

The emergent global economy also nurtures increased size. Many corporations now believe that they must compete in all sub-markets of the global economy in order to prosper. Furthermore, when embarking on global competition they must compete with huge institutions with immense resources. As a practical matter of fact, such pressures can be addressed only by institutions of considerable size.

But, in another part, large institutions will continue to grow and prosper because they are the only structures capable of meeting the demands of contemporary life. Hospitals, governments, and manufacturing concerns *must* be large and complex to meet demands made upon them and survive in competition with other institutions. And, they will survive and prosper only if they meet the demands of individual persons better than other sorts of structures. Large chain stores, though they lack charm, personality, and the dedicated attention of owner/managers, tend to crowd out smaller stores wherever they appear.[10] They do so simply because people prefer to buy from them than from the older, smaller family institutions; people patronize them because the products they offer are generally cheaper and available in broader array than at smaller institutions. In addition, goods, such as automobiles for example, cannot presently be manufactured by small companies in the way that they were manufactured by literally hundreds of small companies in the early part of this century. Small companies cannot address the demands of safety and pollution requirements or the competitive requirements for well-designed, well-constructed, and inexpensive automobiles as the huge corporations can.

But large institutional structures demand that persons shape their lives, their habits, and their skills to accommodate them. Large institutions do not function in the intimate, informal, and personal manner which smaller structures allow. For example, dealing with large institutions entails forms completed, offices visited, procedures followed, and that each step along the way involve dealing with individuals who have little control over the processes as a whole but can carry out only the functions assigned to them. Hence, persons encountering an institution from the outside commonly feel that they have little choice but to accommodate themselves to the institution's demands on them if their needs are to be filled. Often they have no choice in the matter of whether or not to contend with a large institution. Either the institution is government, in which case there is no alternate or the institution is a private commercial enterprise, in which case the alternative is to deal with another which will be much like it.

For those functioning within the institution, the experience will be similar. They too will have to contend with forms, procedures, offices, and other persons who control only a small segment of the larger process and must conform to the structure as a whole – since they will not be able to function successfully if they fail to do so. The circumstance of people laboring within a large institution, in other words, is that they will have a small portion of responsibility and authority, but they must fulfill their responsibilities in ways consistent with the over-all procedures and goals of the institution if they are to successfully perform their tasks. Hence, they will have responsibility but also be unable to control the over-all processes or directions of the institution.

Of course, some individuals within large institutions will have more responsibility than others, and hence more flexibility and freedom to alter the direction of the structure as a whole. Nonetheless, even chief executive officers will be limited in changes they can make. They will lack the freedom or means to radically change the course of the corporation that was possessed by the old-fashioned corporate patriarchs, the Henry Fords or Carnegies of years past. In fact, their anguish over the possibilities of change and the demands on their lives are apt to be greater than those of employees on the lower rungs of command. They are more constrained because the pressures to become certain sorts of people and to function in certain ways increase as they ascend the ladder of authority. Partly this is because the price of gaining high authority in a vast corporate endeavor is that of *being* a particular sort of human being.[11] Moreover, the freedom of chief executives to change the direction of corporations will be constrained by their duties to steer the corporation in certain clearly outlined directions.

Moreover, the manager's ideal is to create a corporate structure that will function as much like a closely integrated organism as is possible; that is, a structure in which all constituents will function in strict coherence with the demands of the whole, in which institutional pressures will keep all constituents smoothly coordinated with one another, fend off external threats, and repair internal breakdown. In other words, the ideal of a smoothly functioning institution, whether corporation or government, is to drain its constituent human beings of their personal autonomy and transform them into functionaries who will devote their energies to the proper functioning of the whole organism. This ideal is compelling because an institution that approaches it closely will be more efficient, smoother running, and better equipped to fend off external disruptions or repair internal breakdowns than an institution more remote from the ideal. Every corporate or institutional manager seeks to create a self-sustaining organism that functions in this way, but, to the extent that the ideal is approached, the autonomy of those functioning within the institution will wither.

Hence, along with mass man, institutional man abounds in contemporary industrialized societies. In fact, institutional man is very probably a more useful paradigm for understanding personal lives and social currents than mass man. This is because the institutions and humans serving them are the most powerful social, political, and economic forces of the present day. Mass man is an impotent epiphenomena of their operation. Mass man is passive and exists to be manipulated, whereas the great institutions and those functioning in their service are working to shape the world to conform with their ideal.

Mass man and institutional man are not mutually exclusive. Both terms may accurately describe the same individual. It is entirely possible to be both mass man and institutional man, though not at the same time nor in the same fashion. However, the models must remain conceptually distinct because their internal workings differ, and they generate differing social and economic and political forces.

The emerging global economy will likely accentuate institutions' importance and encourage them to grow larger. In addition, capitalist economies create pressures on corporations to grow or die. This is exemplified in the experience of the multinational corporations of the smaller nations of Europe.[12] They were among the first to expand into the international arena because they recognized their growth would be limited if they confined themselves within the borders of their home nations. Furthermore, recent developments in communication and transportation allow the creation of institutional structures that can seed themselves across the globe yet maintain tight control over their offshoots. It is also possible that, following the model of vast Japanese corporations that provide housing, marriage counselling, and lifetime employment, these private commercial organizations will become far more important for the individuals within them, that is, more important sources of personal identity and significance, than their national governments.

For the above reasons, the global economy is likely to speed and encourage the development of huge institutions, and hence of the mass and institutional man that accompany them. However, both phenomena erode individual persons' ability to lead their lives as they wish, and, more importantly, to feel that they are in control of their lives. Autonomy will wither not simply because large institutions place barriers in the way of individual self-control but also because the large institutions tend to nurture individuals for whom autonomy is neither a desired nor a viable option. Certainly, they will not have the control of their lives and of their surroundings, or feel the sense of responsibility for themselves and their environment, of a pioneer settler in the nineteenth century United States.

Social and economic conditions can affect the degree of self-direction which individuals are able to enjoy and also the extent to which this autonomy is valued. Future pressures may erode autonomy both as an option for individuals and as a value for them.

Philosophers commonly believe that there is a close link between individual autonomy and direct participation in political affairs.[13] This link is found in the belief that individuals who have slight influence on their nation's political structures, or who are repressed by their national government, have less control over their lives and also lose access to significant human activities, those of making and implementing decisions regarding the nature and direction of the community or the nation. While citizens of the future will have broader opportunity to escape political repression ('repression' in the sense of political infringement on their negative liberty), the arguments of previous sections support the view that they are apt to have less influence on their own nation's governing institutions than at present.

This result may be of small consequence if, as there is some reason to believe, national governments decline in importance. If the domains which national governments are able to control lessen in importance, the benefit from participating in governing activities will diminish and have less connection to the resources of self-direction that individuals are able to enjoy. However, previous chapters also contain the argument that some of what national governments lose will be transferred to a motley of international governing bodies. Moreover, earlier chapters have argued that there is also reason to believe that the international governing bodies poised to shoulder various functions of national governments are apt to be less sensitive to individual concerns than national governments. Certainly, they will be remote from individual lives and lack provision for individuals to participate directly in their operations. They will, rather, continue to have national governments as their constituents and participants. This implies that another important facet of the autonomy of the individual will be removed from access. Furthermore, insofar as large corporations supplant the nation-state as a focus of personal life, the individual's sense of control and ability to influence – or sense of *responsibility* to influence – the surrounding world may be stunted by the tangle of bureaucratic growth.

In light of the considerations offered in this section, it is reasonable to conclude that economic globalization may increase certain aspects of individual freedom (primarily those of negative freedom) but will also diminish the occasion for, and value of, individual autonomy. People will suffer fewer restrictions on their lives resulting from governmental repression. However, the global economy will accelerate and broaden the movement to mass society and the institutionalization of human life. Both currents threaten personal autonomy, which will be further eroded by the impact of the global economy on the relation of persons to their governments. Future perils to individual growth may issue not from vicious political despotism but from a suffocating blanket of social and institutional complexity.

For the philosopher, and also for the ordinary individual, these conclusions raise important issues. For one, they require that the nature and importance of autonomy as a constituent and as a value for human life be reconsidered. Esteem for autonomy is mainly an artifact of Western European philosophy. Most of the world's cultures do not value it, and several philosophical movements of Western Europe dismiss it (the political philosophy of Hegel is a salient example, though even the Greek philosophers did not value autonomy for *all* human individuals). If autonomy is under siege, the first question to ask is whether it should be retained as an important value of human life.

Or, even if it should, the traditional conception of autonomy may be inadequate to current reality. The evidence of this chapter is that it *is* inadequate, for the traditional conception holds that all human beings who are adults and of normal intellectual ability are equally autonomous and that autonomy is a quality each person carries independently of the circumstances of his or her life.[14] The argument of this chapter is that both of these assumptions are false, that different individuals have differing levels of autonomy and that the conditions of a person's life have a direct impact on whether autonomy is available to that person.

Hence, discussions of the value and importance of autonomy must be accompanied by discussions of the conditions which promote autonomy, which persons should enjoy autonomy, and what sort of autonomy people should seek to enjoy. It is entirely possible that further investigation will reveal that complex answers must be given to these questions, far more complex answers than have been given in the past – for it may be the case that differing sorts of autonomy will be available to differing sorts of individuals and that there may be no single, universal autonomy available to all.

DISTRIBUTIVE JUSTICE

The world's economic unification will have implications relevant to matters of distributive justice, that is, the normative principles guiding the allocation of material goods which individuals receive as the result of social endeavor. Distributive justice must be reconsidered because the developing global economy has several important consequences for the ways in which people and nations receive material goods.

One consequence is an emerging fundamental economic distinction between those who are active participants in the world economy and those who are not. Those who are active participants in the global economy, whether individuals or nations, will command the lion's share of wealth, status, and influence. This is because the global economy is the arena of competition of the most advanced and powerful business corporations. The most powerful technology and the most sophisticated business practices are being deployed in this arena.

Thus, the division between the participants in the global economy and those who are not will also increasingly become the division between the haves and the have-nots of the world. At first glance, this distinction reproduces Marx's distinction between bourgeois and proletariat. However, there are important and illuminating differences between the two which are worth exploring for the light which they shed on salient issues of distributive justice.

In stark opposition to Marx's bourgeois, the middle class participants in the global economy are workers rather then owners. The resources controlled by present-day workers are economically insignificant, other than when massed together in consumer markets. Hence, contemporary middle-class participants in the global economy are not the owners and controllers of capital that the Marxist bourgeois class was. In fact, the contemporary owners of large institutions are normally not individuals at all. Rather, the owners of the great masses of the stocks of contemporary corporations are other institutions, including insurance companies, pension funds, or investment funds, which get their resources from ordinary individuals, and middle class managers of these funds are generally functionaries within large institutions and must operate within and by means of them. These manager-employees are both captives and beneficiaries of corporations. Though this captivity is often demanding, it is generally benign, since employer-managers are commonly well paid and enjoy an array of perquisites of office. For the most part the Marxist bourgeois has evaporated, and relations of economic power and influence must be understood in different ways from those he envisaged.

Moreover, the have-nots of the present era are not laborers who can plausibly be claimed to be exploited by the haves. The have-nots of the present era do not significantly contribute to the wealth and influence of corporate giants. As argued below, the concept of exploitation does not plausibly apply to the current situation. The have-nots are deprived and helpless because they are shut out of the global economy and not because they are directly exploited by it.

Hence, the analyses of the issues of justice which Marx applied to the economic relations of his day are no longer applicable. In Marx's view, the power and wealth of the bourgeois resulted directly from its exploitation of the proletariat, since the members of the bourgeois gained their wealth by keeping the difference between the market value of workers' production and their wages. Because of this, and because owners were in bitter competition with other bourgeois capitalists, they were *driven* to exploit the workers or face extinction. Those who raised their workers' wages would have higher costs than their competitors and would thus risk being driven out of business, since competing firms would be able to offer lower prices.

For Marx there can be no peace between owners and laborers because whatever wealth owners acquire the laborers must lose. For this reason, the only avenue which will allow workers to escape exploitation, improve their lot, and gain control of their lives is to revolt against owners. Only when there are no owners can exploitation be eliminated and all individuals gain control of their own lives and the prospect of a decent existence, this being the state of pure communism.

The mode of analysis must differ when *all* human participants in the global economy are employees and the major wielders of power are institutions that function in a manner which differs fundamentally from individual patriarchal entrepreneurs. Moreover, because of radical changes in modes of production, the relationship of laborers to their institutions must also change; because workers increasingly require sophisticated skills, they are more important to their institution than the interchangeable laborers of the Industrial Revolution.[15]

Thus, the major issue of distributive justice in the present era is not: What do the exploiters owe the exploited? Rather, it is: What, if anything, do those functioning within the global economy and profiting from their association owe to those who, for whatever reason, are excluded from its largesse? This question, in turn, divides into two questions. The first is that of whether the comfortable participants in the global economy owe assistance to the have-nots, that is, those whose lives are at risk and who have little chance of achieving a minimally decent human existence unless they receive material goods and social assistance from others. However, there is a difference between the requirement to simply provide the minimal needs of a human life and the provision of aid to improve the lot of those who already have decent human lives but minimally so.

It is important to note that this possible obligation is not based on the moral failings or injustice of the privileged. Rather, it is an issue, illustrated by the biblical tale of the Good Samaritan, of whether the comfortable have an obligation to aid others, simply on the ground that the needy require aid and the agents are in position to give it without significant sacrifice. But the issue of what constitutes the minimal requirements of a decent human existence is relative to culture and resources. Hence, indoor plumbing is a minimal requirement of a decent human existence in most advanced nations but a luxury in many parts of the world. Thus, the issue of exactly what criteria are to be used to establish the level of a minimally decent human existence cannot be resolved in sharply-cut and universal fashion.

However, the second major question of distributive justice is whether those participating in the global economy are obliged to attempt to expand the global economy to encompass people and human societies not presently part of it – on grounds that those excluded from the global economy will fail to enjoy the benefits of wealth, power, and influence it offers. One basis for an affirmative answer to this claim could be that individual persons and social groups who are not full participants in the global economy will be sufficiently overawed by, and at the mercy of, those who are that those excluded will not be in command of their own lives. Hence, the argument would be based on an appeal to autonomy and possibly to an obligation to avoid circumstances likely to result in injustice or exploitation.

Once again, there are several complications. One is that many peoples may wish to maintain their indigenous ways of life and do not wish to exchange their traditional lives for ways of life required to participate in the global economy. It is possible that they would rather accept the risk of exploitation, or seek other avenues of redress against the possibility of exploitation and injustice, than forfeit a way of life which is valuable to them.

The second matter is that of what steps would have to be taken to make the global economy accessible to people not already a part of it. The global economy is extending itself across the world and within several decades is likely, of its own natural forces, to encompass the majority of the globe. Hence, the second issue may eventually become moot.

Nonetheless, there are measures the members of the global economy can take to make it more easily accessible to those who are not. Among them are liberalized regulations regarding work permits or help in making educational facilities available to people lacking the skills and personal habits required to become functional members of the global economy. Also, additional steps could be taken to assist nations seeking to gain the attentions of multinational corporations.[16]

Furthermore, there is the important question of the possibilities of injustice and exploitation at the margin of where the global economy intersects the portions of the globe that are not. The danger exists partly because of the vast differential in power and wealth separating the two areas and partly because portions of the globe not presently part of the global economy may be eager to gain its presence and willing to pay a price for doing so, such as relaxing pollution regulations or worker safety requirements. This is an area where nations have gained greater knowledge and self-confidence in the past several decades; most nations are now tolerably well-equipped to deal with multinational corporations as equals.[17] The major difficulty at present is that of protecting vulnerable groups *within* nations from being treated unjustly by their own governments or local elites.

In addition, the impact of the global economy on the distribution of material goods has another facet. One result of the emergent global economy is that decisions made within one nation, in response to the political and economic concerns of the citizens of that nation, will increasingly ripple outward to affect the welfare of citizens of other nations. These ripples will result from decisions about financial matters, rules and regulations regarding the exploitation of raw materials, labor and pollution laws, immigration and emigration policies, rules regarding intellectual property, efforts to gain international investment and win the presence of manufacturing plants and offices of multinational corporations, and decisions regarding trade laws and policies.

Trade laws and policies are a salient example of decisions made in one nation which have an obvious impact on the welfare of those in other nations. Raising tariff rates to restrictive levels in order to keep certain products out will clearly affect jobs and companies in the target nation. Conversely lowering tariff rates and eliminating other restrictions can benefit economies in other nations. Or decisions that ease the import of raw materials but restrict the import of finished goods will aid some nations but harm others.

Governments commonly make their decisions and policies in response to local political pressures or in response to their estimates of what will benefit their own nation. This is relatively innocuous where nations are independent, self-contained economic units. However, in an age of global economic interdependence and a global economy, this narrow focus is not so obviously justified. It becomes questionable when the actions and policies of one nation have marked consequences for the lives and well being of those in other nations. It will not suffice to respond that governments are explicitly obligated to concern themselves with the welfare of their own citizens but have no such obligation to the citizens of other nations, for that commitment is being called into question by the new circumstances of the world. The constrained obligation may have been justified earlier but may not be now that conditions have altered.

Neither is it adequate to claim that governments must always accord greatest weight to the needs of their own citizens. This is so for two reasons. One is that the circumstances of global economic interdependence may call this into question. They do so particularly when, as argued elsewhere, the distinction between citizen and non-citizen and the significance of national borders are of decreasing significance. If governments are no longer the sovereigns of self-sufficient economic units but only of particular sectors of a global economy, this principle loses much of its plausibility. However, even if the principle that government must accord greatest weight to its citizens is upheld, it allows the possibility that the concerns of those in other nations may have *some* weight, so the issue is how much weight they have and whether they may sometimes outweigh the concerns of a nation's citizens. The issue requires reexamination in an era when the distinction between citizen and non-citizen is not as deeply rooted and distinct as in past centuries, particularly, for example, when many of those who are presently non-citizens may become citizens in future years and a significant number of those who are now citizens may migrate. In an era of diminishing national identification, the distinction between 'us' and 'them' no longer holds the plausibility or visceral significance it once had.

For example, Germany has traditionally been strongly concerned about avoiding rekindling inflation. Occasionally, therefore, it raises interest rates in order to dampen what it perceives to be inflationary tendencies in its economy. However, a higher rate of return for the mark has immediate effects on the economies of other nations, since higher rates in Germany make it more difficult for them to lower interest rates on their own currency in efforts to provide stimulus for their economies by making money cheaper to borrow. This applies with particular force to the other nations of Europe who have determined to link their currencies together and who are already closely linked to Germany's economy.

Hence, German battles against inflation immediately affect other nations' economies. In fact, because the global market in currency is the most fully developed and fluid of the global markets, nearly any important financial decisions made by one nation will ripple quickly though the world and rock the economies of other nations.

As a result people can no longer plausibly claim that they are obligated to consider only the welfare of people and institutions within their own national boundaries. This is because their decisions and their policies have an immediate and direct impact on the welfare of others in other nations. But the question that remains is that of how and in what manner these interests and consequences should be taken into account. For example, the claim that governments are obligated to give greatest weight to the concerns of their own citizens is plausible, but it is not clear either how great this comparative weight should be or whether the citizens of other nations may sometimes have concerns of sufficiently great import that they outweigh those of the nation in question.

Therefore, these developments must rekindle old debates regarding distributive justice. Complex questions of the responsibility held by the citizens of one nation for those of another must be reexamined. Further, and more perplexing, the matters of political jurisdiction and sovereignty become vastly more complex. If citizens of one nation can have their lives and welfare sharply jolted by the decisions of those within another nation-state, it may be reasonable to assert that *they* should have some voice in these deliberations.

Similar difficulty will meet attempts to address the difficulties resulting from the divide between those who are members of the world economy and those who are not. It need not be the case that the comfortable will have gained their wealth at the expense of those who have little, since power and influence in the global economy may depend more on the command of information and efficient social organization than on control of physical resources or political or military domination; witness the glowing success of Japan which has gained its present economic prowess without significant military power and without seeking to be a great influence on world affairs. If the differences of wealth and power enjoyed by those within the global economy as opposed to those outside of it do not arise from exploitation, it will not be obvious that those profiting from the global economy have obligations to those who have been passed over.

Another wrinkle is added to the issue of distributive justice by the fact that a substantial portion of these flows of capital and goods will be directed by large multinational corporations. National governments are losing the means of controlling wealth with their nations. National governments are also surrendering perquisites of sovereignty as they seek to join the global economy. Furthermore, governments have discovered that it is in their interest to preserve free trade in the global economy. The international bodies being devised to manage the global economy are directed toward maintaining free trade. The full array of avenues through which corporations will manage this distribution of wealth are not yet apparent. However, one consequence that has emerged is that corporations, if left to themselves, will tend to equalize the distribution of wages and industrialization across the globe. They accomplish this through their efforts to seek out new areas of opportunity and decrease production costs, both of which motivate them to enter new, relatively underdeveloped areas; thus providing jobs and resources for them.

The analyses of this chapter are all too brief and sketchy. They are intended only to illustrate several of the salient ways in which globalism is apt to reshape individual life and offer some idea of ways in which the concepts of freedom, autonomy, and distributive justice must be reconsidered as a result. Hence, the chapter is intended more to open discussion than offer adequate analyses of these matters.

Conclusion

If the claims of the preceding chapters are correct or partially so, future decades will be the scene of distinct changes in the nature of governing and the relation of individual persons to government and society. These changes are being generated by globalization and, more specifically, by global economic unification. In fact, because globalization has been underway for a half century and gained considerable momentum in the past several decades, its consequences have already began to emerge and reshape political relations.

Western European political philosophy must therefore change its perspective. First, it must move away from its traditional individualism and focus more intently on the role of institutions. Further, since national governments are declining in importance and several of their functions being transferred to international bodies, and because national governments are rivaled in wealth and power by multinational corporations, there is much to be said in favor of viewing government as simply one type of powerful human institution which is not radically different from others. Second, since many of the difficulties human beings presently confront result from the absence of institutions with sufficient power or authority to address their problems, political philosophers must move away from their traditional focus on problems of the abuse of governing power and attend more closely to the problems which result from the absence of clear power and authority. In fact, a case can be made for the view that many of the human tragedies of the twentieth century have resulted from a deficiency of responsibility and authority rather than the reverse. Third, political philosophers must attend more carefully to a human alienation which results from the erosion of personal and cultural bonds which accompany the currents of globalism and the increased role of vast institutions in human life. Finally, political philosophers must examine the stresses that will result from the vastly differing fates and prospects which separate those who function successfully as part of the global economy from those who do not.

EMPHASIS ON INSTITUTIONS

Western European political philosophy has traditionally focused on individuals and their relation to government. Most strands of this tradition are strongly individualistic in the sense that individuals are believed to be of ultimate importance and also in the sense that the lives, concerns, values, and actions of individuals must be understood in terms of the efforts of each person who is in turn presumed to be master of his or her own fate. The few exceptions to this general view include those such as Hegel who discount the value of the individual and develop an organicism in which the life of the individual has value only in relation to the social whole, as represented by the nation-state of which the national government is head.

All, whether Hegelian or individualist, have presumed that government is a unified structure which is distinguished from other human institutions by its sovereignty. Governments, moreover, are deemed the self-sufficient lords of their domains.

If the previous chapters' arguments are correct, the above presumptions are seriously flawed. What individuals can or cannot do, the ways in which they think of themselves, the values which they hold, and the lives they are able to lead are determined to a considerable extent by their associations with various large institutions. The life of the individual in advanced nations of the contemporary era is largely a series of encounters with one institution after another. These encounters shape the person's life and prospects. A grasp of the circumstances and issues of contemporary life requires that the role of institutions be understood.

Traditional assumptions that individuals are self-creating and self-sustaining are no longer plausible or useful for addressing the maladies of contemporary life. One group of contemporary philosophers, the communitarians, understand the limitations of individualism.[1] However, they wish to address its deficiencies by advocating a return to the values of community. But, this response amounts to little more than nostalgia. Conditions able to support the communities of fond memory no longer exist (and may never have existed, for such communities may be little more than Rousseauean myth), and belief in their existence will become less plausible as contemporary pressures continue to shape human life. What *is* required is an adequate grasp of the nature and functions of modern institutions and the complexity of the individual's relations to them. What is needed in place of a nostalgic yearning to revive community is a grasp of how to achieve a decent and satisfying existence in circumstances where large impersonal institutions are the major factors that shape human life.

This also implies that the Hegelian alternative is mistaken and will continue to lose plausibility. Nation-states are not organic wholes and will become less cohesive and less important as years pass. The pressures of the global economy are pulling them apart. National borders are losing significance, and national governments have far less *de facto* control over what occurs within and beyond their borders than in years past. Moreover, the factors which once fostered a sense of national identification are disintegrating. The decline of distinctive national cultures, of self-sufficient national economies, and of military force as an instrument of influence in the world, all erode the conditions which form a compelling sense of national identity.

Moreover, the ties individual human beings have to their nation are increasingly superficial. Citizens are often best characterized as little more than fans of their nation, rooters for its success in war, Olympic events, or economic struggles. As elsewhere, the fragility of national identification is likely to increase under the pressures of the global economy. Moreover, as fans of athletic teams switch their allegiances with time and migration, individual persons may come to change their national allegiance and identification as easily. In years to come they may migrate casually from one nation to another much as United States citizens now migrate casually from state to state.

Rather than traditional human communities or Hegelian organic nation-states, an array of large institutions now control human existence. These institutions exist partly because of technological advances in communication and transportation but also because the exploding human population and complexity of human life make them necessary. Human life is not dominated by a single all-powerful institution, that of national government. Rather, human life in advanced industrialized nations is shaped and channeled by a confused welter of institutions. Moreover, government is not a single organic whole but a collection of governing agencies each of which enjoys a degree of autonomy and independence.

Recognition that governing is carried out by an array of differing institutions opens the way for the realization that a spectrum of *international* governing institutions now exists and that they play significant roles in maintaining the order of the world community. These institutions take several guises and hold varying degrees of formal governing structure or authority. What matters is that they exercise significant control over a variety of the world's affairs, and they are likely to increase in number, importance, and authority as the global economy develops. They are becoming the core of a genuine world government, but they are not likely (at anytime in the near future) to coalesce into the single, unified government that visionary thinkers of past years foresaw. Rather, the varied institutions of world government will continue to emerge in fragmentary and ad hoc fashion as they are needed.

National governments will remain, but they, like the medieval church, will lose much of their impact on human life. Their role and their powers will evolve, though their formal legal status, and their *conceptions* of sovereign authority are apt to remain frozen in a glacier of outmoded presumptions. Huge multinational corporations will accumulate power and influence as national governments continue their decline. Two decades ago, some argued that multinational corporations had already outstripped national governments. This view is belied by recent history. National governments have become resourceful at devising ways to cope with the power of multinational corporations and preserving a semblance of control over them.

However, the balance of power between national governments and multinational corporations may change as the powers of national governments dissolve, as functions of government are transferred to a patchwork of international governing authorities, and as a substantial portion of the power of governments to control people and institutions dissolves rather than being transferred elsewhere. The power, wealth, and influence of multinational corporations, however, is likely to continue expanding, for the processes that erode the powers of national governments continue to augment those of multinational corporations. Moreover, multinational corporations have proven adept at entering the global arena and functioning under its circumstances and in accordance with its demands. Governments have been less adroit at reconfiguring themselves to cope with the demands and problems of globalization. They have acted and adapted only when they had little choice. Moreover, their efforts to cling to the perquisites of sovereign authority inhibit their ability to address the problems of globalization. Hence, by default multinational corporations will gain relative power and influence.

As the above paragraphs hint, the very term 'political philosophy' may now be a misnomer. Many of the functions traditionally associated with government are being taken up by bodies of other sorts, and governments and their functions are increasingly intermeshed with and interchangeable with other institutions.

THE TYRANNY OF POWERLESSNESS

The fragmenting powers of governing institutions, the crumbling of government into a variety of different forms and institutions, and the probable loss of a substantial portion of the control governments have enjoyed over individual persons may appear unalloyed benefits. This is because a substantial portion of the suffering the human species has endured during its history is the work of governments. In addition, governments have controlled the instruments of warfare and have not hesitated to employ them in murderous fashion to achieve their ends. The history of the twentieth century is a chronicle of governments' abuse of their own populations and those of other nations on a magnitude and with a brutality that dwarfs the horrors of earlier centuries. John Stuart Mill, right-minded in so many ways, was disastrously wrong when in 1859 he proclaimed that governments had been tamed and that the greatest threat to human freedom came from the intrusions of society.[2]

Though it is difficult to imagine that national governments' *loss* of power could result in human suffering of the magnitude that they have inflicted, serious difficulties attend this loss of power and authority. The difficulties rise to the surface when problems develop or abuses of human beings by other individuals, by huge corporations, or by governments occur which can be met only by some institution or individual with clear authority to give redress. The impotence stemming from lack of power and responsibility can be termed a 'tyranny of powerlessness', a condition where problems cannot be addressed or abuses corrected because no one has clear responsibility or power to do so.

The phenomena of the tyranny of powerlessness is familiar enough to those who must contend with large institutions. Often a mistake is discovered, a defect of procedure revealed, a lapse in authority and responsibility surfaces, or simple injustice occurs which cannot be addressed because no one and no office has clear power or authority to do so.

Furthermore, the tyranny of powerlessness is likely to emerge in grander form and on a wider scale as national governments lose their sovereign authority, and effective governing authority is transferred to a motley of international governing structures. Anarchy is not necessarily the idyllic condition of romantic imagination; this is particularly so when billions of people exist, large and complex institutions shape human life, and a complex web of political and economic relations connects and entangles people. Moreover, the conditions of human life under anarchy are lividly exemplified by conditions in Lebanon during its 15 years of civil war. Lebanese anarchy was no idyllic dream but a nightmare from beginning to end.[3]

Hence, in coming decades clear lines of authority and responsibility must be developed to address pressing issues or to correct abuses. Global pollution is an excellent case in point. It confronts all peoples and all nations of the globe and can be addressed adequately only on a global scale. A salient problem is that there are presently no institutions with the authority or the power to control it. The United Nations seems an excellent vehicle for this office but is hobbled by internecine political battles, inefficiency, and a history of ineffectualness.

But, resort to the United Nations also presents more immediate and more intractable difficulties. National governments do not wish overtly to cede any significant portion of their sovereignty to a quasi-govern-mental international body. They would allow the United Nations to address global pollution only if it loomed as a distant threat that required solemn conferences, concerned study, careful data-gathering, assiduous planning, . . . but no immediate action. However, all are aware that a decisive response to global pollution is necessary, and that 'decisive action' must be understood to mean that regulations and standards which will apply to the entire world must be devised and enforced. These requirements imply that genuine governing power and authority must be passed to whichever entity is charged with addressing the issue – but the governments of the world are not yet ready to take this step.

Hence, the United Nations will likely be circumvented, but there is no clear alternative organization capable of addressing the threat posed by environmental pollution. The nations of the world will therefore continue to rely on high-minded conferences, treaties, and a fair measure of political theater, but they are not apt to take the measures needed seriously to address the matter of global pollution until cold necessity requires them to do so.

The problem highlighted by global pollution, therefore, is *lack* of power and *lack* of authority, and the difficulty is that the solution re-quires creating global authority and responsibility of the sort that the governments of the nations of the world are as yet unwilling to allow.

A variation of the same sort of difficulty was played out in brutal and gristly fashion in the Serbian siege of Sarajavo, only one arena of conflict in the bloody remains of Yugoslavia. A domain that was once a nation (though a most fragile and artificial one) fell apart and became a cockpit of barbaric ethnic conflict. The siege of Sarajavo was only the most visible and dramatic of the many arenas of barbarity in that portion of the world. Furthermore, it was clear to most observers that a peaceful resolution to the conflict – short of military annihilation of one ethnic group or another – required intervention by the outside world.[4]

However, the community of nations dithered ineffectually over the problem for years. This has resulted in a three-sided conflict between the United Nations, the European Security Committee, and the United States. All parties recognized that the slow starvation of the civilian population of Sarajavo accompanied by particularly vicious bombardment was intolerable, but, for several years, they were unable to devise an effective course of action to halt it. And so people continued to suffer and die while the most powerful nations of the globe offered only sympathetic rhetoric.

If a world governing structure were in place with explicit responsibility to address such problems, clear power and authority to undertake a response, and a fully articulated set of principles listing the conditions that require a response and the standards of how and in what manner responses should be made, the dismal situation in Bosnia might possibly have been addressed far more quickly and with far less human suffering.

As in the instance of global pollution, the morass in the Balkans required decisive action by the global community. The fumbling that occured in the Balkans did so simply because there are no institutions with the power and authority to take decisive action. Moreover, as the remnants of the Soviet Empire continue to disintegrate, turmoil akin to the civil wars in the remains of Yugoslavia is sure to erupt elsewhere. Unless decisive measures are taken to create structures, guidelines, and procedures for the global community to address these issues, more people will die horribly and additional states will fly apart.[5] Once again, the difficulty is a manifestation of the tyranny of powerlessness; a set of problems exists which can only be addressed by an institution with clear authority and responsibility, but because the global community lacks the will and the insight to create it, the problems continue to fester.

The tyranny of powerlessness can also appear in other ways and in other guises. As mentioned elsewhere, global governing institutions are being created in ad hoc fashion to address specific issues. Because of their jealous concern to preserve their sovereign prerogatives, national governments are loathe to create an international governing structure independent of their control and thus holding genuine governing authority. A likely result is that, as indicated above, issues will frequently arise which will find no authoritative agency able to address them.

An example of this sort of problem might be a world-wide outbreak of an easily transmitted, highly infectious, and deadly disease that could be adequately fought only if the nations of the world simultaneously undertook carefully coordinated and rigorous measures. There is presently no international machinery with the authority and power to devise and coordinate this sort of complex response. This scenario is not at all farfetched, even though the world has not yet been forced to cope with anything like it. It is plausible because increased human mobility and the thickening web of international commerce are creating the conditions in which a global pandemic could readily occur.[6]

In addition, advances in communication create difficulties and vulnerabilities. Recently pranksters in Australia were found to have penetrated the computer security of institutions in the United States and were thus able to cause mischief from thousands of miles away.[7] The enormous benefits of nearly instantaneous global communication via computers will continue to expand and thicken the network of electronic communication. But as they become more useful, more important, and accumulate more functions, they, because they allow communication so easily, create heightened vulnerability to criminals, terrorists, and ordinary mischief makers. But again, there is presently no international machinery with the mandate or the authority to address these dangers.

Should a major crisis erupt, such as a global terrorist attack on computer lines, the world may awaken to the need for decisive action. For reasons outlined above, they would very likely not rely on the United Nations. If not, however, new international machinery would have to be devised to cope with the difficulty. In consequence, difficulties of the above sorts, or others as yet unforeseen, may continue to fester until they explode into crisis or become so chronically serious that the necessity of decisive action cannot be overlooked. And, once again, a tyranny of powerlessness will prevent a decisive response until crisis requires that at least half-hearted measures be taken.

Additional problems of the same sort emerge when difficulties arise that are not specifically included within the mandate of ad hoc institutions. Much of the frustration involved in dealing with institutions is that they have fixed procedures, established policies, and recognized mandates. By their nature, however, these are general in scope, designed to accommodate usual and foreseen circumstances. Occasionally, however, difficulties arise which are outside the bounds of these structures, but the institution is powerless to deal with them, or deals with them ineffectually, either because no one within the institution has power to make the necessary changes or because the individuals within the institution who are aware of the problem and wish to make corrections lack the authority to do so. An additional source of difficulty is that an institution's procedures may occasionally be flawed, but no individual or body has clear authority to correct them. At other times the institution's structure may simply be too rigid and too narrowly focused to allow the change to be made. Such cases, once again, would be instances of the tyranny of powerlessness.

Additional problems of this sort may occur as a result of the gradual erosion of governmental authority and fragmentation of governing institutions. It may then happen that individuals or private enterprises suffer abuse from others or from rump governing bodies but lack any institution authorized to help them gain redress.

Philosophers and theoreticians have tended to concentrate on the difficulties which arise from concentrated power and authority. Much of the thought and effort of Western European political philosophy is focused on sovereign governmental power, the difficulties it may cause, and the possible grounds for its justification. Given the history of the human race, concern about sovereign power and its dangers is entirely understandable. Moreover, this concern should not be abandoned. However, equal attention should be given to mechanisms for the creation of power and responsibility, on grounds that serious problems are likely to arise if the human race fails to do so.

HUMAN ALIENATION

The theme of alienation was once fashionable among literary figures and existentialist philosophers. However, for existentialists such as Sartre and Camus, alienation is an ontological circumstance of the human species not the particular artifact of the conditions of the contemporary era.[8] The existentialists may or may not be correct in their views. However, there are reasons to believe that the conditions of contemporary life, particularly those engendered by the emerging global economy, are eroding the ties which once connected individual human beings to one another and to their larger societies. Furthermore, there is also reason to believe that the basic condition of human life which is emerging will consist of a series of associations with a variety of large institutions which will not reproduce the full range of human ties persons formerly had with one another.

In this regard, the work of the literary figures, such as Kafka, whose alienation was more felt than thought, may be of greater help than existentialists, for Kafka's work expresses the livid *experience* of being cut-off and alone. If the alienation relevant to this study were an ontological condition, it would not be felt as a distinct experience which might then be compared with other experiences. Furthermore, it would be senseless to ask whether this alienation should be considered a good or a bad thing or whether the circumstances of human life should be altered to cancel some of its effects. It would simply be a permanent feature of our lives, such as possessing heads and tongues, and we could do little about it.

The alienation being generated by the circumstances of contemporary life, and more particularly by the developing global economy, has three primary facets. One is the erosion of the ties binding individuals to one another and to social groups. It would be experienced as the feeling of not belonging if it were experienced consciously by those who underwent it. The second facet is the condition of *powerlessness*. It would be felt as the experience of being unable to make any real difference in the way societies or institutions function and the sense that a given individual is not an irreplaceable and unique element of an organic social setting but is a mere interchangeable cog or part. (Recall that the latter is at least partly a function of the drive all institutions possess of seeking to make themselves into smoothly efficient and self-preserving organisms. To the extent that they succeed in this effort, the individual must lose a sense of self-direction and irreplaceable uniqueness.) The third facet, closely related to the first two, is a loss of individuality by particular human beings, for individuality is also something which is created by particular social circumstances. The experience of the loss of identity would be the experience of a lack of clear definition to one's life, the lack of a feeling that one is unique and irreplaceable.

The impact of these several aspects of alienation is largely negative; that is, humans are apt to be less fulfilled and satisfied, and societies will be less humane and less responsive to the full array of human needs. (That is, societies are becoming quite adept at providing for the physical well-being and comfort of human individuals, but less adept at providing their emotional, normative, and cultural needs.) However, these circumstances result from central features of contemporary human life. They are the products of the mobility, large and complex institutions, the increased human powers generated by technological advance, and the human population explosion. These factors are not going to disappear of themselves, and human beings are not likely to make any serious efforts to destroy them. This is because these conditions result from human structures which are simply too effective at providing people with the things they desire and because they are predominant sources of wealth and power.

Hence, the basic requirement for dealing with the difficulties these conditions pose is to recognize that they are permanent fixtures and that an attempt to mitigate their effects must be consistent with the requirements these elements impose on human life. Any other approach is only utopian day-dreaming or torpid nostalgia. For example, business relationships in Japan are generally still based on personal relationships of trust, mutual respect, and a fund of shared experiences. (The latter is generated by many evening business jaunts to restaurants and night clubs, the purpose of which is to create emotional ties and allow the various parties to business relationships to come to know one another as individuals.[9]) Hence, business relationships are based on what occidentals would view as personal friendship. There is much that is attractive about this approach. It seeks to nurture commercial ties that are warm and personal rather than shallow and calculating; it allows a high degree of informality and flexibility in business dealings (and avoids the complication of legal documents and the convoluting presence of lawyers); it nurtures the distinctly admirable human virtues of honesty, integrity, and trustworthiness.

However, Japanese business culture depends for its viability on the existence of a closed, homogeneous environment for the conduct of business. Hence, it is unsuited to the business conditions of modern life. The vast numbers of business contacts, the transitory nature of business relationships, and the large size of the institutions involved all require that business relationships be less personal, more formal and calculating, and more overtly legalistic. Moreover, the time and expense (both of which are considerable) required to nurture personal contacts in the Japanese fashion channel time, energy, and resources away from other matters which may well be more economically productive. Thus, it can be little more than nostalgia to wish for the creation of a business climate modelled on the Japanese practice.

The point is also illustrated by the desire of a number of contemporary authors to recreate the conditions of genuine community life. However, the sense of identification with a particular community, the feeling of responsibility for what takes place in it, the ties of shared experience with other community members, and the sense of oneself and of others as unique, irreplaceable individuals with whom one has had ties of experience and common values, are all hobbled by the conditions of contemporary life. People's careers, locations, and personal lives are highly mobile. They are likely to shift from job to job, location to location, and marriage to marriage several times in their lives. But genuine community requires years of shared experiences and close ties to nurture a feeling of identification with a social group. Those who view themselves as essentially transient are unlikely to develop the sense of mutual identification and responsibility required for the creation of genuine community. These days people mostly find their personal associations and identification at their place of employment or in their careers and not in the area where they reside.

In addition, at present most local political units contain many thousands of people, a number far too large to allow the sort of intimate association that is likely to foment a genuine sense of association. Furthermore, local governmental leaders of the present age are commonly professionals who move from locale to locale in search of job opportunity. This is not to say that genuine community can no longer exist; it obviously does. However, it can no longer form the template of how the great bulk of people can expect to live their lives.

A second aspect of alienation is the erosion of the ties which individuals have with other persons and with institutions. The ties include the emotive ties of personal attachment, the ties of mutual interest that draw people together into common endeavor, the ties of shared culture and experience, and finally the ties of identification, the sense of being *united* with other people or social groups.

Perhaps a sense of this loss and an effort to address it is illustrated by the various efforts of corporations and institutions to create an occidental equivalent of Japanese bonding experiences. These are ventures including dispatching employees on rafting trips or mountain climbing expeditions in order to generate the shared adventures that will (it is hoped) create more profound ties than can be established by attending committee meetings.[10] Obviously these are pallid substitutes for genuine contexts in which deeply felt shared experiences would arise, but they attest to the sense of loss. Moreover, they illustrate that humans can no longer depend on bonding experiences to occur as a matter of course; they may have to be created by artificial and explicit means.

But it is not obvious that such bonding is required to make contemporary corporations run better or to create more satisfying careers for employees. Corporations appear to function just fine without them. In addition, they may be self-defeating, because of contemporary mobility and because corporate practice often requires cold-blooded decisions about personnel that would be inhibited by the constraint of emotional bonds. So, corporate bonding expeditions are apt to prove a passing fad. However, individual people may continue to feel the loss and wish to create networks through which such experiences can be generated.

Home life is also affected by the present circumstances. Not only are people apt to have several marriages, but child-rearing is increasingly provided by professionals in day-care centers and in schools outside the home. The conditions of modern life generally demand that both members of a couple work, and these circumstances also require that women's careers be as important and demanding as those of men. Hence, child care may become largely undertaken by a series of professionals outside the home. The life of the individual at the present time is likely to be composed of a series of relationships with ragged clumps and clusters of individuals that will endure for a few years and then be replaced by a new group. The bonds of human relationships under such circumstances are fated to be shallow and fleeting.

Hence, the ties of individuals to other human individuals are being eroded by mobility, by the dissolution of distinctive cultures that give cohesion to particular groups, by the erosion of stable, life-long marriages, by the demands of contemporary careers, and by the absence of long years of shared experience and endeavor in the company of a particular group of individuals.

Moreover, the ties of individuals to groups of people, whether cultural groups, families, local communities, or nations are eroding under the same pressures that erode the ties of individuals to one another. The pressures of current life are eroding the significance of these groupings via the mobility of individuals, the erosion of local cultures, and the expanding importance of large institutions. The needs of human life are increasingly being accommodated by professionals, those trained to offer particular sorts of services, from child care to city management. These individuals may be competent, but they will likely base their actions on professional standards not on deeply-felt personal ties to their clients. Moreover, these professionals are largely interchangeable and as freely mobile as other members of societies. Hence, rather than strengthening and preserving the bonds of community in the places of their employment, they are playing a role in crumbling the emotional and experiential basis of community groups. They are playing a role of placing the relations of human life on a basis of professional, business relationships rather than personal ties.

However, the conditions of contemporary life that are severing personal ties are also dissolving the power of the particular individual. Individuals have few resources for dealing with large institutions. Most often vast institutions can only be effectively battled by organizations with equivalent resources. Furthermore, individuals within institutions are normally constrained by the definitions of their roles and by the multiple centers of power within an institution from changing an institution in ways different from those that are sanctioned by the institution itself.

In addition, the scale, complexity, and mobility engendered by globalism impede the development of social cultures of political action or governmental responsiveness that may give individuals opportunity for effective entry to the political process. Informal political cultures or developed institutional means for allowing individuals to reshape institutional functions are not likely to emerge. Even where organizations or structures exist that are formally charged with allowing individual entry into the political process, the transiency and complexity of contemporary life are likely to prevent such measures from being fully effective. Hence, as individuals become increasingly isolated, they will also have decreasing resources to alter the course of human events.

Large and complex institutions and human mobility require that formal legalistic measures develop to prevent abuses or seek redress for those that have already occurred. The law is often a clumsy and artificial instrument, but a legal system, or something like it, is frequently the only recourse individual human beings or informal groups of human beings have against large, overwhelming institutions. Hence, legal institutions may be of greater importance in future decades as means of gaining redress for social malfunction.

Also, it is increasingly the case that persons are losing their individuality. Individual identity in its fullest sense is not an individual's personal possession in the way that clothing or hair styles might be. It is in large measure a product of social circumstances.[11] Particularly vivid and memorable individuals are always found in a distinctive social context. It is the context which allows lively and distinctive characters to emerge. Individuality results from the particular talents, failings, and experiences of the person, but these are a result of the circumstances of the individual's life. Furthermore, an individual's identity is also composed of the array of that person's associations with others – the groups, cultures, and institutions of which the person is a part. But, it is not merely *association* which contributes to a deep sense of identity. The fact that one is a fan of one athletic team or another is a type of association but is unlikely to contribute profoundly to the individual's identity. Association only contributes significantly to an individual's identity if the individual plays a distinctive role in the various groups and institutions. In addition, the person's individuality and uniqueness, or the imprint which the individual makes on others or on the human environment, depend on the response others make to the individual; that is, on their memories, their common experiences, and on their conception of that person's nature.

Each of the above factors is being eroded by the circumstances of contemporary life. Furthermore, it is difficult to imagine circumstances under which the fraying of emotional bonds and loosening sense of national, ethnic, community, or family identification are apt to be entirely reversed. It is also unlikely that either the powerlessness or the loss of distinctive individuality engendered by the fact that individual human beings must continue to lead lives composed of a series of associations with large institutions will be completely reversed.

The human species is increasingly adept at providing itself with comfortable circumstances and satisfying its cravings for material objects, but this competency is achieved at a cost of flattening emotional life and draining individuality. Moreover, these deprivations will not be reversed for the simple reason that people crave the wealth, status, influence, and power contemporary societies offer more keenly than they feel the loss of other things. However, if these deficiencies are to be addressed, they must be addressed in explicit and artificial fashion rather than expecting them to be supplied by the normal circumstances of human life. They can only be addressed, if at all, by establishing explicit structures within large institutions which are designed for the purpose. Nonetheless, it is also very probably inevitable that the efforts will be less than completely satisfactory, both because they are necessarily artificial but also because the conditions of contemporary life work against them.

THE HAVES AND HAVE-NOTS

A continuing theme of this book is that globalism will spread unevenly across nations and within nations. Many nations and many individuals are deeply rooted in the global economy at the present time, others are poised to join it, but many others have been left aside. It is not obvious that sprawling multinational corporations and leading economic powers among nations are seeking to exploit those who have been left out. However, the great differences in resources will certainly allow successful participants to get what they desire and nurture their interests, while those remaining on the fringes will have few means to defend their interests. Hence, abuse and injustice are almost certain to occur.

As a result much of the coming era's political and social conflict is likely to emerge from the tensions between those nations, or those groups within nations, who are able to function effectively as part of the global economy and those who do not.

For example, there is reason to believe that much of the impetus of contemporary militant Islamic movements can be traced to this division. People are drawn to these movements from poverty and a sense that they are dominated by outside forces and lack control of their own fates or lives. They turn to Islamic fundamentalism as a means of reestablishing their identities and regaining control of their lives.[12] However, there is evidence that these movements will be sterile and self-defeating unless they eventually renounce their isolationism and seek to become vehicles for Islamic people and nations to enter the global economy as confident participants. A militant Islamic movement that fails to make this transition is likely to be reduced to impoverished and embittered isolation or itself become a focus of social and political upheaval. The best evidence for this view is Iran which, following the overthrow of the Shah in 1978, fixed a policy of isolation from the world economy coupled with encouraging fundamentalist Islamic movements in other nations. At present, however, Iran has discovered that its bitter isolation has bred impoverished unrest among its citizens and that the only means of addressing its difficulties is to endeavor to rejoin the global economic order.[13]

In addition to conflict between nations, the emergent global economy will generate strains *within* nations, because some groups of people within nations will command the education, flexibility, mobility, and personal habits of self-discipline and skills in dealing with other people which are needed to meet the demands of global commerce. Other groups, however, will not, and they will be doomed to economic and social marginalization if they are unable to gain access to the opportunities offered by the global economy. This development is illustrated by evidence of the emergence of a two class order in the United States, one class able to function within the global economy and hence prosper and flourish, and a second, increasingly marginalized, impoverished, and desperate group of people who have lost social status and economic stability as a result of the developments of the past several decades.[14]

The above paragraphs reveal several of the fundamental assumptions which guide this work. They include the beliefs that possession and distribution of wealth and power is the fundamental question of human political affairs and that the dynamics of globalism will control this distribution. The implication of these presumptions is that conflicts, even those of global scope, involving religion, nationalism, ethnic identity, or the relations between the sexes must be understood as finally based on the distribution of wealth and power and the way this distribution is shaped by globalism. Hence, there is reason to believe that the core of social and political conflict in coming decades will be the vast differences in wealth and power that will separate those who are able to function successfully as part of the global economy and those who cannot.

Political scientists and political philosophers who wish to comprehend the political currents of the next decades must therefore focus their attention on this uneven distribution, the strains and fissures which it causes, and ways of resolving the difficulties it nurtures. Once again, Marx offers useful contrast. Marx also believed that economics would force human beings into two opposed classes – laborers and owners. He was convinced, however, that their common circumstances and grievances would prompt workers across the globe to unite into a common front, and that their common interests would dissolve the divisions resulting from national affiliation, language, and geography. Recent history shows that he was gloriously mistaken, for the past century and a half has been the cockpit of virulent nationalism, and workers across the globe have taken greater interest in the matters that divide them than those that might unite them. It now appears that capitalism has emerged triumphant and globally unified, while labor remains fragmented. Furthermore, those who are left aside by globalism are those who, by definition, cannot command the resources to function on a global scale. For these reasons, the strife of coming decades is likely to remain fragmented rather than become a single mass conflict between those functioning globally and those who are not. Each conflict, therefore, must be understood on its own terms, whether it be civil war in Bosnia, militant Islamic movements in the Middle East, or fringe militia groups in the United States. However, it should also be kept in mind that a common thread unites them all, that of the divide separating those part of the global economy from those who are not.

Marx was also spectacularly and fruitfully wrong on another matter. Along with many others, he held the faith that the forces he observed in conflict would eventually play themselves out and that a global human society completely free from conflict and violence would eventually emerge. However, the regimes inspired by his vision include some of the most ruthlessly brutal institutions to have appeared in human history.

Many reasons for their brutality must be examined, but prominent among them must be their common view that conflict within their societies should be eliminated, often by eliminating the human beings who opposed them. The most humane societies are those that appear to recognize conflict as a permanent feature of human life, make no effort to eliminate it, but, instead, seek to provide nonviolent avenues within which conflict can occur and, with luck, be resolved.

The upshot of this work is that globalism and the global economy will both give a great deal to humanity and remove a great deal. They will offer vast resources of wealth and power, will provide the goods of material life in ample measure, and will play a role in dismantling many of the sources of human woe. However, they will also erode the bonds of human companionship, spread alienation and powerlessness, and erode the foundations of those institutions which have offered much of the order and stability of human life. Individuals will have increased freedom to live their personal lives as they wish, but they will forfeit much of their ability to make changes in the world beyond the edges of their private domains.

Notes

Introduction

1. C.B. Macpherson offers an illuminating and often provocative discussion of these issues in *The Political Theory of Possessive Individualism* (Oxford: Oxford University Press, 1962) pp. 1–4 and 194 ff.
2. See, for example, Graeme Duncan's *Marx and Mill* (Cambridge: Cambridge University Press, 1973).
3. One indication of GATT's importance in politicians' eyes is the efforts of the remnants of the Soviet Union and China to gain membership. See Leah A. Haus, *Globalizing the GATT* (Washington: Brookings Institute, 1992).
4. Certainly there has been trade across political boundaries from the beginning of human history. There is evidence of such trade even in human prehistory, that of sea shells or exotic materials discovered in sites far from their origin. Contemporary hunter-gatherer societies, once thought to be pristine cultures untouched by contact with the outside, have now been acknowledged to contain evidence of long years of transcultural trade. The lurid imperialism of the nineteenth century took a further step of conquering states partly in order to gain access to supplies of raw materials and expanded markets for domestic industry. However, it was only in the period following the Second World War that a genuine global economy began to emerge. This was partly because quantum advances in communications and transportation allowed the creation of genuine global markets and also greatly facilitated corporate efforts to expand their endeavors across national boundaries. But the expansion was also partly a direct consequence of the war. The war left the United States predominant economically as well as militarily and politically. The remaining industrialized nations had largely been devastated during the conflict. The policy of the United States was formulated by those who had a messianic faith in the value of free trade and open markets for creating prosperity and cementing ties among nations. Hence, the international institutions created in that period largely reflected this ideology, and American corporations discovered vast opportunities for expanding abroad. Also, the shattered industrial economies soon discovered that they must rely on export markets for their rebuilding industries because their own citizens were often too poor to buy the products they wished to produce.
5. Joseph J. Fucini and Suzy Fucini, *Working for the Japanese* (New York and London: The Free Press and Collier Macmillan, 1990), especially pp. 23–5, 28–30, and 34–5.
6. Ian Buruma discusses an extreme formulation of this view in, 'Just Say "Noh"', *The New York Review of Books*, 36 (7 December 1989) pp. 19–20.
7. See Henry Shue, *Basic Rights* (Princeton: Princeton University Press, 1980).
8. As Hoffmann says:

What one finds most of the time now is, on the one hand, disembodied ethical teaching, normally done by professional philosophers for specialists of philosophy. One example in this connection would be in the journal *Philosophy and Public Affairs*, in which one often finds political issues discussed with beautiful logic but without reference to the political universe.

Duties Beyond Borders (Syracuse: Syracuse University, 1981), p. 227. Also, see p. 1 for his pronouncement that he is no philosopher.

9. His Chapter 5, for example, titled 'An Ethics of World Order', does not address the issue of whether the entire system of nation-states may be crumbling apart, *ibid.*, pp. 189–232. However, this is a work published in 1981 prior to much of the tumult that has revealed the stresses in the nation-state system. Much of his recent work is devoted to examination of the slow, pained process of economic and political unification of the European Community. This work reveals clear awareness of the challenges to sovereignty and national identity that this process poses, but he does not undertake a sustained conceptual analysis of the impact of these changes for political theory. See, for example, Robert O. Keohane and Stanley Hoffmann, 'Institutional Change in Europe in the 1980s' in Robert O. Keohane and Stanley Hoffmann, (eds), *The New European Community* (Boulder: Westview, 1991), pp. 1–39 or Robert O. Keohane and Stanley Hoffmann, 'Conclusion: Structure, Strategy, and Institutional Roles' in Robert O. Keohane, Joseph S. Nye, and Stanley Hoffmann (eds) *After the Cold War* (Cambridge: Harvard University Press, 1993), pp. 381–404.

10. For example, see Robert Reich, *Tales of a New America* (New York: Times Books, 1987) or *The Work of Nations* (New York: A.A. Knopf, 1991).

11. Stephen Gill and David Law, *The Global Political Economy* (London: Harvester-Wheatsheaf, 1988) and Theodore Geiger, *The Future of the International System* (Winchester: Allen & Unwin, 1988).

12. See Brian Barry, *Free Movement* (University Park: Pennsylvania State University, 1992); Charles Beitz, *Political Theory and International Relations* (Princeton: Princeton University Press, 1979); Michael Walzer, *Just and Unjust Wars* (New York: Basic Books, 1977); Henry Shue, *op. cit.*; Thomas W. Pogge, *Realizing Rawls* (Ithaca: Cornell University Press, 1987); and Stanley Hoffmann, *Duties Beyond Borders, op. cit.*

13. Lazar Volin, *A Century of Russian Agriculture* (Cambridge: Harvard University Press, 1970) or Stefan Hedlund, *Crisis in Soviet Agriculture* (London: Croom Helm, 1984).

14. Carolyn Webber and Aaron Wildavsky, *A History of Taxation and Expenditure in the Western World* (New York: Simon and Schuster, 1986) pp. 428–36 and 490–511.

15. John Rawls, *A Theory of Justice* (Cambridge: Harvard University Press, 1971); Alan Donagan, *The Theory of Morality* (Chicago: University of Chicago Press, 1977); David Gauthier, *Morals by Agreement* (Oxford: Clarendon Press, 1986); Alan Gewirth, *Reason and Morality* (Chicago: University of Chicago Press, 1978); and Ronald Dworkin, *A Matter of Principle* (Cambridge: Harvard University Press, 1985).

16. This is the presumption behind his belief that his principles of justice will serve as an 'Archimedian point' which can be used to assess the justification of any social structure. Rawls, *op. cit.*, pp. 260–3.
17. John Rawls, *Political Liberalism* (New York: Columbia University Press, 1993).

1 The Emerging Global Economy

1. Jagdish Bhagwati, 'Threats to the World Trading Regime: Protectionism, Unfair Trade, *et al*' in Ad Koekkoek and L.B.M. Mennes (eds), *International Trade and Global Development* (London and New York: Routledge, 1991) p. 240.
2. As one commentator notes, 'Nationalism, in Isaiah Berlin's words, is not "resurgent" – it never died'. Tony Judt, 'The New Old Nationalism', *The New York Review of Books*, 41 (26 May 1994) p. 44. Also see Nathan Gardels' interview of Isaiah Berlin, 'Two Concepts of Nationalism', *The New York Review of Books*, 38 (21 November 1991) pp. 19–23.
3. Gary A. Wright, *Archaeology and Trade* (Reading: Addison-Wesley, 1974).
4. See P. Hertner and G. Jones (eds), *Multinationals: Theory and History* (Farnborough, Hants and Brookfield: Gower, 1986).
5. Three scholars make the point as follows:

> The view that the welfare of all, and the particular interests of the United States, required a world of open economic borders permeated the efforts of both the Truman and Eisenhower administrations to persuade hesitant U.S. companies to expand their operations abroad. These efforts were justified on the basis of their contribution to global welfare and security, which would enable host countries to raise their standard of living and move toward prosperity and peace. They were justified on the basis of their contribution to global welfare and security, which would enable host countries to raise their standard of living and move toward prosperity and peace. They were justified on the basis of their contribution to U.S. welfare and security; providing access to raw materials . . . ; promoting the export of manufactured products to a dollar-short world; securing political allies among the recipient countries in a prosperous interdependent world economy. (C.F. Bergstein, T. Horst and T.H. Moran, *American Multinationals and American Interests* (Atlantic Highlands, NJ: Humanities, 1988) p. 310. Also see p. 313.)

6. Paul Kennedy, 'Preparing for the 21st Century: Winners and Losers', *The New York Review of Books*, 40 (11 February 1993) pp. 32–5.
7. See Theodore Draper, 'Who Killed Soviet Communism?', *The New York Review of Books*, 39 (11 June 1992) pp. 7–14; Martin Malia, 'A New Russian Revolution?', *The New York Review of Books*, 38 (18 July 1991) pp. 29–31; and Celeste A. Wallander and Jane E. Prokop, 'Soviet Security Strategies toward Europe: After the Wall, with Their Backs up against It' in Robert O. Keohane, Joseph S. Nye and Stanley Hoffmann (eds), *After the Cold War* (Cambridge: Harvard University Press, 1993) pp. 63–103.
8. Stanley Hoffmann, as he concludes a careful examination of the difficult-

ies besetting Europe's unification, observes, ' . . . there is no turning back'. 'Goodbye to a United Europe?', *The New York Review of Books*, 40 (27 May 1993) p. 31.

9. See Perry Link's 'The Old Man's New China', *The New York Review of Books*, 41 (9 June 1994) pp. 31–6.

10. See Kennedy once again, *op. cit.*, pp. 35–7.

11. The point is also illustrated by Myanmar (previously Burma). For decades, it pursued a policy of strict isolation, and became one of the poorest nations of the world as a result. Now its military leaders are taking tentative (and sometimes clumsy) steps to enter the global economy. See Hugh Honour, 'Burma: Splendor and Miseries', *The New York Review of Books*, 42 (13 July 1995) pp. 56–61 and 'Head of Democratic Opposition Is Released by Burmese Military', *New York Times* (11 July 1995).

12. Gary K. Bertsch and John R. McIntyre (eds), *National Security and Technology Transfer* (Boulder: Westview, 1983) and Mark E. Schaffer, *Technology Transfer and East-West Relations* (New York: St. Martin's Press, 1985).

13. See Jagdish Bhagwati's 'Global Interdependence and International Migration' in Douglas A. Irwin (ed.), *Political Economy and International Economics* (Cambridge: MIT, 1991) pp. 367–402.

14. William B. Johnston, 'Global Work Force 2000: The New World Labor Market', *Harvard Business Review*, 69 (March–April 1991) pp. 115–27.

15. S. Tamer Cavisgul, *Internationalizing Business: Meeting the Challenge* (East Lansing: Michigan State University, 1993).

16. Walter B. Wriston, *The Twilight of Sovereignty* (New York: Charles Scribner's Sons, 1992) pp. 110–28.

17. Recently the *St. Petersburg Times* reported:

> A British teenager was able to tap into sensitive U.S. government computers and monitor secret communications on the North Korean nuclear crisis last spring. The 16-year-old browsed several defense computers over a seven-month period, and was finally caught by special U.S. investigators when he left his terminal online to a U.S. defense computer overnight. He was arrested by British police, and prosecutors will decide this month whether he can be charged.

'Hacker Penetrates Military Network', *St. Petersburg Times* (4 January 1995).

18. Among others, Kenneth A. Oye has recently made this argument. See his *Economic Discrimination and Political Exchange* (Princeton: Princeton University Press, 1992).

19. Robert B. Reich, 'Who Is Us?', *Harvard Business Review*, 68 (January–February 1990) pp. 53–64 and Robert B. Reich, 'Who Is Them?', *Harvard Business Review*, 69 (March–April 1991) pp. 77–88.

20. One news account contains the following observation:

> Amid the pictures of Mr. Kaifu relaxing in Palm Springs were articles giving an indication of why American criticism of Japan often puzzles the Japanese.
> On the one hand, Carla A. Hills, the United States trade representative,

was quoted as saying that Japanese investment in the United States was a matter of concern. On the other, attention was given to comments by people in Palm Springs saying that they hoped the meeting would bring an infusion of Japanese investment to their valley. ('Kaifu Returns to Political Outcry in Tokyo', *New York Times* (5 March 1990).)

21. Stephen D. Cohen, *Cowboys and Samurai* (New York: Harper Business, 1991) pp. 5 and 35–6. It is worth noting that United States trade is in deficit with the rest of the world *only* in the areas of consumer goods and petroleum. In other sectors of international trade, the United States is essentially in balance or in surplus. Albert T. Sommers with Lucie R. Blau, *The U.S. Economy Demystified*, 3rd edn (New York: Lexington Books, 1993) p. 140.

22. As Felix Rohatyn, a senior partner with Lazard Frères & Co. and something of an authority on capital, notes:

> The legal protections [of American capital markets]; the requirements of disclosure; the variety of financial instruments available to investors including stocks, bonds, mutual funds, options, and futures; the technical capacities of the system – all suggest standards that are far from being met in most of the developing countries but will be necessary for the capital markets of the future.
>
> In the developing world, there will be fierce competition for the capital necessary for economic growth; and capital investors will become more and more choosy and will insist on modern legal and credit systems, political stability, and independent central banks to manage currency. ('World Capital: The Need and the Risks', *The New York Review of Books*, 41 (14 July 1994) p. 50.)

23. Rohatyn, *op. cit.*, p. 50 and 'New Mutual Funds to Battle for Russian Mattress Billions', *New York Times* (29 July 1995).

24. 'Bowing to IMF, Yeltsin Takes New Steps to Fight Spending and Corruption', *New York Times* (2 March 1995) and 'IMF, Banking on Reform, Approves Loan to Russia', *Wall Street Journal* (12 April 1995).

25. Stephen Gill and David Law, *The Global Political Economy* (London: Harvester-Wheatsheaf, 1988) pp. 89–95 and 'Why Currencies Move Faster Than Policies', *New York Times* (23 September 1992).

26. There are several reasons for believing that the importance of trade in manufactured goods in international commerce should not be over-estimated. To begin with, manufactured goods account for less than 60 per cent of the value of global trade. 'Adding Up the World Trade Talks: Fail Now, Pay Later', *New York Times* (16 December 1990). Moreover, as one analyst points out, more than half of the merchandise traded internationally consists of transfers within multinational corporations. Walter B. Wriston, *op. cit.*, p. 93. Most important, though, are the facts that trade in services is the fastest growing domain of international trade and that the volume of international currency transactions dwarfs the value of goods traded. Wriston, *op.cit.*, pp. 79–80. The impact of international currency trade is enormous, sufficient to have a direct impact on the decisions

and policies of governments. 'Why Currencies Move Faster Than Policies', *New York Times* (23 September 1992) or 'Stock Market Diplomacy',
New York Times (6 April 1994).

27. For example, the United States is reluctant to use trade sanctions against
China for fear of repercussions to US businesses and workers. 'A Cold-
War Weapon Isn't Used on China and May Never Be', *New York Times*
(3 June 1993). Also, though the United States and Japan have been battling one another for years, most believe it is highly unlikely either will
take steps likely seriously to harm trade relations, because the two economies are so closely linked: 'Trade Ties Bind, Indeed', *New York Times*
(25 May 1994).

28. According to the *1994 CIA World Fact Book*, the United States' Gross
Domestic Product for 1993 totalled $6.379 trillion, exports totalled $479
billion in that year, and imports totalled $582 billion. Hence, international
trade accounted for some 16 per cent of all economic activity.

29. Walter B. Wriston, *op. cit.*, pp. 9–11, 77–8, and 81–5. Also see, for example,
'Nationality of Autos Big Trade Issue', *New York Times* (9 October 1992).

30. Martin Sorrell, 'Merging For Success', *Advertising Age*, 61 (18 June 1990)
p. 70; 'Global Reach Gains Edge Over Talent', *New York Times* (5 May
1989); and 'British Merger Bid Would Create No. 2 World Advertising
Concern', *New York Times* (1 May 1989).

31. Alberto Giovannini, R. Glenn Hubbard and Joel Slemrod, *Studies in International Taxation* (Chicago: University of Chicago Press, 1993).

32. See Werner J. Feld, *Multinational Corporations and U.N. Politics* (New
York: Pergamon Press, 1980) and Isaiah Frank, *Foreign Enterprise in
Developing Countries* (Baltimore and London: The Johns Hopkins Uni-
versity Press, 1980).

33. This confusion apparently extends even to the highest reaches of the
American government. For example, a recent newspaper account reports
that an anonymous official of the Clinton Administration asserted:

> Participants at the meeting [of 'five top Administration officials'] pointed
> out that it was difficult to determine what is an American company
> now when joint ventures and international stock investors mean that a
> company may have many owners in many countries, the official said.
> ('In Shift, White House Will Stress Aiding Foreign Concerns in U.S.',
> *New York Times* (2 June 1993).)

34. This confusion is reflected in recent American policy decisions. See, 'In
Shift, White House Will Stress Aiding Foreign Concerns in U.S.', *New
York Times* (2 June 1993).

35. Joseph M. Grieco, *Cooperation Among Nations* (Ithaca: Cornell University Press, 1990).

2 National Sovereignty

1. The European medieval order shares several features with contemporary
fundamentalist Islamic political movements, those whose views are
exemplified by the late Ayatollah Khomeini of Iran. They avow that states

should be under the firm control of religious leaders and that there should be only one pan-Islamic state created from all those domains in which Islam predominates. The Islamic view differs from the Medieval European in that there is not, even in principle, a distinction between secular and sacred authority; the state should be under the direct control of religious leaders, and no independent secular authority is recognized. Nonetheless, the militant Islamic view is clearly opposed to the perspective of the modern nation-state. Bernard Lewis examines some of these themes in his recent book, *Islam and The West* (New York: Oxford University Press, 1993) pp. 174–86.

2. He says at one point, '. . . a state when composed of too few is not, as a state ought to be, self-sufficient . . .', in *Politics*, translated by B. Jowett in *The Complete Works of Aristotle*, vol. 2, edited by Jonathan Barnes (Princeton: Princeton University Press, 1984) p. 2105. Also see pp. 2104–7.

3. As Michael Walzer asserts, 'The moral standing of any particular state depends upon the reality of the common life it protects and the extent to which the sacrifices required by that protection are willingly accepted and thought worthwhile'. *Just and Unjust Wars* (New York: Basic Books, 1977) p. 54. Aristotle puts the matter somewhat differently, viz., 'For a state is not a mere aggregate of persons, but, as we say, a union of them sufficing for the purposes of life . . .', *op. cit.*, p. 2108.

4. Locke asserts, 'The great and *chief end* therefore, of Mens uniting into Commonwealths, and putting themselves under Governments is *the Preservation of their Property*'. *Two Treatises of Government*, edited by Peter Laslett (Cambridge: Cambridge University Press, 1986) p. 368 and more generally pp. 368–88.

5. He notes, 'Now it is evident that that form of government is best in which every man, whoever he is, can act best and live happily', *op. cit.*, p. 2101.

6. Karl Marx, 'Critique of the Gotha Program' in *Marx & Engels: Basic Writings on Politics & Philosophy*, edited by Lewis Feuer (Garden City, NY: Doubleday & Co., 1959) pp. 126–9.

7. Thomas Hobbes, *Leviathan*, edited by Michael Oakeshott (Oxford: Basil Blackwell, 1960) p. 219.

8. See F.H. Hinsley, *Sovereignty*, 2nd edn (Cambridge: Cambridge University Press, 1986).

9. Alan James' *Sovereign Statehood* (London: Allen & Unwin, 1986) is a sophisticated and useful examination of these complexities.

10. Article 2, paragraph 7 of the United Nations Charter states, 'Nothing contained in the present Charter shall authorize the United Nations to intervene in matters which are essentially within the domestic jurisdictions of any state'.

11. Edward Mortimer, 'Iraq: The Road Not Taken', *New York Review of Books*, 38 (16 May 1991), pp. 3–7; George Bush, 'Continued Pressure on Iraq to Comply With UN Security Council Resolutions', *US Department of State Dispatch 3* (21 September 1992), pp. 718–19; Ronald Newmann, 'Overview of US Policy Toward Iraq', *US Department of State Dispatch 5* (7 February 1994) pp. 66–8; and 'Challenge to Council Resolutions Continues', *UN Chronicle*, 30 (June 1993) pp. 30–3.

12. Ton Zuijdwijk, *Petitioning the United Nations* (New York: St. Martin's, 1982) p. xii.

13. For example, Walzer claims that states' claims to territorial integrity and political sovereignty ' . . . rest ultimately on the right of men and women to build a common life and to risk their individual lives only when they freely choose to do so', *op. cit.*, p. 61.
14. Walzer, *ibid.*, p. 61.
15. Walzer, *ibid.*, p. 61.
16. See, for example, Charles Beitz's discussion in *Political Theory and International Relations*, (Princeton: Princeton University Press, 1979) pp. 77–82.
17. Peter Reddaway, 'Russia on the Brink?', *New York Review of Books*, 40 (28 January 1993) pp. 30–5. However, David Dyker argues that Yeltsin's reforms were never as extensive as is commonly believed. 'Russia's Economy After The Referendum', *The World Today* 49 (July 1993), pp. 122–3.
18. C.F. Cortese, *Modernization, Threat, and the Power of the Military* (Beverly Hills: Sage Publications, 1976) pp. 7 and 21–2.
19. At least one commentator, Christopher Greenwood, argues that there is evidence that international law is beginning to shift and now offers tentative sanction for intervention in some circumstances. See 'Is There a Right of Humanitarian Intervention?', *The World Today*, 49 (February 1993) pp. 34–40, especially pp. 39–40.
20. Stanley Hoffmann makes the point in vivid fashion: 'But in France and in the UK, much of the public remain attached, in a Danish commentator's phrase, to a view of sovereignty as "something like virginity": it is not divisible'. In 'Goodbye to a United Europe?', *New York Review of Books*, 41 (27 May 1993) p. 31. Another commentator, also discussing European unification, claims:

> Sovereignty is at the heart of the debate over Maastricht. Architects of a federal Europe have been operating on a limited and therefore defective notion of sovereignty. . . .
> Those responsibilities that historically have defined the sovereign state have been eclipsed in much of Western Europe since World War II by an ever more intense concentration on economic performance and social welfare. Western Europe has been preoccupied with the practical methods for achieving these economic and social goals. (Michael J. Brenner, 'EC: Confidence Lost', *Foreign Policy*, 91 (Summer 1993) p. 27. Also, see James, *op. cit.*, pp. 1–25.)

21. See S.I. Benn and R.S. Peters, *The Principles of Political Thought* (New York: The Free Press, 1965, c1958) pp. 299–325 for a useful discussion of traditional views and a penetrating analysis of their deficiencies. Charles Beitz, *op. cit.*, pp. 25–7, 76–81, and 121–2 offers a more recent examination of these matters.
22. Though conditions in Europe have evolved rapidly in the past several years, Robert Keohane and Stanley Hoffman assembled a collection of essays, *The New European Community* (Boulder: Westview), published in 1991, which remains a useful introduction to the topic.
23. See, for example, Walter Wriston, *The Twilight of Sovereignty* (New York: Charles Scribner's Sons, 1992) p. 35 ff.

24. 'Seoul Warns on Jet Deal', *New York Times* (11 April 1991) and 'South Korea Seeks Jets', *New York Times* (9 April 1991).
25. Obviously there is more than a little scholarly disagreement on the pace and character of federalization. Kermit Hall argues: 'Since 1868 the balance of authority in the federal system has shifted away from the states and toward the national government. The system remains federal, but the central government has moved into areas that once were exclusively the domain of states'. Kermit L. Hall (ed), *Federalism: A Nation of States* (New York: Garland, 1987), p. x. However, David Walker argues that there was little change in the relation of the states to the federal government from 1790 to 1930, when Franklin Roosevelt's New Deal began to shift the balance to the federal government. Walker argues that there was a dramatic change after 1960. David B. Walker, *Toward A Functioning Federalism* (Cambridge: Winthrop Publishers, 1981) p. xiii. See also Rhodri Jeffreys-Jones and Bruce Collins, *The Growth of Federal Power in American History* (Dekalb: Northern Illinois University, 1983). Daniel Elizar argues in favor of something of a revisionist view, claiming that the relation of power between the states and the federal government is complex and that it is best characterized as a partnership, albeit one given structure by the central government. Daniel J. Elazar, *American Federalism: A View From the States* (New York: Thomas J. Crowell, 1966) pp. v–vi.
26. The phrase 'habit of obedience' is borrowed from another author and another context. It was coined by the distinguished jurist John Austin, and he employed it to account for the hold of the laws of governments on their subjects. John Austin, 'A Positivist Conception of Law' in *Philosophy of Law*, fourth edn, edited by Joel Feinberg and Hyman Gross (Belmont: Wadsworth, 1991) p. 36.
27. Zuijdwijk, *op. cit.*, pp. 2–9.
28. Brian Urquhart, 'The United Nations in 1992', *International Affairs*, 68 (April 1992) pp. 311–19.
29. As evidence of this, the number of UN peacekeeping operations has increased dramatically in recent years. Mr. Boutros-Ghali recently noted:

> Since 1988, the United Nations has created as many peace-keeping operations in four years as it did in the previous four decades. In 1992 alone, United Nations peace-keeping experienced a four-fold increase in the number of troops deployed as well as in the overall cost. By the end of the year, there were over 50,000 peace-keepers deployed with 13 operations at an annual price tag of about $3bn. 'UN Peace-keeping in a New Era' (*The World Today*, 49 (April 1993) p. 67.)

30. For example, the former Director of the Royal Institute of International Affairs, Sir James Eberle, says, ' . . . it seems to me that the use of armed force on a large scale in the future will almost invariably be on the basis of international action'. 'International Boundaries: The Security Angle', *The World Today*, 48 (April 1992) p. 70.
31. See Beitz, *op.cit.*, pp. 71–83.
32. See, for example, Harry Beran, *The Consent Theory of Political Obligation* (London: Croom Helm, 1987); Leslie Green, *The Authority of the*

State (Oxford: Oxford University Press, 1988); A. John Simmons, *Moral Principles and Political Obligations* (Princeton: Princeton University Press, 1979); or Peter Singer, *Democracy and Disobedience* (Oxford: Oxford University Press, 1974).

33. Anthony Hartley provides a useful examination of the basis of the uncertainty European citizens feel regarding the Maastricht Treaty. 'Maastricht's Problematical Future', *The World Today*, 48 (October 1992) pp. 179–82.

34. Charles Beitz argues that citizen consent need not be required for governments to be considered legitimate, so long as those governments uphold basic human rights. *Op. cit.*, pp. 79–83. The bases of his argument are that in most cases governments and their activities cannot straightforwardly be said to execute the will of their citizens and that it is very difficult to demonstrate in any plausible fashion that citizens have given genuine consent to the rule which their governments have over them. The arguments of this chapter allow the argument to be taken even further. If sovereignty is not considered in a 'whole cloth' sense, if bits and patches of sovereign domain are scattered across the spectrum of governmental activity, and if many of these domains have little impact on the lives and rights of individual persons, then there seems little requirement for a lofty and rigorous standard of legitimacy. Furthermore, if these scraps of sovereignty are being transferred to international entities with a narrow range of powers, if the primary authority of these bodies is held over governments rather than persons, and if the activities of these bodies have little to do with the concerns of individual persons, an even looser standard of legitimacy is requisite. If such bodies serve some reasonable purpose and carry out their responsibilities in competent and conscientious fashion, then they have reasonable claim to their authority.

However, there is another aspect to this conception of legitimacy. If the authority and power of such bodies is attenuated, and they have little consequence for the lives of ordinary people, then no very lofty standard need be met to *override* their authority, or dissolve them altogether. Once again, the standard of reasonable purpose and plausible expectation of benefit would suffice.

35. Beitz is likely the author who has worked out this argument most thoroughly. *Op. cit.*, pp. 71–92.

36. 'Voter interviews conducted by Aarhus University indicated that the greatest reason for a "no" vote was fear of loss of sovereignty (24 per cent), followed by dislike of the EC (12 per cent) and knowing too little about the consequences of the Treaty (10 per cent)'. Clive Archer, 'Denmark Says "No"', *The World Today*, 48 (August/September 1992) p. 143.

37. Hartley reports:

> The political union section of the Maastricht Treaty seems, therefore, to have aroused a feeling of skepticism as to its feasibility and of apprehension as to some of the intentions that lie behind it. In the case of a small country like Denmark these fears take on a precise form: dread of being dragged into expensive political and military commitments over matters which the Danes feel are no concern of theirs. (*Op. cit.*, p. 182.)

38. As Urquhart puts it, 'The truth is that governments do not control the major forces which are shaping the future – if they ever did', *op. cit.*, p. 313. Walter Wriston, who has played central roles both in business and government, makes the point in greater detail. He asserts,

> The global market has moved from rhetoric to reality almost before we knew it. The old political boundaries of nation-states are being made obsolete by an alliance of commerce and technology. Political borders, long the cause of wars, are becoming porous. Commerce has not waited for the political process to adjust to technology but has tended to drive it. . . .
>
> With national borders, sovereignty has traditionally entailed the government's power to regulate the leading enterprises of society, from health care to heavy industry. In an economy dominated by products that consist largely of information, this power erodes rapidly. (*Op. cit.* p. 11.)

3 National Identity

1. Eric Hobsbawm states the point clearly:

> And simultaneously, as modern war illustrates, state interest now depended on the participation of the ordinary citizen to an extent not previously envisaged. Whether the armies were composed of conscripts or volunteers, the willingness of men to serve was now an essential variable in government calculations. . . . Obviously the democratization of politics, i.e. on the one hand the growing extension of the (male) franchise, on the other the creation of the modern, administrative, citizen-mobilizing and citizen-influencing state, both placed the question of the 'nation', and the citizen's feelings towards whatever he regarded as his 'nation', 'nationality' or other centre of loyalty, at the top of the political agenda. (*Nations and Nationalism Since 1780* (Cambridge: Cambridge University Press, 1990) p. 83.)

2. Adam Michnik expresses this fluidity and complexity nicely:

> During my entire life, I was, and I wanted to be, a Pole in the eyes of foreigners. That is how I always presented myself, here in the States, in Europe, and in Israel. In all the documents I have had to fill out, in the space for nationality I have always put down 'Polish'. At the same time, whenever the malignant shadow of anti-Semitism loomed over Polish public life, I clearly and unequivocally acknowledged my Jewish origins and my grandparents' membership in the Jewish nation. As a Pole, so far as anti-Semites were concerned, I always wanted to be a Jew. ('Poland and the Jews', *The New York Review of Books*, 38 (30 May 1991) p. 11.)

Of course, being a Pole and simultaneously being a Jew is not impossible, but Michnik clearly illustrates how, given the history of the twentieth century, this dual identification can occur. He asks:

How can one be a Pole of Jewish origin in the country that lived through the pogrom against Jews at Kielce in 1946, the anti-Semitic excesses in 1965, the anti-Semitic campaign orchestrated by the Communist government in 1968, and, finally, the wounding anti-Semitic rhetoric of the last presidential campaign? (*Op. cit.,* 11.)

3. As Edward Keenan notes:

The notion of the nation-state, first given to the eighteenth century Western world by a French royal establishment only roughly half of whose subjects spoke French, rather than Breton, Catalan or Provençal, has profoundly shaped the political thinking of statesmen and simple citizens. It has literally shaped our world. It has spread to every post-traditional culture; for almost everyone who thinks about such matters it seems axiomatic that ethnic groups or nations spontaneously strive to achieve their natural condition, the nation-state. Nations that do so have fulfilled their destiny; those that do not are somehow unrealized. ('Rethinking the U.S.S.R., Now That It's Over', *New York Times* (8 September 1991).)

Also see Yael Tamir, *Liberal Nationalism* (Princeton: Princeton University Press, 1993) pp. 57–77 and E.J. Hobsbawm, *op. cit..*
4. Linda Colley, *Britons* (New Haven: Yale University Press, 1992).
5. As Liah Greenfeld observes:

There were, of course, nativist movements and sentiments which opposed such retention [of original national identity] and resisted the formation of dual loyalties even before the mass immigration and before the Civil War. Later, both Theodore Roosevelt and Wilson inveighed against hyphenated Americans. If America was not a 'jealous nation', there were always plenty of jealous Americans. But, on the whole, nativist sentiments were not widespread and efforts to enforce uniformity on the part of the leadership were half-hearted. Exclusive loyalty was not insisted upon, and the void left by the discreditation of the states as major foci of group loyalty was filled by nationalities of origin without much or strenuous opposition. (*Nationalism: Five Roads to Modernity* (Cambridge: Harvard University Press, 1992) p. 483.)

6. Dimitri K. Simes, 'Russia Reborn', *Foreign Policy*, 85 (Winter '91/'92) pp. 44–5.
7. Brian Urquhart, *Decolonization and World Peace* (Austin: University of Texas Press, 1989) pp. 13–15.
8. John Gray recently observed:

For Marxists, as for classical liberals, nationalism might be an important tool in the struggle against oppression; but it was destined to disappear or to become politically marginal once the old forms of oppression had been overcome. No one imagined that it would become the most potent source of war and atrocity in the closing decades of the 20th century.

'No Nation Is Indivisible', *New York Times Book Review* (27 December 1992) pp. 6–7.

9. Tamir, *op. cit.*, pp. 3–12.
10. For example, Michael Walzer and Michael Sandel are two major communitarian theorists. However, neither Michael Walzer's book, *Spheres of Justice* (New York: Basic Books, 1983), nor Michael Sandel's book, *Liberalism and the Limits of Justice* (Cambridge: Cambridge University Press, 1982), contains any reference to nationalism or national identity in its index, even though some of their discussions would appear relevant to these topics.
11. See his scattered comments collected in *The Philosophy of Edmund Burke*, edited by Louis I. Bredvold and Ralph G. Ross (Ann Arbor: University of Michigan Press, 1960) pp. 49–64.
12. Robert V. Daniels, *Trotsky, Stalin, and Socialism* (Boulder: Westview, 1991) pp. 130–1.
13. In his inimitable fashion, Hegel asserts:

> Actually, therefore, the state as such is not so much the result as the beginning. It is within the state that the family first developed into civil society, and it is the Idea of the state itself which disrupts itself into these two elements. (G.W.F. Hegel, *Hegel's Philosophy of Right*, translated by T.M. Knox (London: Oxford University Press, 1952) p. 183.

14. Liah Greenfield's *Nationalism: Five Roads to Modernity*, has fine material on these matters, though she does not give a great deal of attention to the forces which may *erode* a sense of national identification.
15. See Greenfeld's discussion of the development of German nationalism. *Op. cit.*, pp. 275–395.
16. Garry Wills, *Lincoln at Gettysburg* (New York: Simon & Schuster, 1992).
17. Richard A. Preston, Sydney F. Wise, and Herman O. Werner, *Men in Arms* (New York: Praeger, 1962) pp. 234–54.
18. See, Steven Martin Cohen, *American Assimilation or Jewish Revival?* (Bloomington: Indiana University Press, 1988) esp. pp. 10–18 or Seymour Martin Lipset and Earl Raab, *Jews and the New American Scene* (Cambridge: Harvard University Press, 1995) pp. 173–207.
19. Brazil is often cited as an example of a nation where race and skin complexion count for little. However, there is also evidence that this picture is oversimple. See 'Brazil's Blacks Feel Prejudice 100 Years After Slavery's End', *New York Times* (14 May 1988).
20. Robert D. Kaplan, who apparently has a taste for the apocalyptic, elaborates this argument in chilling fashion in 'The Coming Anarchy', *Atlantic Monthly*, 273 (February 1994) pp. 44–76.
21. G.W.F. Hegel, *op.cit.*, pp. 210–11.
22. This argument is put forward in a number of recent studies. See, for example, J. Mueller, *Retreat from Doomsday* (New York: Basic Books, 1989) or Carl Kaysen, 'Is War Obsolete?', *International Security*, 14 (Spring 1990) pp. 42–64.
23. Some years ago, Raymond Vernon noted: 'A country determined to shape

its future no longer has much opportunity for choosing splendid isolation, except at a cost most nations would reject'. *Storm Over the Multinationals* (Cambridge: Harvard University Press, 1977) p. 146.

24. Keenan, *op. cit.*

25. James Cantalupo, chief executive of McDonald's International, quoted in 'Overseas Sizzle for McDonald's', *New York Times* (17 April 1992).

26. 'Rethinking the National Chip Policy', *New York Times* (14 July 1992).

27. See Gerard Elfstrom, *Moral Issues and Multinational Corporations* (London and New York: Macmillan and St. Martin's, 1991) pp. 111–12.

28. 'Coke Income Rose 18.6% in second Quarter', *New York Times* (18 July 1990).

29. 'Lopez Elopes', *The Economist*, 326 (20 March 1993) p. 70.

30. 'Corporate Culture Clash', *New York Times* (5 May 1989). Evidence that Pickens' quixotic effort has been followed by others is found in 'Exporting Shareholder Activism', *New York Times* (16 July 1993).

31. For example, Jaguar, the epitome of British automobiles, is now owned by Ford and is seeking financial assistance from the British government on threat of assembling a new model in the United States if the money was not forthcoming. 'Jaguar to Get State Aid to Build Car in Britain', *New York Times* (15 July 1995). In addition, the United States has discovered that many of its corporations are enthusiastic partisans of the foreign nations where they have corporate ties. 'Foreigners Find New Ally in U.S. Industry', *New York Times* (2 November 1993).

32. Vladimir Shlapentokh, *Soviet Ideologies in the Period of Glasnost* (New York: Praeger, 1988) p. 28.

33. A recent news account quotes two students of management: 'In their report Dr. Hambrick and Dr. Fredrickson said, "Executives who perceive international operations as shelves for second-rate managers are unsuited for the year 2000, or indeed for managerial jobs today"'. 'Training 21st-Century Executives', *New York Times* (20 June 1989). Also see, 'Helping Foreigners Adjust to Social Subtleties', *New York Times* (29 November 1989).

34. 'Iranian Workers Find Bliss in Japan as Nation Ignores Their Illegal Status', *Wall Street Journal* (6 May 1991).

35. Stephen Castles, *Migrant Workers and the Transformation of Western Societies* (Ithaca: Center for International Studies, Cornell University, 1989) especially pp. 1–2.

36. See Tamir, *op.cit.*, pp. 57–77.

37. Aristotle, *Politics*, translated by B. Jowett, in Jonathan Barnes (ed.), *The Complete Works of Aristotle*, Vol. 2 (Princeton: Princeton University Press, 1984) pp. 2031–3.

38. Once again, Aristotle observes, 'For law is order, and good law is good order; but a very great multitude cannot be orderly: to introduce order into the unlimited is the work of a divine power. . . .', *op. cit.*, p. 2105.

39. The administration of President Bill Clinton recently adopted a policy of favoring foreign nations seeking to expand production in the United States over the efforts of American corporations to expand operations overseas. Part of the rationale for this change was the difficulty in determining which corporations are American and which are foreign. One news account notes:

'Participants at the meeting pointed out that it was difficult to determine what is an American company now when joint ventures and international stock investors mean that a company may have many owners in many countries.' 'In Shift, White House Will Stress Aiding Foreign Concerns in U.S.', *New York Times* (2 June 1993).

40. Aristotle says, 'But in practice a citizen is defined to be one of whom both parents are citizens . . .', *op. cit.*, p. 2024.

41. C. Nicolet, *The World of the Citizen in Republican Rome*, translated by P.S. Falla (Berkeley and Los Angeles: University of California, 1980).

42. John Locke, *The Second Treatise of Government*, edited by Thomas P. Peardon (Indianapolis: Bobbs-Merrill, 1952) pp. 70–3.

4 The Structures of Government

1. For example, this is clearly implied by the 1971 *Oxford English Dictionary* definition of government as: 'The action of governing'. *The New Columbia Encyclopedia* makes the point explicitly when it asserts that government is 'a system of social control under which the right to make laws, and the right to enforce them, is vested in a particular group in society'. Aristotle also appears to have this meaning in mind when he says 'The words constitution and government have the same meaning, and the government, which is the supreme authority in states, must be in the hands of one, or of a few, or of the many', in *Politics*, translated by B. Jowett, in *The Complete Works of Aristotle*, edited by Jonathan Barnes (Princeton: Princeton University Press, 1984) vol. 2, p. 2030. It is also implied by John Rawls in the passage 'In establishing these background conditions the government may be thought of as divided into four branches. . . . These branches do not overlap with the usual organization of government but are to be understood as different functions'. *A Theory of Justice* (Cambridge: Harvard University Press, 1971) pp. 275–6. It seems clear that this presumption that government must be a unity is founded on the prior assumption that sovereign authority must also be unitary. However, the arguments of Chapter 2 must at least put this notion in doubt.

2. S.I. Benn and R.S. Peters state the view as follows:

> . . . the special theory, associated particularly with the names of Bodin, Hobbes, and Austin, that in every state there must be a determinate sovereign, i.e. that sovereignty must be located in some determinate person or body of persons, exercising 'supreme power over citizens and subjects, unrestrained by law'. (*The Principles of Political Thought* (New York: The Free Press, 1965, c1959) p. 301.

3. See Theodore C. Sorensen, *Decision-Making in the White House* (New York: Columbia University Press, 1969, c1963) especially pp. 22–42, or Hugh Heclo and Lester M. Salamon (eds), *The Illusion of Presidential Government* (Boulder: Westview, 1981).

4. There is an enormous body of literature on the issue of the expanding power and influence of the United States Supreme Court. Shirley M. Hufstedler has a concise and helpful discussion in her 'Comity and the

Constitution', in Norman Dorsen and Archibald Cox (eds), *The Evolving Constitution* (Middletown: Wesleyan University, 1989) pp. 149–68. Alepheus Thomas Mason's *The Supreme Court* (Baton Rouge, LA: Louisiana State University, 1979) is a more detailed study.

5. This diversity is vividly illustrated by the case of the ill-starred FXS fighter plane. project. The FXS was to be designed and produced in Japan by the Japanese. The understanding was that it would be based on the technology of the American F-16 fighter plane. The agreement came under attack from many directions because the American Congress, Department of Defense, Department of State, Commerce Department, and White House had differing interests and concerns at stake in the project. See Harrison M. Holland, *Japan Challenges America* (Boulder: Westview, 1992) pp. 115–20.

6. See Moshe Y. Sachs (ed.), *The United Nations* (New York: John Wiley & Sons, 1977) or Jeffrey Harrod and Nico Schrijver (eds), *The UN Under Attack* (Aldershot, England: Gower, 1988), especially Jeffrey Harrod's article 'United Nations Specialized Agencies: From Functionalist Intervention to International Co-operation?', pp. 130–44.

7. One news account observes:

> In fact, neither the United States nor Mexico was initially keen on Canada's participation, fearing Ottawa would only complicate already fiendishly difficult negotiations. But Canada insisted on joining because of its 'vital interests', a term Ottawa used repeatedly. (*New York Times* (22 July 1992).)

8. Representative works include: Inis L. Claude, Jr., *States and the Global System* (New York: St. Martin's, 1988) and James A. Yunker, *World Union on the Horizon* (Lanham: University Press of America, 1993). Both Claude and Yunker presume that a world federal government would take the place of our present system of nation-states.

9. A representative sampling of recent work on legitimacy includes: Rodney Barker, *Political Legitimacy and the State* (Oxford: Clarendon, 1990); Harry Beran, *The Consent Theory of Political Obligation* (London and New York: Croom Helm, 1987); William T. Bluhm, *Force or Freedom?* (New Haven: Yale University Press, 1984); James Fishkin, *Tyranny and Legitimacy* (Baltimore: Johns Hopkins University, 1979); and Joseph Raz, *Authority* (New York: New York University, 1990).

10. Charles Beitz has a useful discussion of these issues in *Political Theory and International Relations* (Princeton: Princeton University, 1979).

11. 'Going Crazy on the House Bank', *New York Times* (29 April 1992).

12. Douglas Henwood, 'The Issue Whose Name They Dare Not Speak', *The Nation*, 255 (20–27 July 1992) pp. 105–6.

13. Geoffrey Brennan and Loren Lomasky, *Democracy and Decision* (Cambridge: Cambridge University, 1993) or Michael Dummett, *Voting Procedures* (Oxford: Clarendon, 1984).

14. For example, though the Canadian government believed its national interest required that it become party to the North American Free Trade Agreement, a sizeable majority of Canadian citizens opposed it. 'U.S. Trade Pact a Spur to Canada', *New York Times* (22 July 1992). European voters

have been lukewarm at best to politicians' efforts on behalf of the European Community. 'European Leaders Promise to Heed Voters' Concerns', *New York Times* (22 September 1992); 'European Community Weighs a 10th Amendment', *New York Times* (18 October, 1992); or Stanley Hoffmann, 'Goodbye to a United Europe?', *New York Review of Books*, 41 (27 May 1993) pp. 27–31. Lastly, American workers were fearful that both the North American Free Trade Agreement and the GATT agreement would cost them jobs. 'Job Worries at Root of GATT Fears', *Chicago Tribune* (27 November 1994) and Ann Reilly Dowd, 'Ross Perot Is Wrong About NAFTA', *Fortune*, 128 (15 November 1993) pp. 13–14.

15. See Ton J.M. Zuijdwijk, *Petitioning the United Nations* (New York: St. Martin's Press, 1982).

5 The Role of National Governments

1. This, of course, is the reason most commonly given to explain the collapse of the Soviet Union. See, for example, Theodore Draper's 'Who Killed Soviet Communism?', *New York Review of Books*, 39 (11 June 1992) pp. 7–14.

2. David Braybrooke, *Three Tests for Democracy* (New York: Random House, 1968).

3. See Harold J. Berman's illuminating study *Justice in the U.S.S.R.*, Revised Edition (New York: Vintage Books, 1963).

4. As Carolyn Webber and Aaron Wildavsky point out, 'Over time, every democratic, industrial, rich nation has spent proportionately more than it did before on social welfare, and on government as a whole'. *A History of Taxation and Expenditure in the Western World* (New York: Simon and Schuster, 1986) p. 569.

5. This is Hobbes' view, of course, and Locke's as well, but its roots are far older than either, and it retains influence to the present day. See Michael Walzer, *Just and Unjust Wars* (New York: Basic Books, 1977), especially pp. 3–20 and Charles Beitz, *Political Theory and International Relations* (Princeton: Princeton University Press, 1979) pp. 13–66.

6. Brevet Major General Emory Upton, *The Military Policy of the United States* (New York: Greenwood Press, 1968, first published in 1904) p. ix. The United States fared somewhat better in its second century, managing three years of peace for each year of war. (Its record would have improved considerably were it not for the extended war in Vietnam.) The result is sobering nonetheless, as it demonstrates that a large portion of America's history is taken up by armed conflict. Similar calculations for the other substantial powers of the world would very likely yield similar results. War is a distressingly common instrument of political endeavor.

7. Hence, during the period when the Soviet Union was one of the world's military superpowers, its citizens generally lived in poverty, but during the same period West Germany and Japan, losers in the Second World War and lacking significant military power, prospered enormously and greatly improved the conditions of their citizens' lives. Indeed, as noted elsewhere, the Soviet Union's dismal economic performance was a major element of its collapse.

8. See S.I. Benn and R.S. Peters, *The Principles of Political Thought* (New York: The Free Press, 1965, c1959) pp. 299–315.

9. For example, this is the way Norman E. Bowie and Robert L. Simon frame the issue in their *The Individual and the Political Order* (Englewood Cliffs: Prentice-Hall, 1977) pp. 9–28. Their approach is typical of Anglo-American academic philosophers of the present day. However, it is perhaps worth noting that this is not a universal view of the relation between government and citizens. In the theory of Medieval Europe, governments gained sovereign control by virtue of the power of God, so their status did not reside in their own power of coercion but that of the deity. In the traditional Chinese view of these matters, based on the arguments of Confucius, the ruler gains authority through moral rectitude rather than the force of arms. A ruler who loses rectitude will lose the mandate of heaven and hence will also forfeit governing authority.

10. See Sven Steinmo's study *Taxation and Democracy* (New Haven: Yale University Press, 1993) especially pp. 50–155.

11. Carolyn Webber and Aaron Wildavsky, *op. cit.*, pp. 428–559.

12. See Alan Buchanan's concise and useful discussion of contemporary work on distributive justice and its role in the political philosophy of the past several decades. 'Justice, Distributive', in Lawrence C. Becker and Charlotte B. Becker (eds), *Encyclopedia of Ethics* (New York: Garland, 1992) vol. 1, pp. 655–61.

13. For example, this is the central message of a recent book by the present under secretary of commerce of the United States, Jeffrey Garten. See his *A Cold Peace* (New York: Times Books, 1993, c1992). Also see, 'How Washington Makes a Sale', *New York Times* (19 February 1995) or 'Stock Market Diplomacy', *New York Times* (6 April 1994).

14. One result, military metaphors being unavoidable it seems, is that discussion of military battles is being replaced by discussion of economic battles. Jeffrey Garten's book, *op. cit.*, is only one example, but the title 'Next: Cold War of the Capitalists', *New York Times* (6 March 1992) makes the point also. However, at least two authors, George Friedman and Meredith LeBard, argue the United States and Japan face the prospect of war in the literal sense. *The Coming War with Japan* (New York: St. Martin's Press, 1991).

15. Also, see Carl Kaysen, 'Is War Obsolete?', *International Society*, 14 (Spring 1990) pp. 42–64. The idea is vigorously denied by Donald Kagan in *On the Origins of War* (New York: Doubleday, 1995).

16. A small sign of the declining significance of citizenship for individual persons is revealed by two developments in the United States. On the one hand, some wealthy Americans are renouncing their citizenship in order to avoid paying taxes, while, on the other, large numbers of immigrants are applying for citizenship in an attempt to insure that they will continue to enjoy the benefits of government programs. In both instances calculation of financial advantage, rather than ties of national allegiance, are the primary considerations. See, 'Tax Report: "Benedict Arnold Billionaires"', *Wall Street Journal* (19 April 1995); 'Some Rich Find a Passport Lost is a Fortune Gained', *New York Times* (12 April 1995); and 'Legal Beat: More Legal Aliens Seeking Citizenship to Keep Benefits', *New York Times* (6 March 1995).

17. The most influential members of this group appear to be Michael Sandel [see *Liberalism and the Limits of Justice* (Cambridge: Harvard University Press, 1982)] and Michael Walzer [in *Spheres of Justice* (New York: Basic Books, 1983)].

18. Carolyn Webber and Aaron Wildavsky make the point as follows:

> ... federal government before the Civil War was tiny. Between 1800 and 1860, ... federal expenditures rose from nearly $11 million to $63 million in total. More than half of this supported the Army and the Navy. The general category of 'civil and miscellaneous' included a substantial amount for the postal deficit, thus covering everything except defense, pensions, Indians, and interest on the debt. ...
>
> The Civil War changed all that. The government grew from tiny to small. It promoted the interests of businessmen and farmers, sometimes aiding railroads and at other times intervening to regulate railroads in the interests of farmers. (*Op. cit.*, 383.)

19. One sign of this is that the United Nations has become far more active in the years following the collapse of the Soviet Union and is vigorously involved in peace-making and peace-keeping operations across the world. Its record is distinctly uneven at this juncture. Its failures, such as in Bosnia or Somalia, are painful, but it has enjoyed success as well, such as in Cambodia. See, 'The United Nations comes of Age, Causing Some Anxiety', *New York Times* (5 August 1990); 'A U.N. Success Story', *New York Times* (28 April 1995); 'U.N. Falters in Post-Cold-War Peacekeeping, but Sees Role as Essential', *New York Times* (5 December 1994); and Frederico Mayor, 'War and Peace in the Minds of Men', *The Unesco Courier*, 46 (March 1993) pp. 44–5.

6 Individual Lives

1. Isaiah Berlin, *Four Essays on Liberty* (Oxford: Oxford University Press, 1969). This distinction has been roundly criticized. Henry Shue's *Basic Rights*, (Princeton: Princeton University Press, 1980) pp. 35–64, is an example. Shue argues that the distinction between positive and negative freedoms is not as clear-cut as Berlin would have us believe. Nonetheless, the force of his criticism can be accepted while retaining the claim that the distinction is a useful analytic tool.

2. A number of commentators argue that the increasing ease of the collection and dissemination of information will allow governments *greater* control of human individuals. This argument is compelling. An astounding quantity of information about individual persons is presently stored in computers, and it is not difficult to combine these disparate bits of information into a single document containing a detailed portrait of individuals' lives. Moreover, the quantity and detail of this information, as well as the range of its sources, is apt to burgeon in future years. Information regarding an individual's health history, financial dealings, educational status, traffic violations, goods bought and sold, group memberships, subscriptions to periodicals, etc., etc., is being stored in computers which can easily be

linked to one central processing point and then be made available to governments, corporations, or private individuals.

The above prospect is obviously disconcerting. However, the major question is that of the degree to which the above information will enable governments to *control* individual persons, that is, compel citizens to act in ways
they would not otherwise desire or avoid behavior they do desire. The
ominous prospect is an invasion of privacy which may result in embar-
rassment, greater difficulty avoiding the consequences of past mistakes,
or vulnerability to blackmail. However, these are not extraordinarily powerful
tools for controlling individual behavior; they certainly rank far below
police states' torture chambers and prisons. They only facilitate gathering
the same information which determined governmental agencies can already
obtain. Hence, there is potential for abuse, but it is not the sort of danger
that necessarily presages an era of vastly more effective police states.

Furthermore, and more importantly, the above argument ignores the economic pressures which give powerful incentive for governments to grant
increased negative liberty to individuals participating in the global economy.
The issue, in other words, is not the *means* available for political control
of individuals, but the *political will* to do so, and it is likely that economic pressures will erode the political will of even the most authoritarian
governments, such as that of mainland China, to control the activities and
lives of individuals.

3. See Perry Link, 'The Old Man's New China', *New York Review of Books*,
   41 (9 June 1994) pp. 31–6 or John King Fairbank, 'Why China's Leaders
   Fear Democracy', *New York Review of Books*, 37 (28 September 1989)
   pp. 32–3.
4. See Paul Kennedy, 'Preparing for the 21st Century: Winners and Losers',
   New York Review of Books, 40 (11 February 1993) pp. 32–5.
5. Eric A. Kreuter, 'Doing Business in the New Russia', *Secured Lender*, 51
   (Jan/Feb '95) pp. 10 and 59; 'World Wire: Investors Wary of Russia',
   Wall Street Journal (6 December 1994); 'World Wire: Russian Business
   Code Advanced', *Wall Street Journal* (24 October 1994); 'Why Investors
   Aren't Rushing to Russia', *Washington Post* (29 October 1994); and 'Doing Business in Russia? For Now, No.', *New York Times* (7 August 1994).
6. It is partly because large retail chains threaten small family stores that
   the Japanese resisted the efforts of the huge toy retailer, Toys 'R' Us, to
   enter Japan. See 'Japan Sees Revolution in Retailing', *Los Angeles Times*
   (13 January 1992) or Susan Moffat, 'Toy Wars in Japan', *Fortune*, 121
   (12 March 1990) p. 11. In the past several decades, large corporations
   have essentially driven small family businesses from the scene in areas as
   diverse as agriculture and hardware sales.
7. This is vividly exemplified by the experience of Ronald Reagan's administration in the 1980s. Reagan claimed to be inexorably committed to par-
   ing away the social welfare programs of the United States, but political
   pressure prevented him from touching the programs that offered benefits
   to the politically formidable middle class. As this chapter is being written, a Republican majority in the US Congress claims once again to be
   ready to eliminate or truncate social welfare programs. However, the par-
   liamentary wrangling has as yet produced few detailed plans for budget

trimming. Any serious effort to eliminate budget deficits is likely to require cutting entitlement programs which benefit middle-class voters. It remains to be seen whether it will succeed once middle class voters recognize that *their* perquisites are threatened by these measures.

8. Rupert Wilkerson (ed.), *American Social Character* (New York: IconEditions, 1992); Gabriel Marcel, *Man Against Mass Society* (Chicago: Regenery, 1962); Seymour Martin Lipset, *Political Man* (Garden City: Doubleday, 1962) or David Riesman, *Individualism Reconsidered and Other Essays* (New York: Free Press of Glencoe, 1964, c1954).

9. As an executive of one Japanese corporation noted when announcing an alliance with a US corporation: 'It is becoming increasingly difficult to succeed if a company plays by itself'. An executive of the allied American corporation asserted: 'Now all global competitors – be it I.B.M., Siemens, Toshiba, A.M.D. or Fujitsu – recognize that it's better to take on a partner and earn a return'. See, 'U.S. Maker of Chips in Alliance', *New York Times* (14 July 1992).

10. Hence, the huge discount chain, Wal-Mart, has driven many small stores out of business when it appears in a new location. Sandra Stringer Vance and Roy Vernon Scott, *Wal-Mart* (New York: Twayne, 1994).

11. Charles M. Kelly, *The Destructive Achiever* (Reading: Addison-Wesley, 1988) or Robert Jackall, *Moral Mazes* (New York: Oxford University Press, 1988).

12. See P. Hertner and G. Jones, 'Multinationals: Theory and History' in P. Hertner and G. Jones (eds), *Multinationals: Theory and History* (Farnborough, Hants and Brookfield: Gower, 1986) p. 8.

13. See, for example, S.I. Benn and R.S. Peters, *The Principles of Political Thought* (New York: The Free Press, 1959) pp. 407–21 or Norman E. Bowie and Robert L. Simon, *The Individual and the Social Order* (Englewood Cliffs, N.J.: Prentice-Hall, 1977) pp. 127–55.

14. See Thomas E. Hill, Jr.'s article, 'Autonomy of Moral Agents' in Lawrence C. Becker and Charlotte B. Becker (eds), *Encyclopedia of Ethics* (New York: Garland, 1992), vol. 1, pp. 71–5, especially p. 74.

15. As Walter Wriston points out, automation often increases the value and the responsibilities of laborers. *The Twilight of Sovereignty* (New York: Charles Scribner's Sons, 1992) p. 106.

16. James D. Wolfensohn, newly appointed president of the World Bank, offers one example of how this may be done. He has stated that he believes that the World Bank should undertake a vastly expanded effort to provide the expertise underdeveloped nations need in order to become part of the world economy. 'A New World Bank: Consultant to Third World Investors', *New York Times* (27 April 1995).

17. C.F. Bergsten, T. Horst, and T.H. Moran, *American Multinationals and American Interests* (Washington: The Brookings Institution, 1978) pp. 322, 323, 328, 337, 338–9, 341, and 349.

Conclusion

1. See, for example, Michael Sandel, *Liberalism and the Limits of Justice* (Cambridge: Cambridge University Press, 1982).

2. John Stuart Mill, *On Liberty*, edited by Alburey Castell (New York: Appleton-Century-Crofts, 1947, first published in 1859) pp. 1–5.
3. Robert Fisk, *Pity the Nation* (New York: Atheneum, 1990) and Dilip Hiro, *Lebanon: Fire and Embers* (New York: St. Martin's, 1992).
4. Most commentators, Misha Glenny among them, appear to have assumed without question that outside intervention is a necessary requisite for ending the carnage in Bosnia. It is significant that at least one Serb leader shares this belief. Glenny reports:

> As such he [Milorad Pupovac, the leader of the urban Serbs in Croatia] argues, there can be no solution to the Bosnian question without the participation of the UN as the country's arbiter, with, if necessary, a military force large enough to enforce agreements by military action. Pupovac explains that unless that happens, the fighting can end only with the liquidation of the Muslims in the republic. ('What Is To Be Done?', *New York Review of Books*, 407 (27 May 1993) p. 15.)

5. For example, Brian Urquhart, sometime Undersecretary-General of the United Nations, has argued that only a standing UN armed force will prove sufficient to the peace-keeping and peace-making responsibilities that have been increasingly thrust on the United Nations. He claims:

> Whether or not it is too late to relieve the tragedy of Bosnia, it is essential to give the necessary authority and strength to the Security Council to deal with such situations more effectively in the future. The capacity to deploy credible and effective peace enforcement units, at short notice and at an early stage in a crisis, and with the strength and moral support of the world community behind them, would be a major step in this direction. ('For a UN Volunteer Military Force', *New York Review of Books*, 40 (10 June 1993) p. 3. Also see, 'A UN Volunteer Military Force – Four Views', *New York Review of Books*, 40 (24 June 1993) pp. 58–60.

6. Laurie Garrett, *The Coming Plague* (New York: Farrar, Straus and Giroux, 1994); Richard Preston, *The Hot Zone* (New York: Random House, 1994); and Richard Horton, 'Infection: The Global Threat', *New York Review of Books*, 42 (6 April 1995) pp. 24–8.
7. '3 Arrests Show Global Threat to Computers', *New York Times* (4 April 1990).
8. The topic of alienation is sprawling and decidedly untidy. However, Ignace Feuerlicht has a useful survey of the topic. See his *Alienation* (Westport: Greenwood Press, 1978), especially pp. 3–17. Morton A. Kaplan offers extensive argument in support of the claim that much discussion of alienation is based on views of ontology. See his *Alienation and Identification* (New York: Free Press, 1976) p. 131.
9. One observer puts the point nicely. David Watts notes, 'In some respects, perhaps more important than what happens in the board-room is the after-hours entertainment', p. 34. He supports his claim by pointing out that 'One of the most successful British stockbrokers in Tokyo made his name

not through his ability to make deals but because he could wow a night-
time audience of tipsy Japanese punters with his karaoke singing'. *The
Times Guide to Japan* (London: Times Books, 1993) p. 133. Also see,
pp. 133–40. Much the same points are made, albeit in less colorful fashion, by Michael Jenkins and Joyce Jenkins in *Cassell Business Briefings:
Japan* (London: Cassell, 1993) pp. 239–40.

10. 'To Drumbeats (Boom.) They Race (Boom.) in Dragon Boats (Boom.)',
    New York Times (4 June 1995); 'About Those Team Building Retreats',
    Wall Street Journal (12 April 1993); or 'Future MBAs on the Ropes',
    Atlanta Journal Constitution (11 September 1993).
11. That is, the ways in which individuals view themselves or change their
    view of themselves is influenced enormously by what other people think
    of them and the social roles they inhabit.
12. Shaul Bakhash notes that:

    But in many parts of the Islamic world, certainly in the Middle East,
    there is widespread belief that European domination continues, this time
    through the control of economic resources, superior military power, science
    and technology, and through the pernicious influence of Western cul-
    tural values and ways of life. Thus, Lewis writes, large numbers of
    Muslims have recently reverted to a militant form of religion and seek,
    through a reinvigorated Islam, to defend themselves against a Western
    cultural onslaught and to assert their own, unique identity. ('Intimate
    Enemies', *New York Review of Books*, 40 (7 October, 1993) p. 43.)
    Also see, Bernard Lewis, *Islam and the West* (New York: Oxford Univer-
    sity Press, 1993).

13. See, for example, Cyrus Bina, 'Farewell to the Pax Americana: Iran, Po-
    litical Islam, and the Passing of the Old Order', in Hamid Zangeneh (ed.),
    Islam, Iran, and World Stability (New York: St. Martin's Press, 1994)
    pp. 55–6.
14. Robert B. Reich, 'Workers of the World, Get Smart', *New York Times*
    (20 July 1993).

References

BOOKS

Aristotle, *The Complete Works of Aristotle*, edited by Jonathan Barnes (Princeton: Princeton University, 1984).

Barker, Rodney, *Political Legitimacy and the State* (Oxford: Clarendon Press, 1990).

Barry, Brian, *Free Movement* (University Park: Pennsylvania State University Press, 1992).

Becker, Lawrence C. and Becker, Charlotte B. (eds), *Encyclopedia of Ethics* (New York: Garland, 1992).

Beitz, Charles, *Political Theory and International Relations* (Princeton: Princeton University Press, 1979).

Benn, S.I. and Peters, R.S., *The Principles of Political Thought* (New York: The Free Press, 1965).

Beran, Harry, *The Consent Theory of Political Obligation* (London: Croom Helm, 1987).

Bergstein, C.F., Horst, T. and Moran, T.H., *American Multinationals and American Interests* (Atlantic Highlands: Humanities, 1988).

Berlin, Isaiah, *Four Essays on Liberty* (Oxford: Oxford University Press, 1969).

Berman, Harold J., *Justice in the U.S.S.R.*, Revised Edition (New York: Vintage Books, 1963).

Bertsch, Gary K., and McIntyre, John R. (eds), *National Security and Technology Transfer* (Boulder: Westview, 1983).

Bluhm, William T., *Force or Freedom?* (New Haven: Yale University Press, 1984).

Bowie, Norman E. and Simon, Robert L., *The Individual and the Political Order* (Englewood Cliffs, N.J.: Prentice-Hall, 1977).

Braybrooke, David, *Three Tests for Democracy* (New York: Random House, 1968).

Brennan, Geoffrey and Lomasky, Loren, *Democracy and Decision* (Cambridge: Cambridge University Press, 1993).

Burke, Edmund, *The Philosophy of Edmund Burke*, edited by Louis I. Bredvold and Ralph G. Ross (Ann Arbor: University of Michigan, 1960).

Castles, Steven, *Migrant Workers and the Transformaton of Western Societies* (Ithaca: Center for International Studies, Cornell University, 1989).

Cavisgul, S. Tamer, *Internationalizing Business: Meeting the Challenge* (East Lansing: Michigan State University, 1993).

Claude, Inis L, *States and the Global System* (New York: St. Martin's Press, 1988).

Cohen, Stephen D., *Cowboys and Samurai* (New York: Harper Business, 1991).

Cohen, Steven Martin, *American Assimilation or Jewish Revival?* (Bloomington: Indiana University Press, 1988).

Colley, Linda, *Britons* (New Haven: Yale University Press, 1992).

Cortese, C.F., *Modernization, Threat, and the Power of the Military* (Beverly Hills: Sage Publications, 1976).

Daniels, Robert V., *Trotsky, Stalin and Socialism* (Boulder: Westview, 1991).

Donagan, Alan, *The Theory of Morality* (Chicago: University of Chicago Press, 1977).

Dorsen, Norman and Cox, Archibald (eds), *The Evolving Constitution* (Middletown: Wesleyan University, 1989).

Dummett, Michael, *Voting Procedures* (Oxford: Clarendon Press, 1984).

Duncan, Graeme, *Marx and Mill* (Cambridge: Cambridge University Press, 1973).

Dworkin, Ronald, *A Matter of Principle* (Cambridge: Harvard University Press, 1985).

Elfstrom, Gerard, *Moral Issues and Multinational Corporations* (London and New York: Macmillan and St. Martin's, 1991).

Elazar, Daniel J., *American Federalism: A View from the States* (New York: Thomas J. Crowell, 1966).

Feinberg, Joel and Gross, Hyman, *Philosophy of Law*, 4th edn (Belmont: Wadsworth, 1991).

Feld, Werner J., *Multinational Corporations and U.N. Politics* (New York: Pergamon, 1980).

Feuerlicht, Ignace, *Alienation* (Westport: Greenwood Press, 1978).

Fishkin, James, *Tyranny and Legitimacy* (Baltimore: Johns Hopkins University Press, 1979).

Fisk, Robert, *Pity the Nation* (New York: Atheneum, 1990).

Frank, Isaiah, *Foreign Enterprise in Developing Countries* (Baltimore and London: Johns Hopkins University Press, 1980).

Friedman, George and LeBard, Meredith, *The Coming War with Japan* (New York: St. Martin's Press, 1991).

Fucini, Joseph J. and Fucini, Suzy, *Working for the Japanese* (New York and London: The Free Press and Collier Macmillan, 1990).

Garrett, Laurie, *The Coming Plague* (New York: Farrar, Straus and Giroux, 1994).

Garten, Jeffrey, *A Cold Peace* (New York: Times Books, 1993).

Gauthier, David, *Morals By Agreement* (Oxford: Clarendon Press, 1986).

Geiger, Theodore, *The Future of the International System* (Winchester: Allen & Unwin, 1988).

Gewirth, Alan, *Reason and Morality* (Chicago: University of Chicago Press, 1978).

Gill, Stephen and Law, David, *The Global Political Economy* (London: Harvester-Wheatsheaf, 1988).

Giovannini, Alberto, Hubbard, R. Glenn and Slemrod, Joel, *Studies in International Taxation* (Chicago: University of Chicago Press, 1993).

Green, Leslie, *The Authority of the State* (Oxford: Oxford University Press, 1988).

Greenfeld, Liah, *Nationalism: Five Roads to Modernity* (Cambridge: Harvard University Press, 1992).

Grieco, Joseph M., *Cooperation Among Nations* (Ithaca: Cornell University Press, 1990).

Hall, Kermit (ed.), *Federalism: A Nation of States* (New York: Garland, 1987).

Harrod, Jeffrey and Schrijver, Nico (eds), *The UN Under Attack* (Aldershot: Gower, 1988).

Haus, Leah A., *Globalizing the GATT* (Washington: Brookings Institute, 1992).

Heclo, Hugh and Salamon, Lester M. (eds), *The Illusion of Presidential Government* (Boulder: Westview, 1981).

Hedlund, Stefan, *Crisis in Soviet Agriculture* (London: Croom Helm, 1984).

Hegel, G.W.F., *Hegel's Philosophy of Right*, translated by T.M. Knox (London: Oxford University Press, 1952).

Hertner, P. and Jones, G. (eds), *Multinationals: Theory and History* (Farnborough, Hants, and Brookfield: Gower, 1986).

Hinsley, F.H., *Sovereignty*, 2nd edn (Cambridge: Cambridge University Press, 1986).

Hiro, Dilip, *Lebanon: Fire and Embers* (New York: St. Martin's Press, 1992).

Hobbes, Thomas, *Leviathan*, edited by Michael Oakeshott (Oxford: Basil Blackwell, 1960).

Hobsbawm, Eric, *Nations and Nationalism Since 1780* (Cambridge: Cambridge University Press, 1990).

Hoffmann, Stanley, *Duties Beyond Borders* (Syracuse: Syracuse University Press, 1981).

Holland, Harrison M., *Japan Challenges America* (Boulder: Westview, 1992).

Irwin, Douglas A. (ed.) *Political Economy and International Economics* (Cambridge: MIT, 1991).

Jackall, Robert, *Moral Mazes*, (New York: Oxford University Press, 1988).

James, Alan, *Sovereign Statehood* (London: Allen & Unwin, 1986).

Jeffreys-Jones Rhodri, and Collins, Bruce, *The Growth of Federal Power in American History* (Dekalb: Northern Illinois University Press, 1983).

Jenkins, Michael and Jenkins, Joyce, *Cassell Business Briefings: Japan* (London: Cassell, 1993).

Kagan, Donald, *On the Origins of War* (New York: Doubleday, 1995).

Kaplan, Morton A., *Alienation and Identification* (New York: Free Press, 1976).

Kelly, Charles M., *The Destructive Achiever* (Reading: Addison-Wesley, 1988).

Keohane, Robert O. and Hoffmann, Stanley (eds), *After the Cold War* (Cambridge: Harvard University, 1993).

——, *The New European Community* (Boulder: Westview, 1991).

Koekkoek, Ad, and Mennes, L.B.M. (eds), *International Trade and Global Development* (London and New York: Routledge, 1991).

Lewis, Bernard, *Islam and the West* (New York: Oxford University Press, 1993).

Lipset, Seymour Martin and Raab, Earl, *Jews and the New American Scene* (Cambridge: Harvard University Press, 1995).

Lipset, Seymour Martin, *Political Man* (Garden City: Doubleday, 1962).

Locke, John, *The Second Treatise of Government*, edited by Thomas P. Peardon (Indianapolis: Bobbs-Merrill, 1952).

——, *Two Treatises of Government*, edited by Peter Laslett (Cambridge: Cambridge University Press, 1986).

Macpherson, C.B., *The Political Theory of Possessive Individualism* (Oxford: Oxford University Press, 1962).

Marcel, Gabriel, *Man Against Society* (Chicago: Reginery, 1962).

Marx, Karl, *Marx & Engels: Basic Writings on Politics & Philosophy*, edited by Lewis Feuer (Garden City: Doubleday & Co., 1959).

Mason, Alepheus Thomas, *The Supreme Court* (Baton Rouge: Louisiana State University, 1979).

Mill, John Stuart, *On Liberty*, edited by Alburey Castell (New York: Appleton-Century-Crofts, 1947, first published in 1859).

Mueller, J., *Retreat from Doomsday* (New York: Basic Books, 1989).

Nicolet, C., *The World of the Citizen in Republican Rome*, translated by P.S. Falla (Berkeley and Los Angeles: University of California, 1980).

Oye, Kenneth A., *Economic Discrimination and Political Exchange* (Princeton: Princeton University Press, 1992).

Pogge, Thomas W., *Realizing Rawls* (Ithaca: Cornell University Press, 1987).

Preston, Richard, *The Hot Zone* (New York: Random House, 1994).

Preston, Richard A., Wise, Sydney F. and Werner, Herman O., *Men in Arms* (New York: Praeger, 1962).

Rawls, John, *Political Liberalism* (New York: Columbia University Press, 1993).

——, *A Theory of Justice* (Cambridge: Harvard University Press, 1971).

Raz, Joseph, *Authority* (New York: New York University Press, 1990).

Reich, Robert, *Tales of a New America* (New York: Times Books, 1987).

——, *The Work of Nations* (New York: A.A. Knopf, 1991).

Riesman, David, *Individualism Reconsidered and Other Essays* (New York: Free Press of Glencoe, 1964, c1954).

Sachs, Moshe Y. (ed.), *The United Nations* (New York: John Wiley & Sons, 1977).

Sandel, Michael, *Liberalism and the Limits of Justice* (Cambridge: Cambridge University Press, 1982).

Sangeneh, Hamid (ed.), *Islam, Iran, and World Stability* (New York: St. Martin's Press, 1994).

Schaffer, Mark E., *Technology Transfer and East–West Relations* (New York: St. Martin's Press, 1985).

Shlapentokh, Vladimir, *Soviet Ideologies in the Period of Glasnost* (New York: Praeger, 1988).

Shue, Henry, *Basic Rights* (Princeton: Princeton University Press, 1980).

Simmons, John, *Moral Principles and Political Obligations* (Princeton: Princeton University Press, 1979).

Singer, Peter, *Democracy and Disobedience* (Oxford: Oxford University Press, 1974).

Sommers, Albert T. and Blau, Lucie R., *The U.S. Economy Demystified*, 3rd edn (New York: Lexington Books, 1993).

Sorensen, Theodore C., *Decision-Making in the White House* (New York: Columbia University Press, 1969, c1963).

Steinmo, Sven, *Taxation and Democracy* (New Haven: Yale University Press, 1993).

Tamir, Yael, *Liberal Nationalism* (Princeton: Princeton University Press, 1993).

Upton, Brevet Major General Emory, *The Military Policy of the United States* (New York: Greenwood Press, 1968, first published 1904).

Urquhart, Brian, *Decolonization and World Peace* (Austin: University of Texas, 1989).

Vance, Sandra Stringer and Scott, Roy Vernon, *Wal-Mart* (New York: Twayne, 1994).

Vernon, Raymond, *Storm Over the Multinationals* (Cambridge: Harvard University Press, 1977).
Volin, Lazar, *A Century of Russian Agriculture* (Cambridge: Harvard University Press, 1970).
Walker, David B., *Toward A Functioning Federalism* (Cambridge: Winthrop Publishers, 1981).
Walzer, Michael, *Just and Unjust Wars* (New York: Basic Books, 1977).
——, *Spheres of Justice* (New York: Basic Books, 1983).
Watts, David, *The Times Guide to Japan* (London: Times Books, 1993).
Webber, Carolyn and Wildavsky, Aaron *A History of Taxation and Expenditure in the Western World* (New York: Simon & Schuster, 1986).
Wilkerson, Rupert (ed.), *American Social Character* (New York: IconEditions, 1992).
Wills, Garry, *Lincoln and Gettysburg* (New York: Simon & Schuster, 1992).
Wright, Gary A., *Archaeology and Trade* (Reading: Addison-Wesley, 1974).
Wriston, Walter B., *The Twilight of Sovereignty* (New York: Charles Scribner's Sons, 1992).
Yunker, James A., *World Union on the Horizon* (Lanham: University Press of America, 1993).
Zuijdwijk, Ton, *Petitioning the United Nations* (New York: St. Martin's Press, 1982).

ARTICLES

Archer, Clive, 'Denmark Says "No"', *The World Today*, 48 (August/September 1992) pp. 42–3.
Bakhash, Shaul, 'Intimate Enemies', *The New York Review of Books*, 40 (7 October 1993) pp. 43–5.
Boutros-Ghali, Boutros, 'UN Peace-Keeping in a New Era: A New Chance for Peace', *The World Today*, 49 (April 1993) pp. 66–9.
Brenner, Michael J., 'EC: Confidence Lost', *Foreign Policy*, 91 (Summer 1993) pp. 24–43.
Buruma, Ian, 'Just Say "Noh"', *The New York Review of Books*, 36 (7 December 1989) pp. 19–20.
Bush, George, "Continued Pressure on Iraq to Comply With UN Security Council Resolutions', *US Department of State Dispatch 3* (21 September 1992) pp. 718–19.
'Challenge to Council Resolutions Continues', *UN Chronicle*, 30 (June 1993) pp. 30–3.
Draper, Theodore, 'Who Killed Soviet Communism?', *The New York Review of Books*, 39 (11 June 1992) pp. 7–8, 10, 12–14.
Dyker, David, 'Russia's Economy After the Referendum', *The World Today*, 49 (July 1993) pp. 122–3.
Eberle, Sir James, 'International Boundaries: The Security Angle', *The World Today*, 48 (April 1992) pp. 68–71.
Fairbank, John King, 'Why China's Rulers Fear Democracy', *The New York Review of Books*, 37 (28 September 1989) pp. 32–3.
Gardels, Nathan, 'Two Concepts of Nationalism', *The New York Review of Books*, 38 (21 November 1991) pp. 19–23.

Glenny, Misha, 'What Is To Be Done?', *The New York Review of Books*, 41 (27 May 1993) pp. 14–16.

Greenwood, Christopher, 'Is There a Right of Humanitarian Intervention?', *The World Today*, 49 (February 1993) pp. 34–40.

Hartley, Anthony, 'Maastricht's Problematical Future', *The World Today*, 48 (October 1992) pp. 179–82.

Henwood, Douglas, 'The Issue Whose Name They Dare Not Speak', *The Nation* 255 (20–7 July 1992) pp. 105–6.

Hoffmann, Stanley, 'Goodbye to a United Europe?', *The New York Review of Books*, 40 (27 May 1993) pp. 27–31.

Honour, Hugh, 'Burma: Splendor and Miseries', *The New York Review of Books*, 42 (13 July 1995) pp. 56–61.

Horton, Richard, 'Infection: The Global Threat', *The New York Review of Books*, 42 (6 April 1995) pp. 24–8.

Johnston, William B., 'Global Work Force 2000: The New World Labor Market', *Harvard Business Review*, 69 (March–April 1991) pp. 115–27.

Judt, Tony, 'The New Old Nationalism', *The New York Review of Books*, 41 (26 May 1994) pp. 44–51.

Kaplan, Robert D., 'The Coming Anarchy', *Atlantic Monthly*, 273 (February 1994) pp. 44–76.

Kaysen, Carl, 'Is War Obsolete?', *International Security* 14 (Spring 1990) pp. 42–64.

Kennedy, Paul, 'Preparing for the 21st Century: Winners and Losers', *The New York Review of Books*, 40 (11 February 1993) pp. 32–44.

Kreuter, Eric A., 'Doing Business in the New Russia', *Secured Lender*, 51 (Jan/Feb '95) 10 and 59.

Link, Perry, 'The Old Man's New China', *The New York Review of Books*, 41 (9 June 1994) pp. 31–6.

'Lopez Elopes', *The Economist*, 326 (20 March 1993) p. 70.

Malia, Martin, 'A New Russian Revolution?', *The New York Review of Books*, 38 (18 July 1991) pp. 29–31.

Mayor, Frederico, 'War and Peace in the Minds of Men', *The Unesco Courier*, 46 (March 1993) pp. 44–5.

Michnik, Adam, 'Poland and the Jews', *The New York Review of Books*, 38 (20 May 1991) pp. 11–12.

Mortimer, Edward, 'Iraq: The Road Not Taken', *The New York Review of Books*, 38 (16 May 1991) pp. 3–7.

Newmann, Ronald, 'Overview of US Policy Toward Iraq', *US Department of State Dispatch 5* (7 February 1994) pp. 66–8.

Reddaway, Peter, 'Russia on the Brink?', *The New York Review of Books*, 40 (28 January 1993) pp. 30–5.

Reich, Robert B., 'Who Is Them?', *Harvard Business Review*, 69 (March–April 1991) pp. 72–88.

——, 'Who Is Us?', *Harvard Business Review*, 68 (January–February 1990) pp. 53–64.

Rohatyn, Felix, 'World Capital: The Need and the Risks', *The New York Review of Books*, 41 (14 July 1994) pp. 48–53.

Simes, Dimitri K., 'Russia Reborn', *Foreign Policy*, 85 (Winter '91/'92) pp. 41–62.

Sorrell, Martin, 'Merging For Success', *Advertising Age*, 61 (18 June 1990) p. 70.

'A UN Volunteer Military Force – Four Views', *The New York Review of Books*, 40 (24 June 1993) pp. 58–60.

Urquhart, Brian, 'For a UN Volunteer Military Force', *The New York Review of Books*, 40 (10 June 1993) pp. 3–4.

——, 'The United Nations in 1992', *International Affairs*, 68 (April 1992) pp. 311–19.

Index

alienation, 7, 155, 163–9, 194n
  aspects of, 164
  and bonding experiences, 166–7,
    194n
  consequences of, 164–5
  and ethnic identity, 73–4
  and the global economy, 164
  and Kafka, 163–4
  and national identity, 73–4
  ontological, 163–4
apartheid, 43
  see also South Africa
applied philosophy, 4
  and business ethics, 4
  and medical ethics, 4
Aquinas, 100, 113
Aristotle, 46, 89–90, 91, 103, 113,
    114–15, 124, 187n
  and citizenship, 84, 85, 87–8, 125
  and the nation-state, 40–1
autonomy, of the individual, 7, 141–7
  and freedom, positive, 138
  and globalism, 146–7
  and institutions, 144
  loss of, 146
  and political activity, 146–7
  and the will of the people, 44–6
Austin, John, 181n, 187n

Balkans, 74–5, 161, 171 194n1
Barry, Brian, 5
Beitz, Charles, 5
Berlin, Isaiah, 133, 175n
Bhagwati, Jagdish, 13
Bodin, Jean, and sovereignty, 42,
    48, 63, 187n
Burke, Edmund, 68
Bush, President George, 24, 46

Camus, Albert, 163
capital, global market for, 20, 26–8,
    31
  and regulations, 26, 31

capitalism, 9, 15, 17
China, 173n, 192n
  and freedom, negative, 134–5
  and the global economy, 18–19,
    23
citizens, 182n, 190n
  and national governments, 50,
    122–5, 125–8, 130
citizenship, 2–3, 18, 83–90, 152,
    157, 187n, 188n
  aspects of, 88
  changing character of, 87–90
  and clients, 88–90
  consent and, 88
  and the global economy, 123
  and national identity, 65
  and participation in government,
    87–8
  and the states of the United
    States, 83–4
clients, 88–9
  and citizenship, 88–90
Coca-Cola, 33, 78–9
Cold War, 22, 54, 116, 120, 131
  and global economy, 14, 15, 17,
    20
  and the United Nations, 96
communitarians, 125–6, 156–7, 185n
computers
  and the global economy, 21–2
  and national boundaries, 22
  and national governments, 22
consent, 102–3, 182n
  and citizenship, 88
  and sovereignty, 58, 106

Denmark
  and the European Union, 60–2,
    182–3n
  and the global economy, 62
democracy, 10–11, 100, 103–10
  as accountability, 104–10
  definition of, 103

democracy *cont.*
　direct, 101, 127
　extended sense of, 109–10
　and international government,
　　105–10
　representative, 104
disease control, 131, 162
　and sovereignty, 52, 54
distributive justice, 7, 118–19,
　　147–55
　and exploitation, 148–50
　and the global economy, 147–8,
　　150–1
　and labor, 149–50
　and a minimally decent life,
　　149–50
　and multinational corporations,
　　153–4
　and political philosophy, 11
Dworkin, Ronald, 12, 68

ethnic identification, 68–9, 72–4,
　　76, 77, 160–1, 171, 183–4n
　as black, 72–4, 185n
　and colonial liberation, 74
　defined, 66
　erosion of, 73–4
　and international culture, 80
　as Jewish, 72–4, 183–4n
　and militarism, 74
　and national identity, 65–6, 70
European Conference on Peace and
　　Security, 56
European Economic Community, 18,
　　174n
　and international government, 97
　and sovereignty, 48, 49, 182n
　and Thatcher, 47–8
European Union
　and Denmark, 60–2
　and the Maastricht Treaty, 182n,
　　182–3n

Feinberg, Joel, 68
Flat Rock, Michigan, 2–3
Ford Motors, 2–3, 78, 186n
free trade, 15, 97–8, 154
freedom, 133–41
　and globalism, 146–7

　of the individual, 7
　negative, 133–7, 191n; defined,
　　133; and immigration, 137;
　　and information, 136; and the
　　global economy, 133–4
　political, 139–41; defined, 139;
　　negative, 140; positive, 140;
　　positive *v.* negative, 139
　positive, 137–9, 191n; and
　　autonomy, 138; defined, 133;
　　and the global economy, 138–9
　religious, 12

Gauthier, David, 12
Geiger, Theodore, 5
General Agreement on Tariffs and
　　Trade (GATT), 1, 25, 35, 97,
　　98, 99, 173n, 189n
　defined, 35
　see also World Trade
　　Organization
Gewirth, Alan, 12
Gill, Stephen, 5
global economy, 1–3, 5, 8, 9, 12,
　　13–38, 23–5, 118, 172
　and alienation, 164
　and capital, 20, 26–8, 177n
　and China, 18–19
　and citizenship, 123
　and the Cold War, 14
　and computers, 21–2
　cost of isolation from, 18–19,
　　60–2
　development of, 1–2, 7, 13–17,
　　173n
　and distributive justice, 146–7,
　　150–1
　and economic power, 55
　and education, 139
　expansion of, 150–1
　and freedom, 133–41; negative,
　　133–7; political, positive, 140;
　　positive, 138–9
　and injustice, 151, 169–70
　and institutional man, 142
　and institutions, 145
　and intellectual property, 31–3,
　　49–50, 136
　and international government, 98

and Islam, 37, 170, 178–9n, 195n
and labor, 20–1, 30, 81–3
and mercantilism, 23–5
and military power, 55
and multinational corporations,
   33–5
and Muslims, 9
and the nation-state, 3, 5, 41,
   59–62, 71–2, 98
and national governments, 18–19,
   23, 50, 128, 183n
and national identity, 72, 86
participants *v.* non-participants,
   135, 138–9, 148–54, 169–71
and political conflict, 170
and protectionism, 19, 25, 28, 29
and the role of government, 124
and services, 30–1
and sovereignty, 49–50, 61–2
and technology, 1, 14, 18, 21–2,
   28–9, 32, 49–50
and the United States, 14–15
and warfare, 71–2
and the welfare state, 139
and the World Trade
   Organization, 35
global unification, 1, 7, 13, 17,
   17–22, 23–5, 77–83
and multinational corporations,
   23–5, 77–9
and political philosophy, 3–4
and technology, 1, 14, 16
globalism, 1–3, 169, 172
aspects of, 1
and autonomy, 146–7
and freedom, 146–7
and power, 171
globalization, 6, 12, 168
Gorbachev, Mikhail, 15
government, 91–2, 102–10, 159–60,
   183n, 191–2n
fragmented nature of, 92–3, 126,
   156
and the global economy, 120
and human rights, 131–2
and human suffering, 159
and institutions, 127–8
international, 95–100, 157–8; as
   fragmented, 95–100, 108–10;

and democracy, 105–10;
development of, 95–100; and
the European Economic
Community, 97; and the global
economy, 98; and human rights,
106; and individual persons,
129; legitimacy of, 129; and
national governments, 107–8; as
organic whole, 121–2; regional
structures, 97; and sovereignty,
95–9; and transnational
corporations, 129–30; and the
United Nations, 94–7
and military force, 120
as organic whole, 92, 99, 110–11,
   187n
responsibility of, 130–2, 152–3
size of, 93, 191n
and sovereignty, 92
see also world government
Group of Seven, 96, 119

hazardous wastes, and sovereignty,
   52, 54, 57, 62
Hegel, G.W.F., 69, 75, 147, 156
and citizenship, 84–5
and national identity, 84–5
Hobbes, Thomas, 40–1, 59, 86–7,
   89–90, 91, 100, 113, 114, 120,
   189n
and sovereignty, 42, 48, 187n
Hoffmann, Stanley, 4, 5
is no philosopher, 4
human rights, 102, 106
and governments, 131–2
and legitimacy, 59, 101–2, 182n
and sovereignty, 56

immigration, 18
individuality, loss of, 168–9
Industrial Revolution, 1, 10, 12, 70,
   149
institutions, role of in contemporary
   life, 126–8
International Monetary Fund (IMF),
   27, 35
and Russia, 27
International Arbitration Panel, 36
International Court of Justice, 36

institutional man, 141–2
  and the global economy, 141–2
  and mass man, 144–5
institutions, 7, 141–7, 155, 156–8,
  164
  and autonomy, 144, 156
  and demands of modern life, 143
  and individual lives, 7, 143–7
  and the global economy, 145
  size of, 142–3, 192n
Iraq, 95
  and sovereignty, 43

Japan, 3, 15, 27, 78, 120, 153, 192n
  business culture of, 165
  and labor, 81–2
  and national identity, 41
  and the US, 2–3, 23–6, 94–5,
    120, 176–7n, 178n, 188n, 193n

Kafka, Franz, 163–4
Kaifu, Prime Minister Toshiki, 24,
  176n
Kennan, Edward, 76
Keynes, John Maynard, 118
Khrushchev, Nikita, 15

labor, 21, 27–8
  changing role of, 149
  and exploitation, 149–50
  and the global economy, 20–1
  global market for, 29–30
  mobility of, 20, 29–30, 81–3
Law, David, 5
legitimacy, of governments, 6, 11,
  39–40, 100–3, 110–11, 122,
  182n, 190n
  and consent, 58–9, 85–6
  criteria of, 101–3
  and fragmented nature of
    government, 100–1
  and human rights, 60, 101–2
  and illegitimacy, 102
  and the Medieval Church, 39–40
  and sovereignty, 42, 58–9
Lincoln, President Abraham, 70
Locke, John, 1, 10, 40, 68, 86–7,
  91, 100, 113, 114, 179n, 189n
  and citizenship, 85

and national identity, 89
and sovereignty, 42

Maastricht Treaty, 182n, 182–3n
Marx, Karl, 1, 10, 13, 40, 68, 113,
  124, 148–9, 171–2, 184n
  as fruitfully wrong, 8
  and labor, 171–2
mass man, 141–2
  and institutional man, 144–5
Mazda Motors, 2–3
McIntyre, Alasdair, 68
mercantilism, and the global
  economy, 23–5
Michnik, Adam, 183–4n
Mill, John Stewart, 159
Mueller, John, 120
multinational corporations, 27–8,
  33–5, 158
  development of, 14–17
  and distributive justice, 153–4
  and the global economy, 23–5,
    33–5
  and labor, 30
  and national governments, 16, 17,
    123, 129–30, 186–7n
  national origin of, 24, 34–5,
    78–9, 178n
  and nationalism, 16
  and services, 31
  and transnational corporations, 78
  and the United States, 14–15, 16
Muslims, and global economy, 9

nation-state, 4, 13, 39–40, 55–6,
  157, 174n, 184n, 185n
  and armies, 46
  as artifact, 70, 85–6
  and citizenship, 87–90
  and collective action, 56–7, 62
  definition of, 41, 66
  and economic bounds, 77
  and the global capital market, 27–8
  and global economy, 3, 5, 98
  and individual persons, 40
  and the Industrial Revolution, 70
  and the Maastricht Treaty, 182n,
    182–3n
  and militarism, 74, 116–17

and multinational corporations, 78, 123
and national identity, 41
and political philosophy, 40–1
and sovereignty, 39, 50
and technology, 71
and war, 116–17
national boundaries, 13, 18, 19, 20, 41, 76, 119, 123–4, 152, 156, 183n
and computers, 22
and economic boundaries, 55
and economic forces, 71–2
and freedom, negative, 136
and the global economy, 71–2, 76
and national identity, 65
and sovereignty, 51
national governments, 6, 11, 27–8, 59, 60–2, 70, 85–6, 93–9, 129, 158, 192–3n
and citizens, 50, 59, 122–5, 125–8, 130, 157
and computers, 22, 191–2n
defined, 66, 187n
and their economies, 117, 118
and emigration, 53–4
and ethnic identity, 70
fragmented nature of, 93–5
and the global capital market, 26–8
and the global economy, 18–19, 41, 50, 119–21, 128, 183n
and international government, 106, 107–8, 121–2
and international law, 36
and intellectual property, 49–50
legitimacy of, 39–40
and multinational corporations, 33–4, 158, 186–7n
and regulations, 117–18
responsibility of, 130–2
role of, 5, 6, 40–1, 113–32, 155, 179n, 189n; and distributive justice, 118–19; evolution of, 117–19, 123–4; and the global economy, 124; internal, 114–15; and pollution, 128; traditional view of, 114; and the welfare state, 124; and the United States, 115

and sovereignty, 42, 48–9
transformation of, 3, 10–11
usual view of, 91
and the will of the people, 45
and world government, 91
and the World Trade Organization, 35
national identity, 2–3, 4, 5, 6, 18, 40, 61, 65–90, 174n, 185n
and citizenship, 65
and colonialism, 71
dynamics of, 69–74, 185n
erosion of, 73–4, 86, 152, 157
and ethnic identity, 65–6, 70, 73
and the global economy, 72, 75–7, 86
and Great Britain, 66–7
and Hegel, 84–5
and the individual, 68
and Japan, 41, 66
and labor, 82–3
and militarism, 74–7
and the nation–state, 41, 89
and national boundaries, 65
and popular culture, 79–80
and the Soviet Union, 67
and the United States, 3, 67, 70, 83–4, 90
and war, 74–5
nationalism, 13, 68–9, 76, 171, 175n, 184–5n, 185n
and ethnic identity, 73
and modern war, 183n
and multinational corporations, 16
North American Free Trade Agreement (NAFTA), 98, 188n, 188–9n
Nozick, Robert, 113, 114

Organization for Economic Cooperation and Development (OECD), 119

Pickins, T. Boone, 79, 186n
Plato, 103, 113, 114–15, 124, 125
Pogge, Thomas W., 5
political philosophy, 3–5, 8, 10–12, 146, 155, 158, 163, 170–1, 173–4n

political philosophy *cont.*
  and circumstances of human life,
    3–5, 6, 7–8
  and distributive justice, 11,
    118–19
  and global unification, 3–4, 8
  and national identity, 68–9
  and the nation-state, 40–1
  timeless validity of, 4, 11–12
pollution, 11, 98, 106, 128, 131,
  151, 160
  and sovereignty, 54, 57, 58, 62

Rawls, John, 12, 68, 113, 118–19,
  175n, 187n
  and timeless validity, 12
Reagan, President Ronald, 118,
  192–3n
Reich, Robert, 5
Rousseau, Jean-Jacques 91
Russia, 45
  and the IMF, 27

Sandel, Michael, 68, 185n, 191n
Sartre, Jean Paul, 163
Shue, Henry, 4, 5, 191n
social contract, 85
  and legitimacy, 85
socialism, 10–11, 17
  and the United States, 10
South Africa, 43, 44
  and sovereignty, 43, 46
  see also apartheid
South Korea, 140, 141
  and freedom, negative, 135–6
  and freedom, political, 140–1
  and the United States, 49–50
sovereignty, 4, 5, 6, 8, 39–63,
  100–3, 158, 174n, 180n
  and collective action, 62
  and consent, 58, 59, 60–2
  and control of currency, 48, 61
  and disease control, 52
  and economic power, 54–5
  erosion of, 48–50, 51–3, 53–7,
    57–9, 121–2
  and the European Economic
    Community, 49, 182n
  external aspect of, 42–4, 53–7

features of, 42
fragmenting of, 58–9
and the global economy, 49–50,
  61–2
and government, 92
and hazardous wastes, 52, 57, 62
and human rights, 56
internal aspect of, 42, 44–6, 51–3
and international bodies, 52
and international government, 96
and Iraq, 43
as legal fiction, 47
loss of, 59, 98–100, 106–7, 154,
  183n
and legitimacy, 42, 58–9, 100–3
and military power, 54–5
and national borders, 51
and national governments, 42,
  48–9
overridden, 46
and pollution, 57, 58, 62
recognition of, 43
and South Africa, 43, 46
and the states of the United
  States, 51–2, 123–4
and technology, 49–50
and Thatcher, Prime Minister
  Margaret, 47–8
and the United Nations, 42, 44,
  53, 54, 179n
whole cloth view of, 47–8, 58–9,
  180n, 182n
and the will of the people, 44–6
Soviet Union, 10, 12, 15, 16, 22,
  114–15, 116, 120, 124, 173n,
  189n, 191n
  and ethnic identity, 72–4
  and national identification, 67,
    68–9
Stalin, Joseph, 69
state, definition of, 41

Thatcher, Prime Minister Margaret,
  47–8, 118
  and the European Economic
    Community, 47–8
Toyota, 33, 78, 81
  transnational corporations and
    multinational corporations, 78

Trotsky, Leon, 69
tyranny of powerlessness, 7, 159–63
and anarchy, 159–60
defined, 7, 159
and the erosion of the power of
national governments, 159
and institutions, 162–3
and pollution, 160
and the siege of Sarajavo, 160–1

United Nations, 1, 17, 36, 56, 99,
107, 109–10, 129, 160–1, 162,
191n, 194n
and the Cold War, 96
General Assembly of, 96, 99
and international government, 95–6
peacekeeping missions, 181n,
194n
Secretary-General of, 96
Security Council of, 96
and sovereignty, 42, 44, 53, 54,
179n
United States, 3, 11, 23, 28, 30, 54,
80–1, 116, 120, 161, 162, 170,
173n, 176n, 177n, 188n
and citizenship, 83–4, 190n
Congress of, 94, 104
and ethnic identity, 3, 72–4, 90,
184n
and free trade, 175n
government of, 94–5, 126–7,
191n
and intellectual property, 32, 45,
56
and Iraq, 43
and Japan, 2–3, 23–6, 94–5, 120,
176–7n, 178n, 188n, 193n

and military power, 54, 55
and multinational corporations,
14–15, 129–30
and national identification, 67, 70,
82–3, 90
and participation in government,
88
President of, 94
and the role of government, 115
and socialism, 10
Supreme Court of, 94, 187–8n
and South Korea, 49–50
and war, 189n
Upton, Brevet Major General
Emory, 116, 189n

Walzer, Michael, 5, 68, 185n, 191n
will of the people, 44–6, 106
and individual autonomy, 44–6
and national governments, 45
Wills, Garry, 70
Wolfensohn, James D., 193n
World Bank, 27, 35, 193n
world government, 51–2, 91–2, 99,
100, 110, 188n
and control of disease, 162
as fragmented, 95, 110–11, 158,
161–2
role of, 161
see also government
World Trade Organization (WTO),
25, 35, 97
and the global economy, 35
see also General Agreement on
Tariffs and Trade

Yeltsin, Boris, 45, 180n